The Nehantucket

Books by Robert S. Foster

The Granville Hermit

The Nehantucket

Robert S. Foster

Old Orchard Farm Press
East Lyme, Connecticut

The Nehantucket
Robert S. Foster

Old Orchard Farm Press
East Lyme, Connecticut

oldorchardfarmpress.com

Copyright © 2025 Robert S. Foster

All Rights Reserved. No part of this publication may be reproduced, distributed, or transmitted in any form or by any means, including photocopying, recording, or other electronic or mechanical methods, without the prior written permission of the publisher, except in the case of brief quotations embodied in critical reviews and certain other noncommercial uses permitted by copyright law.

Photo Credits: Gallery photos by Robert S. Foster with permission from the collection owners. Photos from the Norris Bull Collection used with permission from his grandsons Lewis Bull and Jim Littlefield.
Inside Cover Map of Connecticut circa 1625: UConn Library MAGIC, CC BY-SA 2.0 <https://creativecommons.org/licenses/by-sa/2.0>.

Front cover art © Susan Leppla, Waitsfield, Vermont
Inside back cover art: Howard Estes, Niantic, Connecticut

Book design by Kitty Werner, RSBPress LLC, Waitsfield Vermont

Library of Congress Control Number: 2024920549

ISBN 978-1-7379525-2-7 tradepaper
ISBN 978-1-7379525-3-4 ebook

Printed in the United States of America

Contents

Preface | vii
Introduction | viii
1 Eons Ago | 11
2 Living River | 14
3 Summer's Quest | 15
4 Prana | 17
5 Migrants | 20
6 Cairns | 22
7 Lay lines | 24
8 Mahigan | 26
9 Animal Guide | 28
10 Enchanted | 30
11 Sachems | 34
12 Shelters of the Earth | 36
13 Elders Council | 39
14 Abenaki | 43
15 Ancient Knowledge | 47
16 Synchronistic Acquaintance | 49
17 Soul Mate | 50
18 Shared Interaction | 54
19 Carnivores | 57
20 Last Behemoth | 60
21 Down Time | 63
22 Unseen Realms | 66
23 Paying Forward | 69
24 Connective Thought Energy | 73
25 A Secluded Mystical Place | 78
26 Living Earth Speaks | 83
27 Canoe Craft | 86
28 Nordic | 89
29 Sachem Contemplation | 98
30 Message of No Words | 100
31 The First Contact | 103

32 An Arduous Journey | 107
33 A Meeting in the Sand | 110
34 Monolithic Axe | 114
35 Power of the Stones | 117
36 Shifts of Time and Sand | 121
37 Insights Shared | 126
38 Living in the moment | 130
39 Birthrights | 133
40 Skills of Living in the Moment | 136
41 Primeval Passions | 140
42 Winter Village | 143
43 A Discreet Return | 146
44 Sacred Places | 150
45 In Ritual | 153
46 Nature Encounters | 155
47 Danger Close | 157
48 Hunter or Prey | 160
49 Skill of Lure | 162
50 None the Hero | 165
51 Sachems and Secrets | 168
52 Orientation | 172
53 Sacred Ecstasy | 174
54 Sleeping In | 177
55 Enlightenment | 182
56 Portal Visions | 187
57 A Distant Future | 191
58 In the Present | 193
59 Rights of Passage | 195
60 Permissions Manifested | 198
61 Transitions of Season | 204
62 Seasons to Come | 211
63 A Return | 217
64 Of Pipe and Peace | 222
65 Of Tale and Lore | 227
Then to Now | 231
Photo Gallery | 239
Dedication | 245
Acknowledgments | 247
About the Author | 249

Preface

Through a series of synchronicities, a human gift, that is a birthright that many of us know, has reopened. Information about, and insights into, the ancient Nehantucket culture have manifested for the creation of this story.

We find in these past times it is important to remember how to recognize, feel, and move through the shifts of energy and, more importantly, to utilize the energy to manifest and remain in connection with the earth and the universe. Most important is to remain connected to one's true self.

The ancient Nehantuckets lived, walked, and breathed the power of magnetic attraction and synchronicity in their daily manifestations subconsciously without thought or wonder of it. It was a knowingness within the soul, an understanding, and an ancient teaching of human birthright. The people lived, prospered, and flourished for thousands of years in harmony and connection with the Mother Earth spirit. They gave homage, tribute, and thanks for all their bounty; and paid it forward to each other, the animals, the earth, and the stars. Signs of their culture abound in the land. Cast in stone, the spirit of these ancient Nehantuckets lives in the stone structures they created so long ago. The builders may be gone now, but their spirit remains as they have ascended to a higher dimension.

For these reasons and according to preserved teachings, this writing serves to enlighten, commemorate, and remember a truth about a special native tribal people:

The Nehantucket
"On point of land"

Introduction

Within these pages unfolds a historical account of an ancient era long gone by brought to life through storytelling. It is a perceptional account of personal experience, enriched by encounters and beliefs through the eyes of a few ancient individuals, native tribal men and women.

A tribal culture inhabited the shoreline setting of New England, including the bay and short river with their pristine waters known now as Niantic a borough in the town of East Lyme, southeastern shoreline of Connecticut. During ancient times there existed a cultural people who, during their migratory journeys, discovered a milder climate along this seasonal shoreline and as they acclimated to the region's climate its bounty brought them prosperity. Theirs was a tribal community living in complete harmony with nature and its seasons. We will speak of their peaceful interactions with neighboring tribes all speaking variations of the same Algonquin language.

Our tale concentrates on a little-known tribe of natives of kind disposition, who are not often mentioned within any documents prior to or after colonial encounter. It is an account of an ancient Indian culture who inhabited these shores for thousands of years, in ways that prior to European contact existed in natural harmony with the earth's rhythms. In this era, the people were cherishing and worshiping and thanking the sun as it rose in the eastern sky and set in the far western horizons, beginning and completing a daily cycle.

The moon, with its various phases, set a dependable form of time that was significant to their harvests, planting, and hunting cycles. Its position in the sky and its noted distance marked the important seasonal changes as they learned to adjust and prepare accordingly.

Prevalent within many of their stone structures, ceremonial chambers and offering sites, there remains today a depiction and a deep understanding of an ancient knowledge of the four seasonal equinoxes. Within many of the stone alignments we find intentional crevasses created carefully and purposely to allow the sun's beams to illuminate on and into these stone structures. With a careful eye many other stone mounds and animal effigies can be found throughout the now forested shoreline summer and the inland winter sites.

Many mounds seem to be arranged in such a manner as to depict certain star constellations, Pleiades, Orion, and Alpha Centauri. They were laid out on the ground or on the slope of a hill as the constellation would have appeared to the natives on pristine clear nights. Perhaps by the construction of these mounds they would invite the knowledge, energy, and return of the Starr People, where their deceased ancestors ascended to and reside. Sacred burial mounds would allow passage to the stars for the spirit of great tribal leaders, sachems, medicine men and women, shamans, and all tribal members with great ceremony at their time of ascension.

Stone effigies of serpent, tortoise, woodland bison, birds and migratory creatures, remain lying undisturbed always nearby these ceremonial sites and spring water sources. They seem to pay tribute and gratitude to Earth's bounty and spirit. The stars, the constellations pristine in the night sky, perhaps connected them to a higher dimension, a universal energy that they could sense and feel and manifest.

The earth at this time may have been on a slightly different rotation from its axis as we know it today. The Aurora Borealis, colors of light bands, natural hues wafting through the night sky would have been exquisite and incredibly majestic to our natives who beheld and understood that all of these phenomena as guides for their spiritual beings.

Let us now introduce an important and untold lost story of a New England native culture, let us now introduce:

The Nehantucket

1 Eons Ago

Over twenty-one thousand years ago, a melting glacier of solid ice with immense crevasses and torrents of melt water still covered New England. It churned and ground its weight into the hills and ledges as it receded, moving back slowly over the original continental shelf remaining beneath, some of the oldest granite bedrock on the planet. Its height was over a mile above the solid earth. It carved and scraped the landscape below its belly, dragging huge boulders and depositing them teetering on ledges like marbles as it melted and receded inland and slowly moved northward.

As the green vegetation reemerged in the soils eighteen thousand years ago, so did the migratory beasts, birds, and fishes of the coastal waters that rose, turning the once mountain peaks into small coastal islands. Envision immense saber-toothed cats, woolly mammoth herds—genetically different from the larger mastodon, massive herds of migratory elk and caribou. Including white tail deer, immense beaver, and teaming schools of freshwater fish filling the stream beds and rivers.

The massive flocks of birds that inhabited the coastal marshlands and inland grasslands were one hundred-fold the population we know of today and included geese, ducks, gulls, terns, partridge, turkey, and doves, just to name a few. The migratory gatherings along the shoreline encompassed not just an acre or so, but over ten and up to one hundred times the open acreage along these shores creating a moving sea of wild fowl flocks as seen from a high standpoint.

Abundant predatory and carnivorous creatures easily stalked their prey during the various seasons, flourished, and maintained a healthy and well-balanced population. The grey and red fox, coyote, mountain lion cats, dire timber wolves, and the massive, short-faced bear, over twice the size of any grizzly or black bear, were also indigenous to the shoreline.

Perhaps ten to thirteen thousand years ago, small tribal bands of early humans, those we consider native people, finally migrated from even further northern regions and found themselves able to flourish along this coastal area of southern New England. This would have been during the Paleo-Indian Period. Adapting quickly, they enjoyed the seasonal climate and adapted well to its variety and bounty, from the coastal marine life to the migrating herds of caribou and elk. They learned the applications of the natural fauna of wild plants, roots, and herbs well. These combinations sustained the people with a well-balanced diet of nutrients and protein not available to other inland tribes even just fifty miles inland and northward.

This civilization thrived during the Middle Archaic Period, some eight thousand years before the present (BP) and continued to thrive through the very early Woodland Period, which began some five thousand years ago. The Paleo-Indian adapted and evolved over those thousands of years to become the original indigenous natives of our story, which begins now, fully into the Woodland Period. Imagine these natives at a time of five thousand years ago.

The Nehantucket were a handsome people, of clear, smooth complexion, with straight teeth. They were tall in stature, from five-foot-six to six-foot tall. They had long straight dark amber hair, some with a tinge of reddish trait, others with darker browns and blackish hues. Their skin tone was that of a lighter olive hue. This was most likely due to an evolutionary adaptation to the seasonal southern New England climate that existed approximately six thousand years ago.

Adornments of polished beaded seashell, bird feathers, and shaped bone trinkets were important to individualism in a way that highlighted the individual's persona and beauty. Adornments were also significant to one's stature within the tribal band, endorsing his or her accomplishments and skills, as well as personality. These were people of deep spiritual connection to the earth, her energies and cycles. They had a deep understanding of all the creatures that they co habituated with in their surroundings and shared a universal respect, giving tribute to them as part of their daily rituals. The Nehantuckets bore a genetic trait of a kind, giving, and sharing disposition. Quiet and mild of manner, there was no need or concept of want or ownership!

In the warmer spring and summer season, only a light loin cloth was worn perhaps with a hide wrapping for leggings to protect from underbrush along with a simple type of moccasin. In the warmer summer seasons women were bare breasted as there was no understanding of shame in the human body. Males would at times paint part of the body with various pigments, colors of blue, greens, and reds derived from plant and okras. These pigments would also highlight the masculinity in males as well as bring out the inner beauty and magic mystical part of the feminine.

With a colder winter season upon them, fur skins were prepared, cured, and worked to a soft flexible texture, to endow their warmth on the people. Once fit to size, these garments could last an adult for many seasons of daily use and were generally handed down to growing children as the need arose.

No part of an animal ever went to waste. Bone was shaped into tools, implements and adornments; sinew was used for sewing and lashings, and hides were tanned into clothing and water shedding covers for their dwellings. These long houses, known as wigwams, were proven efficient shelters constructed of sapling tree bows, reeds, and over-lapped tree bark slabs.

The Nehantucket interactions with neighboring tribes, all speaking variants of the Algonquin tongue, was of the same kind and sharing nature as within tribal groups. At these important rendezvous gatherings, there was no concept of animosity between tribal neighbors to the north, west, or east.

There existed only a respectful trade alliance in the sharing of stone tools, hunting technology, utensils, and finally the much sought after "wampum." These were beads of shaped quahog shells of exquisite colors of blue, purple, and pinkish hues made exclusively by the Nehantucket.

2 Living River

The sun gleamed separate beams of yellow light through the foliage from the canopy of the treetops illuminating the leaves and mosses in patches on the ground. It was early morning—just as the sun was poking in full splendor over the tree-topped eastern horizon.

From his vantage point high above the western edge of the river, now known as the Niantic River, although Ne-han-tuk-it was how the tribal people pronounced it, Lone Wolf looked down at the shimmering water. He could see the northern uppermost channel where the wider river narrowed between the ledges at the river's beginning thread. Here fresh waters flow into the river's body, sourced by the upland brook known today as Latimer Brook.

He could also see the mid-southern, wider, mature body of the river known then as the Inner Bay. To the south the river flowed and ebbed with the tidal influence of saltier brackish waters rising and subsiding in their tidal cycles. It was as if breathing, filling its lungs with life-giving nutrients, and exhaling, flushing out into the narrow deep gut of the ocean salt bay, with the influx of the fresh water from its uppermost source.

This river was and is alive with life not only in and under the sands of its belly, but up along both sides of its broadness, the sloping woods, and embankments. The river teemed with fish, crabs, mussels, clams, oysters, scallops, and lobster. Along its shores were the muskrat, fisher cat, bobcat, and beaver, just to name a few. Uphill into the river's wooded parts in the area on the eastern shore of the Oswegatchie flatland, woodland creatures abounded. Upon the western shore, the area known today as Oswegatchie Hills, another wooded forest was home to all walks of animal life to include beaver along the freshwater stream beds and marshes.

The Algonquin-speaking Nehantuckets called this river "living waters." It teemed with life, this river, alive and breathing. The young man called Tibamahgan, meaning "Lone Wolf," named so by his people after his demeanor, could feel the essence of the river as part of his body and soul.

3 Summer's Quest

Tibamahgan was completing and returning from a twelve-day upland trek that began at the larger summer village along the waterfront shore of the great bay. We know this area today as Crescent Beach.

Off in the distance across the bay's horizon, one could see the islands, mountaintops whose slopes were well below the water's surface. These islands protruded above the surface of the ocean bays much higher than present day, being uneroded some five thousand years ago, just to recall our timeline.

This village was just a series of smaller outlying villages situated along the Nehantucket River, the bay, and shore along the western points of higher land that jutted toward the bay. A large stone circle was used as a main gathering location for council meetings and ceremonial events.

From his high vantage point, Tibamahgan could also overlook these "crescent sands" that held a deep significance to this culture, emulating the moon's beginning and ending cycles. Nearby were the sacred burial grounds, now known as McCook Point Park.

Lone Wolf was designated by the sachem council of elders as a "mashkiki," a medicine scout, whose task, due to his acknowledged skills, was to locate and prepare the best seasonal winter village locations five and ten miles inland. He would survey the game trails of migratory herds, woodland bison, elk caribou, and the non-migrating, whitetail deer.

Winter villages enabled the tribal majority to better withstand harsh winds, snows, and ice annually gusting inward from the ocean and bay beginning in December at the winter equinox. The village always wanted to relocate as close to the grassy meadows and trails that these migratory animals would use so that hunting parties would only need to spend three to four days further upland from the winter village.

In the winter, they would base their diet on the various meats from game animals and stored dried maze and herbs. Their diet included fall-harvested gourds, varieties of pumpkin, squashes and freshwater fish caught and dried on racks. The inhabitants salted fresh meats and fish well, to preserve them. They harvested the salt itself by boiling down the bay seawater to dehydrate it.

Along with the fresh meats brought in from the men's hunting camps, the Nehantucket people flourished far better than tribes located further inland. Those tribes were used to going hungry for longer durations of time. The Nehantucket people, over many hundreds of years learned and passed down techniques in hunting, growing, processing, and applying the bounties of the earth. This included its healing plants and herbs, seasonal and perennial harvests, and its creatures. These were bounties that they would give thanks for, cherish, and give tribute for.

4 Prana

As he sat atop this overlook along the river, surveying its beauty, Lone Wolf reflected on his last few days scouting the upland areas some five miles or so distant by today's measurement, utilizing the streambed of the brook now known as Latimer Brook at the location we call Flanders. It was a good site for this winter's camp, being far enough inland for protection from the shoreline winds, and close to the grassy flatland features of the terrain with its gentle slopes and wooded knolls.

The brook's waters flowed further inland, nicely meandering with the grassy flatlands mostly along its miles of western embankments with the secluded wetland areas and natural ponds whereby all forms of game were abundant. The eastern embankments rose into rock ledges long since scoured and scraped by the glacial movements and recessions, leaving massive boulders oddly placed, teetering like marbles from giants' games!

The brook, rather wide in some locations, harbored native trout, speckled and rainbow, many more than thirty inches long; salmon enough to walk on; and schools of sea bass looking to spawn in the first couple of miles or just a "mornings walk" away in the measurement used in those times. Lone Wolf determined this should be the winter's camp area for his people; he was certain that the migratory herds would pass through this section of lush vegetation in the spring and the perennial game would be abundant. The grasses vibrated greener and richer here this season than further to the western part of the wooded forest known today as the Nehantic forest. The village migration would take only a few days and some smaller clans could utilize the older hovels just a few miles westward along Pattagansett Lake and again along the brook known today as Four Mile River.

Lone Wolf reflected on how at one time during his annual trek, while not far from the streambed, he encountered not one but two massive bull moose. Antlers of well over six-feet wide with webbed-horn growth, over ten inches in width were remembered in his mind's eye, the larger bull with clumps of moss and grasses hanging from its antlers.

Just a few moments before this encounter, Lone Wolf was blowing on a split reed he had pulled from the grass patch. With two fingers, he split it slightly and pulled it taught horizontally and blew air from his lips in a whistle style that caused the reed to vibrate a bleating sound mimicking a deer grunt. With this trick he could scout the abundance of deer in the area. The bucks would respond to the bleats of a doe in heat. Hunting parties would only take bucks, to ensure nature's balance of deer population, understanding that if there are no does there are no babies!

Deer would use various grunts and bleats to communicate their presence with each other. Does would bleat to let the bucks know they may be present and interested during the rutting season. The bucks, especially the dominant, would scrape and rattle their antlers on tree bark. They would also scrape two-foot oval patches of ground, leaving their scent in many locations within their territory. Does would leave their scent in the scraped ground patches as well.

The bull moose would do similar scrapings, tearing up larger sections of ground and limbs. Apparently Lone Wolf's grunting tones, being much deeper and longer this day, drew an unintended outcome! It was just as he noticed this difference, reading the signs and the hoof tracks in the bare dirt that the energy subtly changed.

With an instant premonition, a flash of intuition of what was about to occur, he perceived in his core a knowingness of what was about to unfold. It was just a feeling or inner sense. Expecting a buck, he instinctively started to crouch a little lower. But there was not enough notice. His intuition came too late.

Within a split moment, a loud crack sounded. A heavy snapping of large branches nearby revealed two large dark brown silhouettes charging toward him just twenty yards downslope! He did not have the time to reach the spear strapped over his shoulder.

Nor was he able to even pull the stone axe from its sheath at his waist before the pair of massive beasts bounded up and around his position. The larger more dominant bull digging in its hooves to an abrupt halt just three feet from him. The bull loomed high over Lone Wolf who was standing just slightly down from the top of knoll. Just a few seconds later, the second bull trotted up to him from the opposite side and stood his ground approximately eight feet off.

Now, this was an extremely dangerous predicament. With the bulls deep into the rut and Lone Wolf in *their* mating territory, their testosterone levels were raging and causing unpredictable behavior. One or both could charge at any moment. If they perceived him as a threat or a rival bull he would not fare well from those antlers.

All animals can sense, feel, and even smell fear. Lone Wolf's first impulse was to raise his spear into position or reach for the axe. With no time, his second thought was to pull the wood-handled bone knife from its shoulder-strapped sheath. Still there was no time and both of those thoughts he instinctively knew were fear-based.

Instead, something deep within his core, an inner knowingness, an ancient wisdom, told him to surrender, to suppress the fear emotion and transform it into an energy of tranquility, quietness, and gratefulness for this experience as it unfolded.

The hot breath hit his face from the snorting exhale of the closer bull; the other snorted as well, not expecting the human scent. Another loud long snort from the closer bull filled his senses with the breath and scent of the animal.

The shaman within him filled his essence. Some ancient memory and wisdom came forth in a form of divine timing. Whether he forced it forth from his inner being or, if it was through his natural sense of the earth connection from the soil beneath his feet he was suddenly connected with the massive animals, their essence. He instantly felt relaxed and centered.

Intuitively he put it out to them, focusing on the closer bull, that he was no threat. He meant them no harm. Slowly, he knelt on one knee bowing his head slightly. Lone Wolf relaxed his tense posture, lowered his shoulders, and in a simple gesture, held both of his hands out forward from his body toward the large bull.

With palms up, instinctively he put forth prana. A universal energy, warm and magnetic, it flowed from the palms of his hands. Intention and thought focused on only how majestic the animal was, its beauty and power. Then he spoke softly, saying *meegwetch*, meaning "thank you."

The two bulls, after a few moments, snorted out a mist of breath. Then there was a long moment of silence throughout the woods. Tibamahgan felt their acceptance as the energy shifted with the moment of shared prana. Suddenly, they both crashed off through the woods and were gone.

5 Migrants

Tibamahgan knew and felt this would be the best winter village site. The deer population was abundant, moose most definitely abound, and turkey sign was everywhere: tracks and feathers and leaves in the hardwood areas were ripped up in their quest for acorn and beechnut.

"Pijaki," or woodland bison, tracks were recent along the meadowy edges of timber hardwood. They would migrate somewhat through the region but could and would sustain well into the winter foraging on grasses under the snow. The pijaki were massive animals, generally in small herds of ten to fifteen or so. Just one of these creatures could sustain the entire village for a half-moon, many days, but the hunt would require many skilled hunters and a coordinated strategy.

After locating the area where the pijaki were grazing, usually a day or two prior to any hunt, the Nehantucket would first align many of the people, women and young adults alike, along the entrance of a two-sided steep ravine. Then the agile hunter drivers, sometimes six to ten abreast and thirty to forty feet apart, would push the herd into the narrows.

This is where it would become even more dangerous for the drivers. If the lead bull bison decided to double back or stand ground, the closest drivers in the forest could and did sometimes sustain great injury or death in being charged and mauled by the enraged pjaki's huge horns.

Tibamahgan, Lone Wolf, reflected upon these past bison hunts as he sat on the overlook of the river. In the last season the hunt went well enough. Most of the small herd were forced into the ravine, where they turned and broke through the drivers and escaped back into the forest, leaving only two straggler pijaki trapped by the swarming Nehantucket, who closed the escape route with their numbers and with their spears.

Usually, the Nehantucket spears were made and shaped from the hard and straight white ash wood. Sharp pointed stone spear heads were mounted and lashed at the split end of a long straight shaft. At the opposite end of the shaft, they learned to fasten a beveled butterfly-shaped stone counter weight that would provide a better and more level aerial flight path more accurately to its target. These newer spears proved to be a vast improvement over their predecessors.

In addition, they made two-foot throw arrows or darts from the ash wood, tipped with sharp-edged quartz points, along with two turkey feathers mounted opposite each other at the blunt end to provide better flight control. These long darts were launched with great and accurate force from a wooden canoe-shaped sling rod of the same ash wood. The atlatl, as we call it today, was found to provide double the leverage of the hunter's arm could provide and a shorter spear shaft was quicker and easier to make and carry in a simple quiver that was strapped over the hunter's shoulder and back, leaving arms and hands free to carry the longer spear.

The Nehantuckets developed these tools over hundreds of years and learned to be very skilled with these hunting implements. The force of impact and penetration of these projectiles could pierce the vital organs of the large game and bring it quickly down to its knees.

Other migratory hooved animals such as elk and caribou were hunted very much in the same manner, utilizing the combined effort of many tribal members or by select smaller hunting parties. Younger boys coming of age would be allowed to accompany the senior experienced men on these important excursions, in this way the knowledge was passed down to the next generation.

Winter hunting parties would go off from the winter village for upwards of four to five days at a time, two to four miles into the forested areas. There, they would usually set up small encampments on knolls or higher terrain in and between two stream beds, utilizing the terrain to their advantage as they hunted game in these areas.

Throughout the Nehantic forest and today's current farmlands, ancient fire pits of these encampments have been found at depths of eight to twelve inches, exposing remnants of charcoal and quartz chips and shavings. Here one can imagine the prowess of these hunters sitting around the evening fire working and chiseling new points for their spear shafts and arrows.

Over time they learned to fashion a bow from hickory or ash with a string of sinew strip that would propel a longer arrow than the earlier atlatl arrow or dart. The bow and arrow with turkey or partridge feathers to guide its flight was found to be more accurate at further distances than the atlatl. This technology proved to be more efficient for hunting the more elusive, non-migratory game, such as the independent deer and smaller game.

6 Cairns

Tibamahgan recalled that only the larger of the two *pijaki* or woodland bison was brought down to slaughter as dictated by their ancient code of honor. This held true for all game hunted in this manner. It was a sacrilege for these people to take any game above what was needed. It was based on an ancient universal law, not to be violated. This also retained the natural balance of the earth's bounty and the people's connection to it.

All would give thanks, in group ritual and in individual ritual. The animal's spirit was released back to the earth and the stars so that it could return. The people were spiritually connected to the earth and stars.

Throughout the forested areas today and within the open farmsteads and wooded areas, one can find, with a keen eye, mounded structures, piles of moss-laden stone of various sizes situated in many different forms. Some mounds reveal lengthy serpentine wall forms with no obvious purpose to the layman. In fact, these structures were built with a much deeper intent than the casual observer might understand. Usually with a large serpent head stone at one end, they would point southward or be in circular formations giving tribute to the summer and winter equinoxes and solstices. Some openings within the structures would serve as portals to the other dimensions. Others would be as large mounds in silhouette shapes of animals or tortoises. Still others would be purposely set as small chambers whereby offerings would be made to the great spirit, to give thanks back to the earth and the stars.

These cairns, mounds, and chambers can be found throughout the woodlands of the Nehantic state forest, as well as throughout all of New England's coastline and interior. Situated on and within the state and governmental preservation and forest lands as well as private woodland lots and farmsteads, they have withstood and remained intact over many recent centuries, and thousands of years. Holding the secrets of the ancients' spiritual belief system, they depict a story, unfolding truths of the indigenous Nehantucket peoples and their relationship with the earth and heavens' bounties.

This writer has now developed a greater understanding with deeper insights as to their meaning, uses, and purposes; a connection and passion for this ancient culture, these ancient and perhaps more humane of beings.

7 Lay Lines

Sitting quietly at his overlook viewing the river's water gleaming in the sunlight, Lone Wolf's thoughts returned to a time when he was much younger, still a boy by our reckoning, about the age of perhaps twelve years old, just to provide a reference. He reflected on his "kawagwedjit" experience, the spiritual revelation during his vision quest.

Tribal people did not conceive of any age lines utilizing months or years as any form of reference. Instead, age was determined through experience, stature, and demeanor. Thus, when a young boy or girl was ready, as it was taught and passed down from the elders, they would quietly venture out into the forest or the shore on their own vision quest, a "kawagwedjit," for a duration of days or even weeks.

While on this rite of passage, the boy, later to be known as Tibamahgan, found himself miles northward of the summer's coastal encampment. For some reason he was drawn to an area just northwest of the Four Mile River and the eastern part of what is now known today as Old Lyme. Here amongst the steep ledges and deep ravines, were bear caves situated within the glacial tumble of boulder and ledge slab etched and jaggedly eroded by the eons of climate changes. Other dens and smaller chambers provided a haven for all forms of wildlife, including the timber wolf.

While searching a particular spot to shelter and set his temporary camp for his quest to unfold he became enchanted with the vast rock ledge formations and boulder tumble left behind by the retreat of the glaciers. Every few hundred yards it seemed like a new landscape to explore, another unique terrain that could reveal another habitat area for some creature!

More, there was some alternate sensation here in this area that felt like an inner magnetic attraction. The tops of the massive pure granite ledges, smoothed and rounded only at their crests seemed to vibrate somehow.

Some small areas had beautiful blankets of green moss. As he laid upon the soft moss, looking straight up at the clouds for a quick rest and contemplation, the boy becoming a man could feel a vibration or a vortex of energy that emitted upwards and back down through the stone again.

Lay lines of magnetic energy form a grid, throughout the earth, energy vortexes erupt and intensify in areas within these lay lines. The solid granite ledges that hold certain other mineral deposits within them create and intensify these magnetic grids and vortexes.

This particular lay line was part of the reason these granite and mineral ledges rose fifty and one hundred feet higher than the lower terrain just a quarter or even a half mile away on either side of the high ridges that run straight north- and southward.

Formed eons ago much before the great glacial age, these lay lines are part of the earth's energetic life force. They exist throughout the entire planet, the very living lifeforce vibration connecting the family of galactic star systems.

As he lay there on the carpet of moss atop this massive monolithic rock ledge, the boy could feel the energy surging through his body and soul. It brought clarity to the teachings and ancient knowledge passed down from the elders' stories that stemmed from even older generations.

The youth arose refreshed and inspired to continue his adventure, his spiritual walk, atop these high ledges. He could not get enough of the feeling and the vortex energy intensified as he went along. Atop one higher point he could clearly view "Nehantucket" Bay and the distant islands of Long Island Sound. He continued on his way.

8   Mahigan

As the boy becoming a man, on his "kawagwedjit" quest, came up over a ledge formation, he suddenly heard snarling sounds echo through the still air! Just down to the side of the outcropping, he creeped on his belly to view the ruckus with just his short spear in hand.

There, a massive, short-faced bear, standing on hind legs, towered three to four times over a timber wolf. She was snarling ferociously at the immense bear and lunging at his exposed abdomen with her teeth gnashing. The bear had one of her pups in his mouth, with its body partially dangling out on the side, and another gripped in its massive four-inch claws.

Mother wolf, "Mahigan," was desperately attempting to protect her other three remaining cubs, two of which watched amongst the rocks just outside the den trying to decide how to hide or escape. The third remaining cub managed to scramble up and over the smooth ledge surface and down the opposite side. Not even noticing Lone Wolf laying on his belly, the cub ran just a foot past his position.

With the large mother wolf's final and fatal lunge, her gnashing fangs would not and could not be near enough to defeat this immense carnivore. With a mighty swipe of the bear's free open forepaw and its immense deadly claws, it ripped the huge wolf's body open almost in half and flung her fifteen feet from the torn-up terrain just below her den that was just a large crevasse at the base of the broken ledge.

The short-faced bear flipped and crunched the cub already in its mouth, devouring its little body in one swallow. It then tossed the other cub into its maw letting it dangle there in its mouth while descending on all fours.

With one bound it leaped the span to the gasping mother wolf and picked it up with one powerful forearm. Looking toward the den where the other two cubs had apparently retreated, it seemed to decide that it would save them for another future meal.

Then within a flash, on three legs it bounded off, down slope into the thick lowland ravine, out of sight. The youth, remaining still and quiet, could hear the branches breaking off in the distance. It was then silence that filled the air, only to be broken by a faint sound, a slight yelp that came from a distance halfway down the opposite slope.

9 Animal Guide

Cautiously, the youth peeked out from his hidden spot. There it was! Just down the craggy, steep western slope of the ridge, he could hear the little wolf pup's whimpers and short yelps of pain it emitted as it continued to struggle. With its rear leg wedged in the rocky narrow crevasse, the scared and stressed timber wolf pup, barely four weeks old, was trapped.

The youth, not much older by comparison, he thought, made his way down to the pup, all the while emitting a persona of quiet and peaceful intent so as not to instill any more terror into the little pup's day. Lone Wolf surmised that the pup would survive no more than two days at best, dying by starvation or another carnivore's hunger. The yelping would not work for survival either. So, he made his way down the rocky terrain.

His silhouette and upright stature initially caused fear in the pup, being a similar form as the bear. The pup crouched as low into the crevasse as it could, whimpering and expecting to meet his fate as his siblings had.

Lone Wolf calmly reached with both hands, placing one over the pup's eyes, holding his head snug and firm while the other hand followed the trapped leg down to the crevasse. Easing the leg forward and sliding the ankle part of the pup's foot toward the wider part of the rock, he was able to free the leg. Then with one motion he scooped the pup up from under its hind quarters and placed it into his deerskin satchel strapped over his shoulder and proceeded back up onto flatter ground.

Placing a cover over a creature's eyes eliminates fear and prevents them from thrashing around during the instinctive survival mode. The needle-sharp teeth of the pup could have caused some severe lacerations to his hands without a doubt.

After a couple hours of travel, the youth settled into a makeshift camp for an early overnight far away from the den, and hopefully the bear. He built a small fire. Finally, he opened the pouch just enough for the afternoon light to reach in and allow the pup's head to poke out.

There was no scent of bear or the carnage at the den to alarm the pup any further. Lone Wolf pulled a tidbit of dried jerky venison from his other pouch and held it to the pup's nose as its mother may have done with a kill brought back to the den. Apprehensive of the morsel, the pup cowered back into the safety of the satchel.

Thoughtfully, the youth had gone down to the carnage and salvaged a small remnant of the mother timber wolf's fur and hide that had been torn away by the bear and placed it into another small pouch, before he left the den area. Now the boy placed the mother's scented remains near the pouch opening. The pup immediately poked his head out again, this time with less fear, and licked at the dried morsel of meat. Soon he was eating out of the boy's hand.

The pup's leg healed from the sprain after riding in the boy's pouch for a few days. Then able to walk on its own, it followed the youth just about everywhere, although keeping its distance. Over a short time, the timber wolf readily learned his new pack mate's hand gestures and body language, obeying well as it accompanied him on his continuing kawagwedjit.

Upon returning to his people, because of this relationship with the wolf pup now fairly grown, members of the tribe began to whisper about this wild and feared companion the new man of the tribe had adopted on his lone vision quest. They told stories about the tamed wolf, thus earning the young man respect and the conception of his adult name now agreed upon by the elders, "Tibamahgan," meaning "Lone Wolf."

Remaining as Tibamahgan's companion of sorts, the pup was always free to return to the wild, which it did occasionally for days at a time, hunting and fending for itself. Somehow, this young wolf never seemed to be too far off, always a silhouette in the distance. When Lone Wolf went out on his excursions beyond the village alone the normally reclusive young wolf would walk alongside him companionably.

10 Enchanted

Tibamahgan was exploring along the ridge above the river on one of his excursions. As if in a vision, there she was with her baskets, wading knee deep along the river's edge. Her long reddish-brown hair kept falling over her shoulder and was wet at the last six inches as she bent and reached down into the sand below her feet. He could not remember ever meeting her before!

She would pull up two or three four-inch round quahog clams at a time and then walk to the basket to deposit them, surveying up and down the river's edge and up into the wooded slope and ledge tops each time she came back to the basket. She did this four or five times as Lone Wolf watched from his higher perch. He was mesmerized by her form, her slender legs, her bare breasts, and her smile that expressed her joy every time she scanned the embankments. She seemed pleased about life itself, as well as this spot that hosted an abundant bed of clams. He thought he could hear her humming a tune while she splashed the water on her way back to her basket.

There was something about this beautiful young creature, a magic energy that surrounded her essence. He was powerless as it drew him toward her. He could not take his eyes off her; he was totally enchanted.

Lone Wolf decided to move in a little closer, and so did his tame wolf that was now of a more adult stature than the cute puppy he had been. The wolf took a position just up upon the solid ledge precipice where the young woman was bent over, reaching down in the water, with her back to the embankment. This time after depositing her quahogs, she scanned her surroundings and noticed the wolf standing and staring, not twenty yards away. Her smile disappeared, then she saw movement just to her right, about five yards from the wolf. With his fine leggings, his satchel, spear, and quiver strapped over his right shoulder, he held out his hand palm up as a gesture of friendship.

Startled, she glanced back and forth between him and the wolf, not sure if they were aware of each other. Tibamahgan stepped toward her, descending the smooth sloping granite but stopped when he noticed her startled glance at the wolf off to his right.

He motioned with one hand gesturing to the wolf to "stay", as he took a few more steps. He made the same command again and then with two fingers motioned in a downward direction. The wolf immediately laid down, not taking his eyes off Lone Wolf.

She was surprised and impressed all at the same time. Thinking the wolf was the more dangerous wild predator she was always warned about from childhood, she instinctively backed deeper into the water. Tibamahgan motioned for her to come out of the water as he approached, finally jumping down onto the narrow beach sand strip.

Still startled and glancing back up at the wolf, she put up both hands gesturing to Tibamahgan to stop! She did not want him to come any closer until she could find some sense of security. He was, after all, a stranger, although she had heard of him through the village wives and her other friends. She had imagined Tibamahgan to be much older, this man who speaks to wolves.

She was taken in by his masculine features, bronzed skin, chiseled jaw and cheek lines. His eyes were gentle and kind. She could sense his aura and light-body as strong and wise. She felt she knew him from some place beyond the village, a place from another lifetime or dimension. It was an inner knowing although she had never met or seen him at the village or river before this day.

As he sat there, relaxed not seeming to care about the startling encounter, he just smiled slightly and motioned for her to come out of the water again! Looking at him, she cocked her head toward the wolf; then a half smile began to form as she stepped forward from the waist high water. The wolf remained upon the smooth ledge outcrop, laying there as it had been commanded. Her fear dissipated a bit more after realizing Lone Wolf was its master; she was impressed by their unheard-of unique relationship.

"Tibamahgan!" he said as he pointed at his own chest smiling, still impressed, and also intimidated, by her essence and beauty. Fiddling with her basket half full of clams and kneeling in the sand, she shyly glanced at him. Putting her hand upon and between her breasts, she said, "I am called 'Mahkiwasie,' which means Medicine Girl."

Lone Wolf leaned back, instinctively knowing she was special and that is was no coincidence that he came upon her this day as he was making his way back to the village and his small wigwam set just on the outskirts of the village in the area we now know as Pine Grove, near the national guard training site now called Camp Niantic. No, it was no coincidence, it was more of a synchronicity, or a manifestation for him. In the moments before he saw her attractive form down at the river's edge, he had been sensing that a new adventure or experience would enhance his life.

Not so ironically while Mahkiwasie was in the river, humming in her own moment, she had had a similar insight along with a pleasant sensation welling in her loins. Her mother called her "Abetonimi" or "light dancer," when she was younger because she would dance in the morning light beams shining through the smoke flap at the top of the wigwam shelter down onto the floor in a small circular pattern. She would dance in this light beam every morning, the light bouncing and warming her smiling face. As she grew to girlhood she began to understand, feel and see light energy around every living thing. Plants, animals, people, and even the stones and water vibrated with this glow of soft light.

Mahkiwasie learned without any teaching to use this force to heal and to connect with the things in her daily life. Her smile projected this essence that emitted from her inner knowingness and set her apart from the other girls in the village of the same age. Her little plot of garden was an example of this; she would spend hours each day putting light energy with her hands into her plants, talking and humming a tune to even the seedlings. Each plant flourished greener and lusher than others nearby. She would even put the energy into the soil, tilling only the top few inches so that all the natural nutrients would remain undisturbed at the root system level and plants would thrive for many seasons.

They sat in the sand across from each other for quite a while, speaking softly of things of shared interest, especially the fact that they both enjoyed being alone and quiet for long parts of each day. Then there was this quiet moment, just sitting looking out at the water and at each other, sharing and projecting the energy back and forth between them, without speaking, each admiring the beauty in the other's facial features and personas.

Mahkiwasie could see the inner light around Lone Wolf's body that emitted from his solar plexus, hues of gentle blues, greens and yellows, and she allowed his energy to touch and join hers there on the sand. They were smitten with each other on that little sandy beach along the Nehanticut River. "I must go now," she said, smiling as she proceeded to get up. Lone Wolf and Mahkiwasie touched hands ever so briefly, as they both reached for the basket at the same time. Their eyes met as a surge of energy shot through both of them and sealed their connection.

The other women and girls of the village just down river collecting quahogs called out to Mahkiwasie with a high "yip" sound to let her know that they were ready to return to the village. She called back to them letting them know she was on her way. When they saw the legendary and handsome Tibamahgan walking alongside Mahkiwasie, oh, how the whispering and giggling began!

The gaggle of women went ahead with their baskets of clams, little necks and lobsters that were abundant on the rocky shore, each glancing back at the enchanted couple holding hands and trailing well behind the pack. They now had a whole new topic of discussion and innuendo for their fires this night.

Lone Wolf told Mahkiwasie of his own small wigwam located just to the south upon a small pine knoll. He told her about it in the hope that she might venture by in the next day or so. She knew his meaning and smiled coyly as she considered how to do that secretly. She was enchanted by him and began to scheme in her mind. She would need to follow protocols to visit openly, with permissions through the senior women's circle. She did not want to deal with that pecking order.

Perhaps a more secret rendezvous in the forest would be better, she thought to herself. Lone Wolf had a similar thought when he noticed her apprehension. As he thought of a nice mossy covered spot under some ancient pine trees not too far west of the river, she smiled at him again. The women beckoned for her to catch up, as it was time to return to village chores. Mahkiwasie reluctantly bid him farewell, her eyes still smiling and looked back at him three times as she scurried to join the group. He stood smiling in total enjoyment of the day, as the wolf reappeared at his side.

11 Sachems

Lone Wolf was glad to be going back to the village after his last ten days trekking eight to ten miles north of the shore. The cooler ocean breeze and the smell of the salt air was a refreshing change from the woodland heat. Although his small hut was set of a good distance from the main congregation of hovels and longhouses he would enjoy the daily bustling of village folks, children playing and women organizing things.

This village located near what is now known as Pine Grove and another one along Saunders Point were part of a series of summer clan villages located throughout the shoreline points, from both sides of the Niantic River up through today's McCook, Crescent, and Black Points, Giant's Neck and even the modern-day Niantic borough. In this early time, there existed perhaps eight clan villages on the Nehantucket shoreline, each supporting perhaps six to eight wigwams. Upwards of twelve to fourteen families of four made up each clan.

The eldest and wisest of each clan, usually the senior male, or sometimes a grandmother would become "sachem," a wise visionary and/or knowledgeable medicine person. Sachems would be the voice of the clan at the larger tribal gatherings and semiannual meeting councils. They would mandate the number of supplies derived from hunting, fishing and crops, to be put into cached storage for the winter. Sachems would make the final decisions and give permissions for maturing men and women to join and mate. Further, sachems would determine the type of work and position within the tribal community an individual would hold, based on his or her aptitude.

The sachem cataloged trade goods such as furs, stone tools, watertight baskets, hunting implements, and the valuable wampum beads made from polished and strung clam shells, all important council items used to keep good relations with neighboring tribes like the Uncas, Mohican, Hammonasset, and Narragansett. At the annual tribal rendezvous, the Nehantucket sachems would trade and form alliances with these neighboring tribal sachems, discussing hunting territories, techniques, and trading the items that each specialized in. In fact, the wampum beads and jewelry were highly sought after amongst the inland tribes. Wampum was valued as almost a type of currency that only the Nehantuckets were known to produce in the best quality.

Sachems praised and rewarded their skilled and accomplished clansmen and women, such as women like Mahkiwasie who was intuitively skilled in plant and herbal healing medicines. Any knowledge about healing was also valued at these rendezvous. Although she was young, her clan sachem would have her accompany him to the gathering for that one purpose.

The head clan sachem was the ultimate authority, answering only to the lead sachem for the entire Nehantucket tribe. At the "new moon" meeting of tribal elders, the clan sachems would discuss and decide important issues regarding the wellbeing of the entire tribe, holding ceremonies and tributes of gratitude to the "Mother Earth," and to the sun and stars for nourishment and knowledge. These elder sachems were the guides for the people.

12 Shelters of the Earth

Before Lone Wolf returned to his own shelter, he would first bring back some game to be shared with the villagers; it was customary not to return "empty-handed!" Venison was the most logical choice for sharing. As Lone Wolf sat quietly thinking about Mahkiwasie, just to the western side of the craggy slope, the wolf growled slightly a few yards to his right and stared downslope. There in the distant shadows of the trees, the silhouette of a six-point buck stood on the game trail, its antlers still draped in velvet.

Lone Wolf slowly arranged his atlatl, affixing the short bone tipped arrow into the haft. It flew accurately to the target piercing the deer's shoulder and heart with a shocking impact that dropped the hundred and fifty pound animal in its tracks. Soon after, Lone Wolf walked into the main village with the dressed animal slung over his shoulders and presented it at the sachem's long house wigwam. Around the fire pit just outside this main long house sat three of the elder women who were working at their individual stone pestles, wives of the village sachem. They yipped with glee as Lone Wolf dropped the deer down and within moments the whole village knew he was back as word spread incredibly fast! The head women of each family would participate in the processing of the deer as portions of the meat were distributed equally as well as the hide, bone and antlers to whomever bid for them instead of the meat.

Wigwam huts, roundish and oval in shape, were proven structures, strong against wind, rain, heat and cold. Frames were made from long straight sapling poles fixed into the ground and bent over to the top and lashed together at that top point creating a dome effect. Often actual rooted saplings were used.

Generally wide strips of birch bark or oak bark were attached in layers, starting at the bottom and overlapped to shed water. Tanned animal hides were also used in the same fashion, or in sections to create smoke flaps and entry doors. These shelters would range from fourteen to sixteen feet wide and the long house style could be as long as twenty five feet with entry openings at each end. The typical wigwam would house two or three families while the bigger structures would house even more. These shelters were just that, mainly for sleeping, to provide warmth in the cooler evenings from the fire pit in the middle of the floor, and for cooking during rainy or stormy days. Mostly they were used by the occupants for sleeping only as the daybreak chores began quite early.

Each person in the village had specific daily chores to accomplish each day. Wild berries would be harvested in season, mostly by womenfolk, both young and old. The necessary task of collecting dry wood required long treks out into the woodland areas where bundles of deadwood were gathered and hauled back to the village encampment. Sometimes larger bundles would be loaded on drag skids while smaller bundles might be strapped onto a hearty individual's back.

Collecting shellfish along the shore and fishing were shared by men and women alike. Netting was fashioned by weaving reeds and attaching stone plummets as weights. Smaller nets would be thrown out into the streambed, while longer nets would be rolled out at the shore of the river or beach. Long tethers were used to haul these nets back in, dragging the abundant catch. Many times, they would chum the nets with remnants of shellfish or bait fish, like mummies found in the brackish shallows, thus creating a feeding frenzy and drawing in large schools of fish. This technique worked well for both fresh water and saltwater areas.

Hooks were fashioned from bone and were used not only with nets but also cast on lines from dugout canoes further out in the bay. Harpoon points were also fashioned from bone. Seals and larger air-breathing mammals were abundant during these ancient times and hunting them required the use of harpoons and long boat canoes.

Before Lone Wolf retired for the night, he walked through the center of the village to the water's edge, while his wolf companion remained on the outskirts. After shedding his pouches and weapons, he dove into the waist deep water and splashed himself clean from the week's events. He then approached his small hut refreshed.

The crossed sticks on the deer hide flap entrance to his wigwam were intact. This symbol was to warn visitors and passersby not to enter. It was a sacrilege to enter a person's abode uninvited; any violation would bear a dark consequence to the thief or perpetrator whose intent was dishonorable. If a person had good intentions such as bearing a gift, however, they could open the flap to place the article just inside safe from the elements. In that case, they would also place or fasten a personal item on the outside of the flap indicating their visit.

On this day Lone Wolf noticed three items: a smooth rounded stone on the ground in front of the flap, a blue jay feather fastened under the stick cross and a short, braided sinew strap. All these indicated that visitors of good intention had come by. He opened the flap and fastened it to the loop tie at the top in the fully open position.

Just inside on the floor was a small sack of grain meal brought by one of the older women who had mothered him since childhood. The next item was a small packet of three quartz arrowhead points fashioned by one or more of the teen youths, potential students hoping to learn his ways of woodsmanship. Finally, there was a short string of polished, blue-streaked wampum beads, more like a bracelet than a necklace. It had come from a secret admirer. He smiled to himself, hoping the admirer was Mahkiwasie.

The wolf companion appeared at the hovel and took up a position just near the door flap laying in the grass. Speaking to him as if he was a human, Lone Wolf said, "Yes I agree, time to rest a while!" At that Lone Wolf retrieved a piece of dried venison from his pouch and tossed it to the wolf. Then he crouched and entered the hut and lay on the woven bed of reeds.

Just before falling off into a deep sleep, he pictured Mahkawasie in his mind's eye with several blue jay feathers braided on each side into the ends of her long hair that hung down beside her thighs. He slept soundly that night in between intervals of consciousness inundated with thoughts of her radiant smile, her slender form and the shape of her legs. He was overcome with infatuation with her essence. As the morning sun peeked through the entrance of his hut, the flap moved in the dancing breeze and touched his face; semi awake he pictured her smiling. He could not stop thinking of her beauty and her essence. For the first time in his life, he was truly smitten.

13 Elders Council

Just after arising and stretching his bones and peeing in the small pit, a dug hole off a way from the hut, Lone Wolf cut a beech twig from a live tree and with his stone axe, frayed both ends of the twig upon the boulder that had an indentation as a pestle just near his hut. The frayed beech twig he used as a toothbrush; it not only cleaned the teeth by its bristles, but served as a bit of flossing action. The beech also has a minty flavor that lasted for quite a while and one could suck and chew the flavorful twigs bark and all.

Lone Wolf contemplated making a fire in his fire pit at the base of the same boulder and just hanging out near his hut for the better part of the day but he then decided to just take a walk through the village closer to his people and watch them bustle about with their activities. It was after all one of his favorite pastimes when he was back from his loner excursions.

He gathered his pouch, knife and axe from inside the wigwam. As he emerged, backing out of the entrance, standing up and fastening his gear at the waist, he sensed a presence. Lone Wolf turned abruptly; there stood a young teenage boy staring at him wide-eyed with a painted gourd rattle in his left hand. Ironically, his timber wolf was nowhere in sight. Silently the boy handed the rattle handle to Lone Wolf. It had the emblem of the tribal elder chief etched into its dried gourd husk.

Lone Wolf knew this meant only one thing: the senior elder sachem and other council members and shamans requested his presence at the main ceremonial circle up on top of the overlook of the bay. These important meeting events took place at the high sun. The boy pointed at the sun just risen over the horizon and motioned with his right arm extended to the position of the sun where it would be at midday, indicating the time of day for Lone Wolf to be at the council circle.

The boy stood silent still mesmerized in being in Lone Wolf's presence, aspiring to emulate him one day, to be like him as a tracker, hunter, and woodland shaman. He had heard many tales of Tibamahgan's adventures and powers, spoken time and time again around the teaching fires. No one else had the ability to walk with a timber wolf! Lone Wolf was renowned for his knowledge of the forest and was a legend as an animal whisperer. Now the boy stood before the legend himself. Still intimidated and in awe, the thought flashed that if he could befriend this great man, perhaps Lone Wolf would teach him these ways.

Trying to acquire the courage to ask, the boy called "Bird" would first try to gain some form of friendship with Tibamahgan thinking he should do it in a roundabout way. Thus the coy boy spoke softly at first, asking Tibamahgan if there was any message he wanted him to relay back to the elders as he was going back to that part of the other village.

Lone Wolf turned, hearing only a part of the boy's question, and stared at the boy as if to look deep into his soul with intense eyes. "What should we call you, my friend?" Lone Wolf asked. The boy spoke softly again. "They call me Omdah, meaning Bird," he said, thumping his hand on his chest. Lone Wolf cocked his head inquisitively, "And why is it they call you this?"

The boy responded, "It is because I can run very fast like the flight of a bird." Lone Wolf glanced at the sky, "Can you do this in the forest or just on open ground?" "I can do it well in the forest and I use the trees and rocks to bounce off and to conceal me so as not to be seen; I become invisible! But only when I need to, mostly just with my friends when we play hunting games with each other."

"And do they catch you?" "No, never, well, not yet anyway!" replied the boy, shyly twitching a stick with his foot. Then the courage came and he asked, "Where is your wolf companion," as he scanned the tree line in a few directions, "I would like to meet him." Lone Wolf stared at Bird deciding that he liked this boy.

Cupping his hands with his thumbs pressed to his mouth he emitted a warbling whistle, with a vibrating pulse by flapping one finger. The tone pierced the air, a sound Bird had never heard before. "He is never very far," said Lone Wolf. "Do you have fear of anything, animals or people?"

The boy Bird thought for a few long moments, then answered by looking straight into Tibamahgan's piercing eyes, "No I do not believe I do. Because I can run swiftly if there's danger. Mostly because, instead of fear, which I'm not sure what that is, I have just great respect for the creatures in the forest and water, especially those bigger than me!"

Lone Wolf smiled, liking this boy's demeanor and style, thinking to himself that this boy, 'Bird,' would make a good hunter. Soon he might be selected as an apprentice to train in the art and skills with the older seasoned men.

Bird with his keen eye or sixth sense suddenly turned and stared directly at the silhouette of Tibamahgan's wolf who appeared at the tree line. For Lone Wolf this also did not go unnoticed. Lone Wolf summoned the wolf to come to the hut with a short wave motion of his hand. With that and a little apprehensiveness, the wolf slowly approached, scenting the boy and simultaneously watching Tibamahgan.

Lone Wolf tossed Wolf a tidbit of dried venison from his possibles pouch and, speaking out loud with an open hand motion, said to the wolf, "This is Omeday, my new young friend." With that Tibamahgan said, "Would you like to walk with me to the village circle? I must head that way soon now and pay respects to folks along the river on the way." The wolf realized that Bird was now an accepted friend of his master, as was Mahkiwasie, "Medicine Girl," whose scent he was also familiar with.

The wolf walked along side Lone Wolf for quite a distance with Bird before vanishing into the tree line as they got closer to the first clan village where there was the bustle of tribal folk. Bird was in his glory to say the least to be walking with the living legend Tibamahgan. Not many, including elders and adult hunters, could befriend Lone Wolf in this way.

However, Lone Wolf had another motive for wandering into this clan village before making his way to the counsel before the noon sun. As mentioned earlier his favorite past time was to just watch the folks, women and children bustling about in their daily routines, prepping skins or grinding grains with their mortises and pestles, children playing hoops or mimicking animals. But this day he was hoping to get another glimpse of Mahkiwasie, or even better to speak with her again and enjoy her radiance and beauty, her beaming smile, and her long hair cascading down her slender body. He needed to find out more about her, hoping she was not claimed or spoken for by another male, or worse, promised to another by the clan elders.

Then a revelation occurred to him as they sat on a large boulder upon a knoll just uphill from the huts. He gazed towards the boy, "Bird, my friend," he asked, putting his hand on the boy's shoulder, "Do you know of the woman Mahkiwasie?"

The boy gleamed with his eyes, and responded eagerly, "Yes, I know of her a little. She is daughter to the midwife woman who raised her from a young girl, as her real mother had gone with the sky people. She became known to me when she helped to heal a hunter man in my village. He was badly injured by a bear while hunting in the north. She made special poultices for him, against the older medicine women's instruction. Now she is renowned for her healing work. She stays alone mostly now, except when she is needed as a healer."

Bird looked at Lone Wolf with a kind of knowingness; Mahkiwasie was not to have a man for her path as a medicine woman forbade it, at that time. "Sometimes I would watch her from a distance when she was off alone gathering herbs. I think she knew I was there," he said bashfully looking at the ground. "She has a great special power. She is favored by the great spirit."

"Are you in need of healing?" Bird asked. "She only lives just around the bend in that grove of pine", he said, pointing the direction. "Her stepmother is a cranky old hag! We kids were all told to stay clear of that one. Mahkiwasie is always nice and smiling!" Lone Wolf smiled a crooked smile while pondering his response.

"Yes, perhaps I may need some healing!" Lone Wolf stared at the boy for a few moments, enchanted with the knowledge he had just received. Then he stood up, strapping his possibles bag over his shoulder, then motioned with his hand to the wolf and said, "Come, let us head to the council."

14 Abenaki

Arriving at the council circle on time at midday Lone Wolf found the Nehantucket elders who represented the local encampments along each side of the river, as well as most of the outer village seniors from all along the east and western outer shorelines. Some from as far as the area known today as eastern Rhode Island and even Fishers Island. Still others were enroute, and those who could not attend would receive word from today's event and the decisions made.

Some were already sitting at the stone circle as the center fire pits embers were hot and lightly smoking upward. To enter the circle, one would first smudge themselves with the dried bundle of wild sage to purify mind and body and to connect with the great spirit of the earth to speak with clarity and insight from the inner knowingness of self. Each invited person's viewpoint was important and respected for the highest good of the villages throughout.

As Bird was not invited by council, but was in attendance with Lone Wolf, Tibamahgan smudged the boy at the entrance and directed him to sit off in the distance outside the circle of stone and with a stern look urged him to stay quiet! Tibamahgan's wolf also remained patiently off in the distance near the tree line.

Bird was indeed honored to be able to come this far, sensing that Lone Wolf's acceptance of his company meant something. He after all was the message bearer under direction of the local shamans. One day he would also be sitting at the stone circle.

Within the hour all members invited and summoned were present and seated. With gourds of fresh spring water placed beside each attendee, the head sachem for Nehantucket opened the ceremony. He first made an offering to the earth spirit by lighting the long pipe adorned with blue and white feathers and short strings of polished wampum shell, with its carvings of birds and woodland bison and bear. The pipe, filled with a blend of dried herbs and tobacco leaf, was passed to each person.

Standing strong with his arms outward, palms up, Eagle Claw, 'Migi-wishkanj,' chieftain and elder sachem, spoke loudly for all to hear. "We welcome with honor you all today, to share in the knowledge of change and the presence of a people who have traveled to us from the far north where the mountains touch the clouds, mountains made of "shingwakekan," pine forest. This small group of people have journeyed many moons and bring with them much sacred knowledge from our ancestral Starr People, gifts of stone and tools from the high mountain land, the medicine of earth energy which cannot be seen. They bring teachings that will benefit all of our people, young and old."

"They have asked for permission to be welcomed into this village, to visit each of your villages and to walk amongst all the Nehantucket. They have asked to learn our ways and share their knowledge and ways, as they are only just a few of many living much farther north than our kindred tribal cousins. They have never shared or seen the bounty of our sovereign waters or seasons."

Eagle Claw turned and gazed at the contingent, ten men and five women with different adornments and body paint. With his gesture of open hand, they stood up, and he proclaimed, "Let us acknowledge the Abenaki!" The sachem then paused his speaking, set his jaw and surveyed each face in the circle. This is when the murmurs began, small talk and questions abuzz. Some stood, looking to glimpse the new arrivals.

Using his ability of clairvoyant intuition, he could sense which elders were open to this introduction or not; and he knew this was an important event for the entire Nehantucket tribal community along the shoreline both east and west. A majority vote was essential.

The Abenaki spoke a variation of the Nehantucket Algonquin language and thus did not require an interpreter. With that in the Grand Sachem's favor, the council members could next introduce themselves and speak one on one with the members of the Abenaki.

Eagle Claw motioned for the Abenaki clan to enter into the circle center. First forward was the head shaman of the group. Next was the lead scout, Nashkid, Lone Wolf's equal. Then came the hunters and protectors, the high medicine women and finally the spirit women, each bearing pouches filled with various implements, herbs, pendulums, and stone points.

The lead scout held a very intriguing long curved wooden branch hewn and shaped equally on both sides of a center hand grip and wrapped with a wide strip of deer hide. Feathers of turkey and eagle adorned the notched ends. A long strip of sinew hung loose from one end with loops. The Nehantucket saw that this scout also had a long narrow pouch strapped at his back with a number of narrow shafts each with three fine feathers affixed at the notched ends. This article alone commanded the attention of most of the Nehantucket men in the circle, each eager to speak to the Abenakis. Council members began to stand and mill around wanting to break protocol.

Eagle Claw stepped to the center of the circle again with both hands up above his head and spoke loudly to regain their attention. "All be seated! Let us hear the Abenaki sachem's words!" With a commanding downward hand gesture around the circle, Eagle Claw quieted the excitement. The members quickly resumed their sitting positions.

Eagle Claw then motioned the Abenaki sachem to speak to the council, turning the center over to him. In broken Algonquin tongue he began to speak first by raising both hands and turning to greet all. He began facing first to the north, next to the east, then to the south and last to the west, "We give thanks to you all, children of great spirit and Mother Earth. We have journeyed far to greet the Nehantucket people of peace and harmony. We come to you in hope to be welcomed, to live amongst you all and to share our ways. We come to learn your ways and experience the bounties and seasons here in your land."

Introducing himself, he thumped his hand on his chest, "I am Kajagen," meaning mountain cat. He glanced at Eagle Claw and received a nod indicating permission to proceed and bring forth other members of his contingent and to show some of their wares. After a simple display of some certain parcels laid out for the council circle to view, Eagle Claw motioned for them to mingle and approach the visitors with their questions and become acquainted.

Eagle Claw was satisfied that the council members were well receptive of these visitors, which in turn would reverberate through the entire village community. He would now appoint certain council members to engage one on one with visitors of like status and corresponding skills.

It did not take but a few moments for the Nehantucket folk to gravitate to the smiling visitors and engage in light conversation, some even waiting in line to get their chance to interact with the Abenaki visitors. The womenfolk at the council gravitated to the Abenaki women immediately, as did the menfolk to the Abenaki men, towards hunters and scouts of similar status.

With a motion of his hand, Eagle Claw summoned Lone Wolf who had remained sitting quietly at his stone bench during the initial bustle. When he stood and approached, Eagle Claw took him by the arm and walked him directly to the visiting scout and thrust them together, interrupting the waiting admirers, but were still staring and looking at the scout's implements and adornments. Forcing the two to lock forearms, Eagle Claw nodded in satisfaction, intuiting that they were of like mind and skill. Pleased with this important introduction, he then turned and walked back to his seat.

Bird saw this from his distance and could not hold his enthusiasm! He ran towards the circle, almost entering the inner section before catching himself just in time, as he was not allowed. He almost fell inward catching himself. As he stumbled back up, he noticed Medicine Girl, Mahkiwasie, sitting at the inner circle way off at the far end. She was invited as an important medicine woman of her clan, but her shyness had kept her in the background during the excitement of so many milling about. Bird snuck up behind her staying outside the circle and made a "psst" sound with his mouth. After the third try, she sensed his presence and turned. Cocking her head when she recognized Bird, she immediately smiled, her eyes beaming. "Bird! What are you up to? How did you come to be here?"

"I came with Lone Wolf. He asked me after I delivered the summoning rattle at sunrise. We are friends now. We spent the early day talking of things. I think he will teach me some of his skills. His wolf guide likes me too!"

Mahkawasie's mouth dropped open in astonishment. Collecting herself, she had a feeling that Lone Wolf might be here, but out of the fifty or so people with even more outside the circle she had not yet spotted him on the opposite side of the large gathering. "Where is he now, Bird?"

Bird pointed to the far side where Lone Wolf was standing with the Abenaki scout. Mahkawasie focused and then stood, her mind whirling as a sensation welled up in her loins. Why she was suddenly enchanted with Lone Wolf she did not know. It was an emotion she could not control. Glancing around and back at Bird, she quickly suppressed the feeling should someone notice. Bird, however, smiled at her knowingly.

15   Ancient Knowledge

Mahkiwasie, now standing, was then noticed by Eagle Claw's wife, the head spiritual woman of the Nehantucket nation. The spirit woman walked straight up to the Medicine Girl who was still facing Bird, now sensing that he knew her emotional body language. Cocking her head slightly and looking at him from the corner of her eyes with embarrassment, she understood this.

Bird saw the prominent spirit woman approaching Mahkiwasie from behind, who recognized her by her long reddish tinged hair that hung down her back well below her hips. Medicine girl was the only young woman with the red tinge and two adorned braids on each side. Bird betrayed the spirit woman's approach with his eyes, and Mahkiwasie turned with a slight startle not expecting any encounters today.

Spirit woman "Nodinosi," which means "spirit of wind," greeted her, smiling. "Mahkiwasie," she spoke softly as she took the Medicine Girl by both hands, "you have been chosen to be liaison to the Abenaki spirit and medicine women, for the Nehantucket people. It is my great honor to introduce you. We ask you to accept this position, to share and learn new ways that they may offer. It is because of your great power and essence that we have chosen you."

Mahkiwasie, never wanting to be any center of attention, nor expecting this task, glanced at the group of Abenaki women then back at Nodinosi, with some apprehension. She then suddenly had a flash within her being that dissolved the apprehension. It was an instant visional insight, clear and vivid.

The vision was as if she was viewing the scene from above herself, as she was sitting amongst the Abenaki women, part of them. "Nodinosi" was there as well. They were singing as one with one harmonic tone that reverberated through her soul. It was a healing and energy harmonic tone: a universal vibration that came from the core of Mother Earth itself. Everything became lighter and translucent at the same time in the vision.

Mahkiwasie suddenly was funneled back to her physical body. Nodinosi was still smiling and holding her two hands. Bird was still motionless just outside the inner stone circle. She blinked her eyes a few times, refocusing on the spirit women. Collecting herself, she nodded, acknowledging the request, and responded, "What must I do, spirit mother?"

Smiling even more Nodinosi responded, "All you must do is come and acquaint yourself with them. All else from this time forward will unfold in its natural way as is meant to be! Come." As she held her by one hand and led the way, Medicine Girl glanced back at Bird off in the outer section of the inner circle. Lone Wolf, now engaged with the Abenaki scout, for some reason glanced over and caught her eye. He smiled.

16 Synchronistic Acquaintance

Mahkiwasie, if not for her importance and quiet power, would not have been selected for this introduction. With Nodinosi at her side they approached the Abenaki women already engaged in small conversation with other Nehantucket women from the east side of the living river. They were the clan women of stature living in the village along the area today known as Millstone Point in Waterford.

As Nodinosi and Mahkiwasie approached, a silence fell in the circle and the Nehantuckets stepped back a bit, respecting the spirit sachem's presence. Nodinosi looked about the women and gestured, bowing her head slightly she spoke softly, "We apologize for the interruption of your questions and excitements with our new friends from the northern mountains."

"I only wish to introduce Mahkiwasie to our Abenaki friends and for her to share with them knowledge in the days to come. Please resume your discussions," she said as she bowed slightly and backed up a step, a gesture intended to humble her status so as to become an equal amongst the group. After a slight pause they resumed the session with everyone starting to speak at once, smiling and laughing as women do.

Mahkiwasie joined in with her beaming smile and was duly noticed by the Abenaki medicine woman who understood the importance of her introduction. She made a point in the next few moments to acknowledge Mahkiwasie one on one. "I am called Ninikiji," she smiled and held out her hand to the not much younger Mahkiwasie. "My name means 'vibrant voice' to our people."

Ninikiji, liking Mahkiwasie immediately, took her hand and pulled her a distance away from the gaggle of women for more of a one-on-one acquaintance, smiling and rolling her eyes a bit at them. That body language itself intrigued Mahkiwasie, setting her at ease with being in a crowd, as she also became more enchanted with Ninikiji in that simple moment.

Little did the Medicine Girl, Mahkiwasie, realize that she was about to embark on a new and powerful life changing energy that would seal her life work for the Nehantucket people. This new acquaintance and friendship with Ninikiji reverberated with a universal synchronicity.

17   Soul Mate

The excitement of the council circle pow-wow wound down later that evening with celebration well into the night, the center bonfire embers glowing hot and surrounded by the last morsels of food set on the hot flat stones. The varieties of food included baked striped bass, clams wrapped in seaweed, and venison strips, as well as a succotash of mashed corn, bean, and squash. White breast of turkey and turtle were also part of the festive feast.

The villagers who remained in support outside of the inner stone circle began to retreat back to their wigwam hovels, while members of the inner circle slowly retired nearby with their groups under the stars if they came from a distance. They would prepare to trek back to their clan villages over the next few days if they chose.

Others, including the Abenaki, were invited to sleep in or camp just outside of the three "long houses" located at the main village near the point. These were very wide and long wigwam style structures of twelve feet wide and upwards of thirty paces long. Two or even three cook fire pits were situated in the center floors of the long houses and simple lashed stick cots were fixed back-to-back along each side of the long walls. Some were protrusions of the actual framework of the structure utilizing the natural branches of the heavy sapling frame.

Lone Wolf, Mahkiwasie, and even Bird chose to remain at the long houses rather than trek the mile or so back to the clan village or their personal hovels. Daybreak would bring more interaction with their new Abenaki acquaintances as they were so directed by the elder leaders Eagle Claw and Nodinosi. Sleep did not come easily for Lone Wolf nor for Mahkiwasie as they both were very set in their personal solitude style routines.

Before daybreak as the new morning sun poked over the shimmering water horizon, they simultaneously encountered each other at the fire circle. Lone Wolf had a hankering for some of the venison, and Mahkiwasie craved the tasty salted baked sea bass for breakfast.

Lone Wolf, very intimidated by the Medicine Girl's beauty and essence, fumbled slightly for some words, surprised to find her already sitting there. All she could do at first was to smile with her starry eyes and her mouth open in awe of his appearance in the early morning with no other people or peers and, certainly, no crowds.

"I saw you from across the circle last evening," she said in her quiet tone. He said, "Yes and I you," as he gestured for permission to sit next to her. She motioned in approval, sliding over slightly on the wooden log bench.

An awkward long silence took place with only mourning doves cooing in the distance and a fat grey squirrel rustling at the tree line. He munched his venison, and she her piece of fish. Then each started to speak at once, not once, but twice! They resolved the awkwardness with a simple shared laugh, taking in each other's facial features.

"How do you find these people from the north mountains. Mahkiwasie?" Lone Wolf was finally able to blurt out.

She thought momentarily, then almost in a whisper she said, "My sense of them is of goodness, a high vibration and intent. The woman Ninikiji is of good spirit and power. I am to now be her guide during their first weeks here with our people."

Lone Wolf's eyebrows lifted, "I am also to be a guide and companion, to the Abenaki shaman scout, he who is called Nashkid." He called him Nashkid, which is the Algonquin work for Hawkeye.

She touched Lone Wolf's forearm impulsively, now being a little more comfortable with her internal sense and the clear essence of their unspoken attraction. "May I ask of the whereabouts of your wolf companion?" He smiled and knowingly scanned the tree line. With a pointed cross hand motion toward the trees Lone Wolf said, "He is never far. Would you like meet him?" Smiling again and looking straight at her eyes in a playful challenge, he spoke again, "I will summon 'Wolf' to share our breakfast."

Mahkiwasie, a little concerned said, "Yes, I would like that, so long as I am not his morning meal!"

Lone Wolf, with two fingers, shrilled out a short piercing whistle, that surprised Mahkiwasie. She began to scan the tree line apprehensively.

Lone Wolf broke the silence, "I saw you as well at the circle and I wanted to come and sit with you. It was just before Eagle Claw chose me to meet with the Abenaki named Nashkid."

"Yes," she said, "I do not care for so many people at once. I saw my little friend Bird and he made me more relaxed by his friendship. Then Nodinosi brought me to meet the Abenaki women. We spoke well into the sunset and then I found a little spot under a father pine over there and tried to sleep with my rabbit skin covering. I cannot sleep amongst other people well."

"I share the same as you," said Lone Wolf, "to sleep amongst others so close is not restful for me. Is that the same for you?"

"Yes," she replied, looking down at the fire pit and poking the embers with a stick, hesitating as she picked her words. "I don't know why I share this with you, only in hope that you can understand. Being so close to them I get sensations from their spirit relations who have passed over. They keep coming into my mind uninvited, speaking all at once and making noise in my head. So, I must be alone and quiet, and need to listen to the peepers and trees talking."

Lone Wolf suppressed an urge to put his arm around her and hold her, saying "I deeply understand this for you." He allowed his shoulder to touch hers. He then raised his hand and with his waving motion to the tree line, "Wolf" began to walk cautiously toward them, yet remaining ten feet outside the stone circle. Tibamahgan tossed the timber wolf a morsel of venison.

"Mahkiwasie, give Wolf a piece of your fish from your hand; do it like this," he said as he held her hand and together, they tossed the fish to land just a few feet from her. It was the perfect excuse to hold her hand and touch her soft skin. "Now try again, only this time just hold it out with your palm up like so," Lone Wolf said, as he demonstrated with his own open hand.

Wolf cautiously approached her open hand as Tibamahgan spoke in a soft tone, commanding the wolf to be gentle. It was a large and beautiful animal. Seemingly not so wild and fierce as one would expect, it watched and obeyed Tibamahgan's every command and understood his voice tones. Mahkiwasie was apprehensive. Still holding the fish out, with eyes closed she felt the wolf's tongue gently lift it from her palm.

Tibamahgan spoke to her softly. "From here forward Wolf will always respect you. It is an honor for you and him now, to be of acquaintance. If you take my hand, he will know your essence as my friend and he will watch over you when he is nearby. He knows your scent and your kind essence."

She was again in awe with this encounter this sunny morning. Her thoughts were of how she never expected any of this to manifest and unfold in this way. The mere fact that no one else was around seemed magically arranged somehow too, as if everything was meant to be.

Putting aside her timidness, she took his hands in hers, looked into Tibamahgan's eyes and then over at the timber wolf standing there knowingly. When their hands touched, Tibamahgan and Mahkiwasie both felt a surge that cannot be described, the "prana" heat from both of their palms pulsed back and forth, with shared intent. Within the silence of this moment, a powerful spiritual bond was sealed between them both and included Tibamahgan's wolf. It would profoundly connect their lives forever.

Within the next moments, breaking and shattering the silence, Wolf alerted his attention to one side with a short huff. Into view, rubbing his eyes, Bird stumbled into the outer circle. He was a surprising yet welcome interruption as they both just looked at each other, cocked their heads and smiled at his presence.

18 Shared Interaction

Over each of the next eight days, both Medicine Girl and Lone Wolf, as well as others of the Nehantucket met with their appointed contingents of the Abenaki. Over this time they introduced them to the bounties along the shore and river, sharing the techniques used in net and bone hook fishing, basket weaving, herbal and medicinal plants and poultices along with cultivated planting fields and mound techniques.

The wigwam shelters, some of which were in the process of being constructed, were intriguing as they visited the clan villages up and down both sides of the Nehantucket living river, walking the well beaten trails and pathways.

For two of the days, Lone Wolf and a few hunter braves took the Abenaki male scouts seven or so miles inland following game trails and hunting game. Some of the younger agile boys were allowed to come as part of their life training. Bird was among them as Lone Wolf's protege.

As they came upon larger tracks and sign of elk still grazing the lush grasses in the lower wetland and the mossy ledge tops that trapped fertile topsoil, the hunt was organized. The Abenaki shaman scout described how they would ordinarily stalk the prey until getting close enough to utilize a hunting implement.

But not this day. The Nehantucket would organize themselves on either side along the tops of the steep ledges, while the younger would form a line with spears in hand and drive the game into the narrow wetter low section between the ledges. This was done after they located the fresher tracks or visual sighting of the herd.

The hunters used a series of signals, one of which was to cup both hands tightly together with two thumbs pressed to the lips. By gently blowing air through the thumbs, the hollow palms vibrated a tone not unlike a barred owl. By slightly opening the lower fingers, a higher or lower pitch tone was emitted. A rapid alternating tone echoing through the woods meant the game was on the move toward the ledge ravine.

The silence was broken as Lone Wolf and Nashkid, the lead Abenaki scout, sat twenty feet apart on the precipice. Three of the herd of twelve or so elk veered and stopped under the steep ledge just below their position.

It appeared they would bound up the narrow lateral game trail and over the top of the ledge rock. One of the three was the dominant bull, stopping to let the females, the sub herd members and yearlings catch up.

Lone Wolf prepared his atlatl by placing the short dart shaft in its grooved end. The angle for his shot was not clear enough yet, not even for the spear.

He gazed over at Nashkid, who motioned for Lone Wolf to wait still. Nashkid drew an arrow from his quiver strapped to his back in one smooth motion with his right hand. Affixing the notched end to the bow gut string he raised it up and drew back the arrow shaft almost to his eye.

The arrow flew straight, clean, and silent. It pierced the vital heart section of the bull elk with a shocking impact. The bull staggered a few steps back down slope and fell. The two other elk were unaware of what had just occurred but, moved down slope slightly as well, as if to the follow the downed animal.

Lone Wolf, now with a clear shot, launched his shaft with a deadly accurate shot of his own, striking one of the two elk in the vital shoulder section, penetrating the lungs with the shaft's razor-sharp quartz tip.

The third elk bull bolted back down hill and charged off into the thicker, taller sweet grass, where both downed animals, now immobile, lay a few yards from each other. Nashkid and Lone Wolf descended upon them with knives drawn to open a slit at the neck to hasten the bleed out and quickening the journey of the spirits of the animals into the next dimension. Lone Wolf made the deeper tone call with his cupped hands to signal the other members of the hunting party.

Lone Wolf then opened the belly of his elk and knifed out the liver and took a bite holding it up toward Nashkid; the Abenaki not knowing exactly what this gesture meant. The look of confusion in his eyes told Lone Wolf that he did not understand.

"You must always release the animal's spirit in this way, to give it thanks for the life that it has just given to us to sustain and nourish our people and our way," Lone Wolf said. "By doing this we allow this great beast to be reborn again. Only next time he will be just a little smarter!" He smiled with the red blood dripping on his chin. Nashkid slit open the other elk's belly and performed the same offering.

After a moment of contemplative silence, Lone Wolf reached over to admire the long bow and longer shafted arrows with the three feathers at the notched end glued on with hardened pine sap. He had not ever seen anything like this powerful implement before. Impressed with its accuracy and its longer range he was slightly in awe of it but did not want to disclose or reveal his fascination.

Nashkid could sense that Lone Wolf was intrigued with the bow as he caught him studying it multiple times. With a simple expression of acknowledgment and without words he handed the bow and quiver of arrows to Lone Wolf with an abrupt throughsting gesture. Still with no words, Lone Wolf looked at Nashkid with approval, nodding his head in acceptance. Looking at it from a distance is one thing, but to feel it in hand, taking in all details was an enlightening experience.

It would be a sacrilege in both the Nehantucket and the Abenaki cultures to touch, borrow, or steal a man's tools or weapons without permission. These things were personal implements that held the power and energy of the individual.

The same is true regarding the possibles pouch that all native braves carried that contained their personal things that enhanced their spiritual connections. Most men and women would carry these "medicine" pouches with collections of small things such as sacred quartz crystals, ornamental shell, animal claws or feathers, and dried herbs, all of which would bear deep meaning and power for the individual. Within Lone Wolf's pouch amongst his smooth round stones, bear claw necklace, and power crystals were his sharp quartz shaft points.

Raising the bow, Lone Wolf drew the string of animal intestine partially back as he had seen Nashkid do, testing the pull of it. Nashkid reached over, teaching Lone Wolf to lock his left elbow straight and outward at about eye level. Then Nashkid showed him, with no arrow, how to pull the gut string back using only three fingers.

After a few tries, Lone Wolf smiled with the feel of it. Next Nashkid placed an arrow with the notched end into the gut showing Lone Wolf how to hold the bow horizontally out in front of himself so the arrow can rest on top his gripped fore finger and then to raise the assembly back up to eye level with the notched arrow end between his right forefinger and two middle fingers, while all three fingertips were hooked on the gut string.

Embarrassed and laughing at the same time, Lone Wolf fumbled with the procedure multiple times until he mastered it. Over the next hour he learned to shoot the arrow with some degree of accuracy.

Nashkid eyed the atlatl weapon and its various lengths of shafts. In return for the bow and arrow lesson, Lone Wolf then took the time to reach Nashkid the technique of the use of the atlatl.

19 Carnivores

It was a good day of hunting for the other members as well. The evening brought the hunting party members to a closer friendship as they sat around the campfire, swapping stories of the day's event and chipping new points from quartz, which was another art form in itself.

They would razz and jest with each other too, keeping in good humor for the younger boys to learn the importance of camaraderie.

It was the new bow and arrow that mesmerized most everybody in the group. Nashkid demonstrated it a few times before darkness fell upon them. At the fire they passed it around, each testing its pull and admiring the technique used to develop the ability to use it with skill, agreeing about the required practice that would take.

Early the next morn, just before sunrise, the quietness of the night was shattered. Barred owls or even a distant cooing of a black bear were normal nighttime sounds emitting over the crickets, peepers, and bull frogs. This night was quite different, however. The bright moon was waning in almost full splendor, illuminating the midnight sky to nearly daylight. The swishing clouds put on an immaculate display of color, with reds, pinks, and greenish blue hues. The stars were not quite as bright as usual, overcome by the moon's sheen.

The eerie howl of wild wolves shattered the morning dawn, they were not far off, it could be a pack of six or eight. The scent of the day's elk kills, now quartered and hanging up in a tree for the night, were the cause of the wolves' approach. Wolves, in this time were immense animals, standing waist high to any human and weighing over one hundred and fifty pounds, or more! These dire wolves were swift and fearless, coy, and stealthy when hunting in their packs. The alpha, often male, sometimes female, would organize the entire campaign.

Tibamahgan's tamed dire wolf companion appeared at the edge of the camp; his silhouette clearly stood out, to the alarm of some of the other hunters who were now clamoring to gather their spears and weapons.

Lone Wolf whistled to his wolf, and with a motion of his hand, summoned the animal to his side. Then the other men realized that this wolf was the legendary one who accompanied the shaman scout everywhere. The tamed wolf took a defensive position at the camp's outer edge, and stood with its back to Lone Wolf, at full alert, peering intensely into the woods. It was as if the two were of the same mind, an inner intuitive communication and a body language that only occurs with the deepest of bonds. While it occurs in all of earth's creatures, it has unique characteristics in each species.

To Nashkid, this was startling, for very rarely does this type of communication happen between different species. This was one of those rare occasions when he had ever witnessed a bond between a timber wolf and a human. Wolves were only to be respected and avoided as predators with humans on the menu!

The silence in the air became palpable. The peepers stopped their calls, the members of the hunting party were in a circular pattern around the center fire facing outward, the fire now raging higher in flame fueled with the last of the long, dried shafts. They would be used as a last resort if need be. Fire could, at the very least, fend off the wolves if they would not vacate the area despite being out matched and outnumbered.

Bird, a bit apprehensive, sidled up to Lone Wolf, with his spear and sling shot in hand. "What should I do if one comes in?" he asked.

Lone Wolf put his hand on Bird's shoulder briefly, "Stay next to me or Nashkid, show no fear, become the dominant alpha wolf. Stand tall and do not break the animals gaze," said Lone Wolf, as he put his two fingers to Bird's eyes to demonstrate.

Lone Wolf looked at Nashkid, who nodded in affirmation standing at the ready with the bow and two arrows stuck in the ground at his feet. He had had encounters with dire wolves before in the green mountains, but only with one or two at a time, mostly an adult female defending her pups or over a fresh kill.

The moonlit night was a large advantage for the Nehantucket hunting party. The forest trees were illuminated and there was virtually no underbrush to obscure vision for a considerable distance. Movement or silhouettes could be seen twenty thirty yards out in this moonlight. It was the same for the wolves as well, with their keen sense of smell added.

Tibamahgan's wolf began to growl, low, deep tones. It stared out in one direction, then shifted his gaze slightly to another spot. The fur on his shoulders hackled up as he crouched into an attack position, as silhouettes appeared in the tree line.

The alpha, dominant male of the pack, approached our domesticated wolf. They circled each other clockwise, then counterclockwise with fierce aggressive snarling and gnashing of teeth. The wild alpha had not expected this type of encounter. It was one thing to have never encountered the dangerous humans, but to be challenged by one of his own kind, ready for the fight as well, was an entirely new experience. In addition, there was the fire, the flame, the smoke, the humans wielding this new substance at the ends of shafts.

The domestic wolf was slightly larger in stature. Well fed, healthy, faster and angry, he was unafraid and willing to fight to protect his master. He had seen how his mother fought viscously against the flat-faced bear when he was a pup. All this was sensed by the wild alpha through the two animals' body language.

Other members of the wild pack drew closer still, glancing back at the alpha for approval to charge in. Just then, a flaming spear tip launched by one of the older Nehantucket braves pierced the front paw of one of the younger wolves, causing it to yelp in pain. The wolf retreated, to be followed by another yelp as the arrow of Nashkid's bow found its mark. It pierced the hind quarter of yet another younger wolf who'd decided to venture into the kill zone of the encircled humans.

The cries of pain from the two wounded wolves echoed out into the moonlit night creating an eeriness as sound bounced throughout the knolls and dells of the forest.

The wild alpha and the domestic wolves were still in pirouette with each other, standing ground, but not engaging. At that moment, there was a flash of gnashing teeth and with a furious movement, the humans' wolf had a vicious throat hold on the wild alpha. It would have only taken but a quick jerk to rip him open.

There was a purposeful tense moment when the domestic released his death grip. The message clear, the wild alpha backed up a few paces to acknowledge a bewildered defeat.

Yelping sounds of the wounded were now distant, the alpha howled out a tone signaling the rest of its pack to retreat; and the six remaining dire timber wolves disappeared back into the tree line.

The sunrise was now just breaking the horizon. The braves remained in the defensive circle. They all glanced at each other silently while remaining in heightened vigilance.

20 Last Behemoth

The younger boys, including Bird, restocked the fires from within the circle, whispering in excitement about what had just occurred and the bravery of Tibamahgan's domestic wolf.

They all worked together to pack the meat, skins, and antlers onto drag sledges made from sapling bows to begin the trek back to the village. With this cargo, it would now require all of two more days of travel.

Some of the younger boys, including Bird, who was in the lead, mostly due to being Lone Wolf's recognized friend, would now venture ahead as a scout party. They were instructed to remain only a few hundred yards ahead from the main contingent of braves hauling the meat.

These scouts crept up to a ledge peak to scan downslope at a small valley of grasses and brushy meadows. Bird raised his hand in a fist formation for them to stop! He could not believe what he was looking at, nor did he recognize the creatures in his view.

He motioned for the other boys to crawl up to his position quietly. With their faces painted and their spears at the ready, they crept up to the edge of the ledge. A silence of awe overcame them, each with mouth agape! Still on their bellies, they slowly retreated just a few yards into a dell and formed a huddle. In whispered tones, and looking to Bird for answers, they tried to reason as to what these large animals were.

Bird crept up to the ledge again, then he retreated to his crouched friends. He whispered, "I have heard grandfathers' tales of these creatures. They say they are dangerous for a man or even for five men to kill. They are called "Mammototh" and just one can feed a whole village!"

One of the other boys, excited, crept back up to gaze again upon the herd of eight of these huge, massive, hairy creatures. He was joined by the rest who stared in amazement.

As we know today, these animals were the descendants of the great mastodons that roamed in large herds throughout these grassland valleys. This small herd of eight would in fact be known today as "woolly mammoths."

Even at that time, it was rare for humans to come upon these animals, with their massive hulk, ivory tusks as long as a man, and long powerful trunks that were as agile as any human hand. Even for the boys, in their time, these animals were just things of lore around the campfire.

Bird directed two of the boys to quietly report back to the older men of the hunting party and lead Lone Wolf and other senior hunters back to this spot with the utmost stealth and care, knowing that to hunt these mammoth animals and to take down just one would be a massive undertaking, involving, at best, ten of the most experienced braves. They would have set up a gauntlet of spear wielding hunters to try to herd and corner them into a "narrow." To corner one onto a ledge or a in bog could prove fatal for the braves if the mammoth decided to charge. A lethal spear thrust would have to pierce the tough leathery hide and find a vital organ. Even then, other bulls in the herd could and would charge into the puny humans to defend one of their own.

Bird recalled these points from the tales at the campfire. He now was excited just to have been the one to locate these woolly mammoths, or "Mammototh" as the Nehantucket pronounced it, and for the older experienced hunters to bear witness and accredit these young braves for their find: these massive animals, these things of campfire lore!

Within twenty minutes, the two boys hooted out their return with six of the older braves, including Tibamahgan and Nashkid. They cupped their hands to their mouths, imitating the barred owl. Bird motioned for the men to creep up onto the ledge's peak. Lone Wolf and Nashkid creeped up on either side of Bird. It was a sight to behold!

The best part of two hours passed in viewing the immense creatures. The two braves overseeing the cached meats were relieved and able to view the mammoths as well. None had ever seen these creatures before!

Finally, the woolly mammoth herd moved off further upland through the brushy meadows and into parts of the tree line. They were likely beginning their season of migration, grazing as much of the lush grasses and brushy vegetation as possible. Because of the high fiber in this area this particular season, they had chosen to linger here along the shoreline grasses and forested meadows much longer than usual, rather than moving through unnoticed, as in previous seasons.

The thick woolly hair that essentially covered their entire bodies helped them to adapt to the then colder seasonal climate in what we now call New England, even specifically in southern "Konnekticut," meaning "beside the long tidal river," now known as southeastern Connecticut.

They could forage proficiently through deep snows by swishing their tusks side to side and grabbing the frozen grasses with their long trunks. But this work in winter months took much energy and would burn much needed nutrients which were hard to come by in winter months.

Although their populations had been stressed and in decline for many years, adaptations had enabled them to graze the saplings as well. Their teeth and metabolisms became better suited to digest the brushy vegetation, enabling them to forage on the bark and branches of certain trees and saplings.

This small herd was most likely one of the last that these Nehantuckets would ever encounter. Only a few visionary shamans would have foreseen the great woolly mammoth's decline.

The hunting party was honored to have been able to witness these mammoths. They were looking forward to telling the stories of this encounter amongst their village kin, all thanks to a few young boys, led by Bird.

Lone Wolf leaned into him on the ridge, and whispered, "I believe it is time to elevate you to a more powerful name. I shall call you, Mammototh Scout." Nashkid nodded in agreement.

Afterward, the hunting party discussed organizing a strategy to take down one of the behemoths. They asked Lone Wolf his mind on the idea. Lone Wolf pondered for a bit, something inside him sensed a knowingness of the mammoth's plight. He looked at the cargo of elk and answered, "It will not be so, we have no need or want."

21 Down Time

The hunting party made their way back to the village by a slightly alternate trail just a couple miles west of the trail through "Oswegatchie" from which they had come. This less-used trail led them through the area now known as Four Mile River, with its vibrant brook teaming with trout, salmon, and sea bass that would spawn in these upland streams that connect to the ocean.

Word spread throughout the clan villages of their return with the bounty of fresh elk to be dried and shared with all. The hunters were eager to each tell their versions of the elk hunt, the wild wolves encounter, Nashkid's bow and arrow and then the biggest adventure story of the woolly mammototh herd. Woven into story was Bird's ascension into manhood as Mammototh Scout, all due to his disregard of the instructions not to venture too far ahead.

It was not an ordinary hunting excursion by any means. The main contingent dragging the elk cargo continued ahead back to the village. Soon they reached the main shoreline trail intersection near what is known today as the 'Old Stagecoach Road' in Old Lyme alongside the Four Mile River streambed.

Lone Wolf, Nashkid, and Bird decided to hang back and take the eastern trail toward "Pattagansett Lake" and venture back onto the trail in the area known today as Flanders. This trail would bring them through the "Gorton Lake" region and back into "Saunders Point" and "Pine grove."

After some discussion, Lone Wolf, to avoid any fanfare and hoopla with the villagers, simply stated that he would return to his hovel to reflect on the excursion in private, as was his custom. Mammototh Scout and Nashkid, now of like mind and position, both recognized Lone Wolf's point of view and decided to adopt this custom. Being shaman scouts required them to be somewhat humble regarding their skills.

Lone Wolf was eager to find and be with Mahkiwasie. Now that he was near the village his thoughts of her were more prevalent.

Nashkid also was missing his secret love and his own romantic encounters. As it turns out Nashkid and Ninikiji, spirit woman of the Abenaki, were connected romantically, not openly, but as secret soulmates.

This was revealed during a quiet discussion between Lone Wolf and Nashkid at their last campfire along the Pattagansett River. Mammototh Scout had just taken a walk to relieve himself. The domestic timber wolf lay crouched nearby waiting for more roasted elk strips.

Nashkid was impressed by the wolf and the last few days' events as a whole. He finally asked how Lone Wolf came to be with this wolf. After Lone Wolf's brief story, Nashkid lay back using the log as a headrest and asked, "Is she your woman?"

Lone Wolf raised an eyebrow and quickly Nashkid said, "I mean the one with the long hair down to here," tapping his buttocks. "She is with my woman Ninikiji, teaching each other their ways of healing. She is special as is mine, with gifts of the Starr People."

"Ninikiji comes to me in secret. Sometimes at night or, early morn before the sun. She knows when I think of her, and she just comes!" he said. "Is that how it is with you and…" he hesitated, trying to remember.

"Mahkiwasie!" Lone Wolf blurted out, "…not yet." Lone Wolf mumbled, poking the fire with a stick. "Me thinks she will be soon…" he broke off as he stared at his wolf.

"Ahh…," Nashkid nodded knowingly, "You, my friend," pointing his two fingers, "should bring her something special, something for when you are away. Then she can feel you; she will come to you. You will only have to picture her here," he said, as he pointed to his temple, smiling. "And feel her here!" he said, thumping his chest.

Lone Wolf intuitively squinted, half smiling at his new friend. Nashkid reached into his pouch and pulled out a clear three-inch-long quartz crystal of about an inch round.

He held it in his palm outward to Lone Wolf. Tibamahgan took it and held it up to the sky, it was clear through and sparkled with its glassy texture. The sunlight seemed to magnify through it with a focused beam. He looked at Nashkid with awe.

"This is now yours my friend," said Nashkid. "I gift this to you for all that we have shared and the bond that we now have. I know the burden you keep inside."

"Put your thoughts of Mahkiwasie into this and gift it to her with no words. She will come to you! It will hold the power for her and you to be of one mind, she will come to you whenever you think of her, as Ninikiji comes to me," said Nashkid.

Wolf went on alert as Mammototh Scout appeared from the tree line. The men spent this last night under the stars, if only to wind down from the hunt and to gather some quiet time before returning to the bustle of the village clans.

This had always been Lone Wolf's routine after a long stint in the wilderness. It was a form of meditation to prepare him for the energy of the groups of inquisitive people. It was the same for Nashkid back north in the green mountains. He would also need some quiet time.

As for young Bird, or Mammototh Scout, he had learned much over these last days and, unlike Lone Wolf and Nashkid, he was eager to return and share his stories. Waking early, it only took two hours for the group to make the final trek into the village.

22 Unseen Realms

Mahkiwasie and Ninikiji had spent the last four days in each other's company. Each day was spent trekking out to various locations gathering herbs, plants, roots, berries, leaves, and barks. Each variety was taken back to Mahkiwasie's mortise and pestle stone that she kept just outside of her wigwam hovel. There they would grind the herbs into medicinal poultices, pastes, or powders with shared recipes and instructional teaching of the medicinal applications.

Ninikiji took up residence with the Medicine Girl overnights in which the evening campfire discussions ranged from serious herbal comparisons to just light giddy giggling that especially occurred when some of the neighboring women joined the evening fire circle. When the others arrived, they would promptly put aside the remedies, as these things were held as private and sacred knowledge.

On one afternoon, at a quiet secluded bend upriver at the very same location where Mahkiwasie first met Tibamahgan and his wolf, the two women sat on the smooth ledge rock to take a break from the gathering of elderberries. There was a moment of absolute quiet between the two women who had become very bonded as if they were sisters from a previous lifetime reunited. Both were very "old souls."

Staring out over the water, her eyes focused on something distant, Mahkiwasie struggled internally with revealing what she was about to say. Because of the bond they had developed and insights they had shared, she now felt compelled to break the silence.

"It is not only herbs I use to heal," she said softly, holding both of her hands outward toward Ninikiji. She closed her eyes and the two women touched hands as Ninikiji instinctively extended hers.

"When I walk amongst the plants in the forest," she said, "They speak to me. They illuminate with a brightness, and then a feeling of warmness in my hands when I gather them. The trees talk to me; they tell me where the patches of herbs or roots that are needed are."

Ninikiji felt a surge of heat emerge from Medicine Girl's hands, a vibration passed through her as well. Medicine girl was in a trance-like state, her eyes remained distant as she spoke. Ninikiji closed her eyes to allow more of the warm vibrational sensation. Even she had never felt this type of connection.

Deeply centered and focused, Ninikiji intuitively sensed an urge to return energy back to Mahkiwasie. She opened her eyes slightly. As they remained out of focus, the hues of yellows, pinks, greens, and light blues emitted and flowed back and forth between the two. These sensations emitted from their light bodies, spiraling and flowing from the solar plexus of each.

Ninikiji's body became lighter. She felt as if she could levitate if so desired. No words were spoken in this transcendental moment. Never had Ninikiji felt this simple vibration or state of being. Nor had Medicine Girl ever felt the energy returned with such purity.

They both chose to remain touching hands with the light flowing between them for a few more moments, until the tears that streamed down Ninikiji's face dripped onto their bonded warm hands and brought them suddenly back to physical consciousness. They were tears of sheer joy, and she could summon no words. Mahkiwasie smiled her beaming smile in full knowingness of what had just occurred.

"You see now? In this way is how we heal them, in this way is how the herbs want to work."

"When they come to me or, if I am summoned to them, I put hands on them and know what the body needs, what the soul needs and where the deeper cause of the pain is rooted."

"We see what is blocking their center. We can many times clear out the dark energy with our hands and touch. Then the herbs can do their work on the body's wounds. It is then the herbs come alive in this same way."

"I say 'we' because you also have this power within you. It takes no effort, just your intent to do so. Now, do you see?"

Still with tears streaming, Ninikiji summoned her words, "Oh yes, Mahkiwasie, my sister! I now know! It has been within all this time. I give you much thanks for opening it to me. Please let us share again, I think I shall need some practice!"

Medicine girl spoke softly, "Come. We should rest now." Taking Ninikiji's hand, Mahkiwasie led her down to the soft white sand and had her lay with a basket under her head. "Rest now, for a bit. Your first attunement is exhausting for the body."

Medicine girl sat in the sand cross legged and hummed a little tune, chanting in her way to give thanks to the universe for her new friend and the chance to share her magic power with a person of like mind and bond.

Her thoughts suddenly shifted to Lone Wolf, his handsomeness and physique, his demeanor and quiet strength. She reflected back to the morning's ceremony circle when he had touched her hand and the surge of energy that flowed from him into her core. His entire essence swept over and filled her again on the sand.

Ninikiji fell into a deep out of body sleep. She dreamed, although what seemed like a dream felt more like a message of instruction. In her dream, she hummed into a long hollowed wooden tube, creating a low harmonic vibrational sound. She could hear the sound in the background, now with another entity humming into it.

Medicine girl appeared facing her sitting cross-legged and she began to sing her single note from her vocal chords at a higher octave. It was in perfect harmony with lower earth tones in the background. Another human entity took up the vocal tones as well.

Finally, and most important, was a large round singing bowl made from pure rose quartz crystal. Another human entity was circling the smooth outer rim of this bowl with a wooden mallet. The vibrational sound emitted from this sacred crystalline bowl was of such a deep penetrating effect, it's tones alone would raise the vibration of every cell of the body, mind, and spirit.

The dream continued with the two instruments and vocals, as they emitted vibrational tones that harmonized at different octaves. Together, the sound vibrations penetrated, raised and elevated their bodies as they brought both women's frequencies higher. Yet still, they remained grounded to earth in some way. Mahkiwasie was enchanted and smiling in the dream.

Suddenly she was in a vacuum vortex being sucked back into consciousness. Slowly she returned to a half-dazed, yet awakened state, there in the sand. It was clear that Medicine Girl of the Nehantucket was chosen; the synchronicities that brought them together made it so. Ninikiji knew exactly what she needed to share with Medicine Girl, she would now just need to present it at the perfect time in the perfect secluded setting to keep the knowledge sacred.

As she regained her focus directly on Mahkiwasie sitting in the sand, the dream message clearly indicated that Medicine Girl was one of the very select few to receive this ancient Abenaki sacred knowledge of vibrational sound.

Confirmed by the dream vision, Ninikiji was excited and eager now to reveal this technique to her. "Mahkiwasie, there is something very special I now need to bring to you. It comes from the Starr People." Medicine Girl turned from her sitting position looking over the river and smiled broadly again. In a deeply rooted knowingness she whispered, "Yes, I am ready."

23 Paying Forward

The two medicine women lingered on the sandy river spot for almost another hour just relaxing and splashing in the water a bit to cool from the sundry hot day. As early evening approached, lifting the humidity a bit, they headed back to Mahkiwasie's wigwam hovel.

There they would set the fire and prepare the evening meal of crab, dried flounder, and sweet grass. It would be wrapped in seaweed and steamed to perfection over the coals of the fire. With a few clams on the side and a flavorful pine needle tea, this easy meal would set the night's sleep deep and out of body.

Other villagers who were engaged in fishing from their dugout canoes, or collecting shellfish along the abundant shoreline beaches or, crabbing in the rocks, would consolidate their catches, to barter and share the bounties with the clan elders and shaman who contribute in many other ways.

This community lifestyle, beneficial to all, allowed for no need or want. No one would ever go hungry or without shelter. One could simply approach another familiar wigwam fire and be invited to join without question and share a story or two. Perhaps they would share a technique which they used in their skill trade.

Within the clan villages meals were often prepared as a group event in one fire pit centrally located within the hub of the complex. The catch of the day, together with roots, leeks, berries and gathered herbs, were ground or mixed to go further and last for at least a day or two. Many times, portions of these meals would be delivered to the shaman's or healer's hovels. This was the case this evening for Medicine Girl and Ninikiji. Wrapped tightly in seaweed, the ingredients were placed at the wigwam entrance to become part of their more private meal together.

The greater part of the clan would gather around the center fire pit as a group to eat and socialize and organize the chores for the upcoming days, while still others would work on nets, spear points, and tools.

A large pit was dug nearby to discard waste products, bone, shells, and the like. Sand was placed over the daily waste in layers so as not to attract unwanted scavengers and predators. Peeing near the village was forbidden, a path led away from the hovels to smaller pits used for the purpose of relieving oneself, also covered with sand after use.

This day, as Ninikiji awoke at sunrise, she emerged from the hovel to find Medicine Girl sitting at the fire pit facing the east in deep meditation. Apparently, she silently woke before the sun, stirred the coals of the fire's embers, and embraced the sun's energy as it poked above the bay's horizon. Upon the sun's fullness laying low upon the horizon, her meditation pulls in the full power of the earth's vibration, and she is connected, centered, and lifted.

This was and had been Medicine Girl's daily ritual since she was a young girl. Even on a rainy morning it would be the same except she would remain within the hovel. Ninikiji, not wanting to disturb Medicine Girl, slipped out of the village toward the other main village where members of her people were staying.

This day Ninikiji secretly gathered two of the other Abenaki women and revealed to them that she had found the "one" worthy of the secret Starr People knowledge. Then the three Abenaki women began the trek back to Mahkiwasie's hovel. With them they carried a very special hand-crafted wooden box carved with hieroglyphics. Its contents — prized artifacts from the core depths of the green mountains.

Meanwhile, a young girl from the nearby clan village at "Pine Grove" was brought to Mahkiwasie shortly after her meditation, during which she was subtly aware that Ninikiji had arisen and left. Mahkiwasie was nibbling on some of the evening's leftovers when a young girl's mother and older brother approached, the brother carrying the little girl. Setting her down, they explained that the little girl had stepped on a hot coal from the cook fire the evening before.

The brother joked lightly, "No one has ever seen a girl run so swift through the village! It took three of us to catch her just to find out why she was yelping so loudly."

The mother then spoke more seriously, "We checked her all over until finally we found the burn on the bottom of her foot, I put only cool water on it for the night."

Looking at Mahkiwasie, the little girl stopped sobbing momentarily, "It burns deep in," she squeaked, eyes red from her tears.

Mahkiwasie smiled, already knowing the cure. She held her hands toward the mother and brother as if for them to calm down and remain quiet. She then motioned for them to sit as she held the little girl's blistered foot.

"What is your name little one?" As her mother started to speak, Medicine Girl motioned with her hand for her to stop and stay silent. It was the one-on-one connection with the girl she was seeking for administering what was to come next.

"I am "Little Cloud," the girl responded, feeling the kindness of Mahkiwasie's hands as the touch somehow removed the deep burning pain.

"If you can lay still for a moment, I will get my pouch hanging inside," the girl, Little Cloud, now much calmer now, nodded, not taking her eyes off the medicine woman.

She emerged with her pouch and proceeded to the pestle. With the mortise, she crushed a healthy bundle of leaves of plantain into a wet pasty substance. Next, she produced a four-inch roundish comb from a beehive, its cells full of honey.

"Little Cloud, now I am going to need your foot please!" As she knelt at the girl's feet, she could see that the blister was as big around as a little neck clam shell!

Mahkiwasie reached in the pouch and produced her razor-sharp pointy shark's tooth knife, fastened to a short handle of ash wood. She smiled at the girl stating, "Now, Little Cloud, you might feel just a little prick, like a thorn, for just a moment. Soon your burning will be gone, is that okay?" The girl nodded apprehensively.

With the shark tooth knife, Medicine Girl opened the large blister and, with all five fingers around it squeezed and drew the fluid from the wound. She did this two more times, allowing the fluids to drain, then applied the honey into the wound. Honey was anti-fungal, anti bacterial, and would keep infection from setting in.

Next, after a few moments, she applied the plantain paste, now smeared out on a large broad fern leaf. After wrapping the poultice tight with some string hide, she put her hands on the top and bottom of the little girl's foot.

The prana healing energy would penetrate the girl's foot with its powers to heal and release pain. She handed the rest of the paste to mother, "Put this on again tonight. By morning Little Cloud should be back at play!" By now Little Cloud was sitting up smiling happily. She tried to look inside Medicine Girls pouch to see what magic was within, and so did brother. Mahkiwasie calmly closed its flap and held it to her chest. "Now little one, you stay off that foot today. Just use your tippy toes if you must walk and keep that poultice wrapped tight. Mother will check it for you at sleep time." She looked at mother who nodded accordingly. "If your foot feels itchy tomorrow, that means it's getting better! And be very careful, next time around those fire pits, Little Cloud!"

The mother, in full of appreciation, asked Medicine Girl if there was anything she needed. Looking at her son, she said, "My boy here, 'Two Hands,' would be glad to gather you a bundle of firewood!" Offering her son's labor was not to his liking, Mahkiwasie could see by the look on his face. So, Medicine Girl smiled kindly, declining the offer, "Oh no, that will not be necessary. I am happy to help Little Cloud. I do not require any compensation."

The mother insisted that she felt obligated to in some way return the gift of healing. Medicine Girl simply said that she can help someone else in need as to pay it forward. Mother bowed slightly, acknowledging the gesture. In her silence she had made her mind to weave a nice watertight basket for Mahkiwasie as it was her specialty. The Three departed back to the other side of the village and crested a knoll, now well out of sight of Medicine Girls hovel. Just then, Ninikiji appeared upon the knoll with the contingent of three Abenaki women, each carrying a basket, a box, and something long wrapped in a soft deer hide. The two groups exchanged a brief greeting and continued on their separate ways.

24 Connective Thought Energy

Medicine Girl had retreated into her wigwam to recenter herself after the healing of the girl Little Cloud. She just needed some quiet time to regain the sense of her own innerness and her thoughts, as always after a healing.

As she sat for a moment her thoughts suddenly shifted to envisioning Lone Wolf; it was as if he was in the room with her. His masculinity, his handsome face and his powerful aura filled her. She felt compelled to lie down as she brought forth a simple fantasy of him appearing at her hovel in an evening setting. With no words whatsoever, he lay beside her.

She could smell his essence, his body touching hers from head to toe, her feet spontaneously wrapped and caressed his while he held his hands upon both sides of her face. With his nurturing eyes gazing into hers, she then felt urges deep in her lower abdomen. It was a pleasurable ache, unlike any she had ever felt before. It crept into her loins, as every part of her felt as if she was at one with him. Her breasts swelled and she groaned as he held her against his broad chest. Then a strong tingling sensation arose within her pelvis.

She spontaneously touched herself and felt so much wetness. Again, the surge of extreme pleasure filled her body as she lay there all a quiver, her fingers felt so good caressing the moistness, all the while imagining Lone Wolf's hardness. Never had she had such a vision, her hand remained upon the spot as the intense sensations subsided some. But still with every fiber of her being still tingling, she wanted to feel the intensity again. Her fingers kept caressing, and the surges swelled again. This time she was more focused on her own hand movements.

She kept his essence in her thought as it was the vision of him through her fantasy that brought her to this new experience. She swelled again with the gentle motion of her fingers. Suddenly another explosive surge filled her and so much wetness emerged upon her hand and thighs. She quivered as her legs raised her torso up off the reed mat in an impulsive reflex at the peak of its explosion. Her body thrust and quivered; she could only moan involuntarily.

She lay back exhausted, with Lone Wolf still holding her now in her mind, just caressing her face and shoulders, nurturing her with his arms wrapped around her entire body as if she was a child, something that she had no memory of in real life. She dozed in and out of a sleep state with each conscious thought being only of Lone Wolf holding her. She never felt so safe and secure as she did in this moment.

At this time, Lone Wolf was at his own hovel, with his timber wolf laying just outside the entrance. For some reason he had returned from starting his day trek to gather his pouch of possibles in which was included the quartz crystal that was gifted to him from Nashkid, his new Abenaki friend and counterpart from the hunting excursion.

He instinctively pulled the crystal from the pouch, remembering what Nashkid had told him of its power, how it can project emotion and thoughts to Medicine Girl or anybody else. Instead of heading back out he sat down holding the crystal for some reason not even he could fathom. Staring at it in his palm, images of Mahkiwasie suddenly filled him, her pretty face and smile, her slender frame, the shape of her legs and bare feet, and finally her long hair that fell below her cheeks to the back of her knees.

The crystal suddenly felt warm in his hand as he felt its smoothness with his thumb. It seemed to glow brighter even though he was inside the dark hovel. He pictured her when they had held hands and thought of her touch at the early morning fire circle so many days ago. The warmth that emitted from her hands was all he could think of ever since then. Her essence penetrated his core even more often lately, each time he thought of her. Even though their wigwams were almost a mile apart, he felt as though she was right next to him.

He submitted to a daydream in that quiet moment, totally out of any normal routine for him. Normally, he would not even be near his hovel at this time on any given day. It was that crystal that called him back, he realized, as he held it in his hand feeling its warm power. Perhaps, he thought, this was because he had found it so alluring ever since he'd obtained it from Nashkid, but he had not had any quiet time to play with it and contemplate it alone. Little did he know that while he sat quietly holding the crystal and thinking of Mahkiwasie, she was now doing the same.

Lone Wolf, in this moment, could feel her essence. His nostrils filled with her subtle scent, and even though his eyes were closed, her face and smile penetrated his mind. He instinctively reached out to caress her face with both of his hands as he felt her softness against his body and he held her closer to his frame as she melted into it. His arms went around her petite body, and he felt her as one with him. She cooed and made subtle sounds that came not from his ears but from his inner mind.

It was an act of oneness whereby she became a part of himself. He sensed something, some inner knowingness that had been missing in his life was now returned. There was no sense of time or space, nor realm of earth, nor any particular place upon it. Suddenly, he was jerked back to physical reality. He refocused, staring at the crystal in his hand in amazement. His manhood was swollen.

A rustling sound from outside entered his ear. His wolf had leapt to its feet, and it began a low soft growl indicating someone's approach. Lone Wolf quickly gathered his possibles and the crystal, stuffing them back into his pouch feeling somewhat intruded upon with his quiet time in this significant moment. The entrance of the hovel was still open, anyone approaching could just peer in. He felt just a little awkward of his stiffness for the first time in his life, and it was not something he wanted to share or explain.

It was Bird who approached, as Lone Wolf referred to him with his first thought. As his head came back into reality he remembered Bird was now called "Mammototha" or "Mammototh Scout." The teenager charged into the camp with his same old excited boyish zeal, calling out Lone Wolf's name as an old friend would do.

"Tibamahgan, Tibamahgan! It's me, Mammototha! You in there?" He peered inside innocently.

Lone Wolf emerged from the wigwam, squinting his eyes in the sunlight, adjusting his pouch strap over his shoulder.

Bird said, "I did not hope to find you here so late in the morning! I have news from the elders that has been revealed by the elder of the Abenaki," as he produced the rattle from his pouch. "Finding you here I do not need to leave the summon rattle now!"

"Do you know of this news, Bird?" Lone Wolf asked.

"Not much yet," Bird replied, "only that Nashkid was summoned as well. It is for the men only, something of strange men from another place. Nashkid knows more as he was the one that spoke of it to me when I saw him this morning. The council Sachem would like you to sit with him and others at the evening circle. I think the Abenaki men will be there as they are the bearers of this news," he beamed a smile, hesitating before changing the subject, "Tibamahgan, I, Mammototha have been invited to sit at this circle!"

Lone Wolf smiled slightly, nodding his head at the same time, "My young friend, you have come a very long way on your path. You have earned the right of this passage. I wish to speak to you of your newfound power if you will allow it?"

Bird, now "Mammototha" replied, remembering his deep respect of Lone Wolf, "Yes I will never stop hearing your words Tibamahgan." He sat cross legged next to the wolf near the fire pit. Lone Wolf sat against the large boulder that served as the back wall of the fire pit, facing Bird, as he still referred to him for some reason, perhaps because it was the boy in Bird that he liked so much.

"Mammototha, to keep respect with others, and especially the elders, you must always stay quiet in your manner. Always hear others when they speak and never speak yourself from a reaction or from excitement or emotion. Make your voice and manner come from within your core here." Tibamahgan thumped his fist on his chest to emphasize the meaning of his words.

"I ask you not to flaunt your new status with your friends, as they will each come into their own power soon and you may sometime be in need of their friendship and brotherly camaraderie. Let me respeak this. You — will — need their camaraderie in the future, just as we did with the hunting party when fending off the timber wolves," said Lone Wolf.

"Remain quiet and humble in both actions and words. Know that there are other powerful forces that work within us and outside us. If you can do this contemplation before speaking out loud, then your words — will — bear the weight of wisdom."

Mammototha sat quiet and said nothing for the longest time to acknowledge Lone Wolf. Many moments passed. It became awkward, then he smiled. Lone Wolf stared at him for a bit then, not standing the silence anymore, finally said, "Bird, did you understand my meaning?" "Bird" just smiled boyishly again and laughed, "Yes," he responded, "I was just contemplating what you said," and laughing again, "I wanted to see how long you would wait! I was practicing!"

Lone Wolf just stared at him with a serious look on his face, not too sure if he had just wasted his time or, if "Bird" the boy was ready to become "Mammototha" the man. He then picked himself up, shifted his pouch and waved a motion at his wolf to follow.

"I will see you at the council this evening," indicating that Bird was not welcome where he was heading. Apparently, Bird got the message, clearly rethinking his little tom foolery. "Where are you going?" Still hoping he could tag along. "I am going to 'Little Sand,' to the fishermen, to see how their new canoe design is coming along."

Lone Wolf was really going to see if Mahkiwasie was around near the shore somewhere. His path would take him near her hovel. Bird realized he was uninvited.

Lone Wolf paused at the outskirts of his camp, hoping Bird would head back first before he departed. He thought to himself about resuming the alone time with the crystal, and then he thought he could do that anytime, anywhere.

Bird said aloud, "I shall look forward to seeing you too at the council. I will now go and find my friends who were at the hunt with us," he smiled in a knowing way as if he knew Lone Wolf was going to the shore beach area to find Mahkiwasie; it was just a flash bit of intuition. Then he dismissed it, and with short wave of his hand turned on his heel and headed back on the pathway.

Lone Wolf wondered as he headed on the alternate path if he had been too harsh on Bird.

25   A Secluded Mystical Place

The Abenaki women with their cherished and secret instruments arrived at Mahkiwasie's hovel. She was not there nor was she near the cluster of village huts as two of them looked and asked for her, while the others waited calmly at the Medicine Girl's hut.

She was, in fact, found by Ninikiji down at the little sandy spot at the river where the ledge touches the water, the same place where Medicine Girl had first met Lone Wolf. Medicine girl had decided to take a walk to her special place to clear her emotions and try to clarify the new dream experience, considering the reality that a relationship with Lone Wolf was forbidden.

"Mahkiwasie, I'm so happy that I found you!" Ninikiji said. "The others are waiting at your hovel; we have a very special gift for you if you can come back with us. We must go to a secluded place to present it to you!"

Medicine girl turned, slightly startled by her approach. She quickly wiped tears from her cheeks with the back of her hand and tried to compose herself. Her demeanor, however, was very noticeable.

"What is it that troubles you, my sister?" Ninikiji asked, as she took Medicine Girl by both hands and hugged her close. "Come now, tell me," she asked, with an intuition of it already.

Medicine girl shook her head and tried to shrug it off. "Oh, its nothing of importance; just frustration with things." Ninikiji looked deeply into her eyes with loving compassion and a knowingness.

"I sense your loneliness, she said, as she held the other girl's face with both her hands, putting her forehead on Medicine Girl's. "I once was lonely too! I once was not allowed to show my attraction to someone." She held Medicine Girl's face again, looking at her eyes for confirmation.

Medicine girl looked down at the ground, "It was a dream, and not a dream." She hesitated, "I mean to say it was so, so, real! We were together alone with each other with such pleasure! We were not here, but in another place and time. No! There was no time as we know it. We were in another dimension, and I was free of earthly bonds." She stared at Ninikiji; tears welled again. "He came to me and held me, and now it tears at me that I cannot see him in this waking time! There is no one to speak with from my people, of my pain."

"Shush, my sister," Ninikiji said, still holding her face. "You have me to talk with. You must now make yourself quiet and know that it is a very simple thing to heal. The universe and your guides will gift you your dream." Ninikiji closed her eyes for a few moments and cocked her head slightly as if listening to a silent voice.

She opened her eyes, smiling. "Yes, they have already made it so for you. All you must do is surrender and release it to them and your dream is about to unfold! Your man seeks for you even now as we speak. He feels for you as you do for him. It is meant to be for you both."

Medicine Girl wiped her tears again, standing up straighter.

"Come now," Ninikiji said. "My women friends have a gift of significant importance for you. They wait for us back at your wigwam. We will need to go to a secret and quiet place, secluded from village folks. Ninikiji took Medicine Girl by the hand, saying "Come now."

On the way back from the water's edge, Ninikiji spoke to Mahkiwasie of her own experience of being forbidden to have a man in her life, of her fantasies and of the secret love affair she had, and still had, with Nashkid. She told how they had to sneak off to a remote place to a small cave overlooking a valley in the mountain far from the main village. There they would spend a few overnights and sundry days in the summer's heat making love and pretending to be husband and wife. Then would come the torturous task of separating before returning to the village to resume the duties of the tribal council. How hard it was for them both to be in the eyes of the village and not be able to show even the remotest affection openly. Even now, they still rendezvoused in secret away from the contingent. Happily, their meetings were not so secret now that they had traveled so far away from their people in the mountains of what is now known as Vermont.

When they arrived back at Mahkiwasie's hut the other three Abenaki women were elated that they had returned so quickly as they were eager to demonstrate the sacred instruments to Medicine Girl. Each greeted and embraced her with unconditional affection as if she had been part of their family forever.

Mahkiwasie was and felt the same of them, a bond of sisterhood that allowed her, for the first time, to be able to reveal her close feelings and quiet abilities with women of sensitive and like mind.

Ninikiji spoke, "We have chosen only you Mahkiwasie, 'Medicine Healer' and 'Sacred Light Worker,' of the Nehantucket people to share in this very ancient and special knowledge. It has been taught and brought to us since our peoples beginning by the very ancient Starr People!"

Ninikiji continued, "We have brought with us, in these baskets, very special and secret instruments. It is our task, and most of the reason why we have traveled so far to your village, to share this knowledge. It has been revealed to us that you, Mahkiwasie, and your people, have been chosen to receive this ancient knowledge, to continue its gift and teachings, so it cannot be lost. Long before our small group ever left the mountains it was through the visions of our powerful elders that we were summoned to make this journey with these gifts."

Mahkiwasie, with her mouth somewhat agape, was stunned and intrigued simultaneously with this revelation. She had never felt so accepted by any human beings like this before and was not sure if she was worthy. She tried to peek into one of the sacred baskets, smiling, as Ninikiji grasped her arm gently and whispered, "Not here, we must go to a secluded place for this!" Perplexed, Mahkiwasie thought for a moment. "I do know of just the perfect place," Medicine Girl revealed. With a motion of her hand, she gestured for them to follow. Then she remembered to grab her own medicine pouch from just inside her hovel.

The four women gathered their satchels and, with Mahkiwasie in the lead, proceeded to the trail that led to a very special and remote place. It was a place that Mahkiwasie cherished as sacred and secret. The trail led them northward toward a small, secluded pond just along the western side of what is today known as Saunders Point Road, heading toward the Oswegatchie hills.

After an hour walk from Medicine Girl's hut along the western edge of a pond, they arrived atop a flat, open, ledged plateau. The sunbeams warmed their faces as they arrived in the center of this beautiful meadow with its sparse young hickory trees sprouting along its outer perimeters.

The tall, four-foot-high fire grasses in the meadow's center, bleached in the sunlight, waved slightly in the breeze as if excited that the women had arrived. The lush green grasses of rye covered the thin layers of topsoil. Lichen mosses carpeted an exposed perfectly flat rock ledge within a hundred fifty foot oval.

Within this magical meadow, for absolutely no known reason, stood eight, four foot pedestal-style boulders in a semi-circle, teetering in place for centuries like the marbles of giants. The women, led by Medicine Girl, gathered and settled themselves in the center on the soft moss and rye grass with the fire grass taller than their heads concealing them as they sat.

Once they settled down in the circle and refreshed themselves from the hour-long hike with spring water, the Abenaki women each commented to Medicine Girl of how magical this site felt, agreeing that "The energy here is strong and penetrating."

The one called Omeday asked Medicine Girl, "How is it you have found this place? Does no one else know of it?"

Medicine Girl responded "I believe no one knows of this place. I have never seen any sign of others here in a few seasons now. I found this place by following a great hawk who spoke to me from a tree branch and flew just a short distance, many times, each time waiting for me to catch up! After many stops, he finally flew in circles around this meadow and perched here on this stone!"

She walked to it and put her hands upon the top flat surface, "I then thanked him for guidance, and tossed him some of my dried fish! I have been coming here many times now to offer thanks to the great spirit for all that I have and all that I shall receive. Then, I sleep deeply and leave my body to go above the earth. This is my place now, given to me by the great hawk spirit. He sometimes comes here to visit me; I believe he likes my fish!!" She giggled loudly as they all did.

After a moment, Ninigret pulled out of her fancy basket, a rather heavy roundish-shaped stone bowl of semi-transparent hues of pinkish quartz, with streams of greens and bluish swirls throughout its inner texture. It was smooth all around the top rim for almost three fingers deep on both the outer and inner surfaces with crystalline protrusions on the lower outer portions. It seemed to have a slightly flat bottom, so as not to rock or wobble. She needed to use two hands to carefully lift its weight and place it upon a pedestal of shaped applewood. She then retrieved a beautifully carved mallet of the same applewood with a ringed handle. Ancient hieroglyphics were carved into its thickest sections. She tapped the rim with the mallet lightly and the quartz bowl rang out a tone that touched Mahkiwasie to her soul.

"Mother earth's voice sings from this instrument!" Ninigret said. She then began to swirl the mallet around the outer rim of the quartz bowl and a monotone sound emerged from it like nothing Medicine Girl had ever heard before! With each revolution the tone became louder and more pronounced so much so that it pierced and penetrated every cell in her body. It was truly nothing less than the voice of the great earth spirit. More, with each revolution at the masterful hand of Ninigret, the tone began to overwhelm all of nature's sounds. Even time stood still to hear it sing! Then with a slowing of the mallet its tone deepened. With the bowl now vibrating on its own, the tone faded as she tapped the rim with the mallet lightly, causing the crystal bowl to ring out like a bell in the same frequency that very slowly faded off. Then even the air became strangely silent as time seemed to stand still.

The tears flowed freely from all five women in this circle as they looked lovingly at one another, smiling through the tears of joy!

Ninikiji took from her pouch a short hollow log with exceptionally fine notches sliced along its bowed top. It had been sealed on both ends with pine sap resin, with just a small slot at the slightly bowed top. With another wooden mallet she began to stroke the bowed top with the fine slots and a wonderful monotone sound reverberated from its core. The even strokes held the low tone, and maintained the earthly sound.

Then Omeday, from her long, woven basket, pulled out another beautifully carved long tubular staff-shaped branch of about three feet in length and perhaps as wide around as one's fist. It was hollow throughout its length. Mahkiwasie first thought it was like the flutes used at the tribal drum circles.

However, the symbols carved into its length all around its outer shape were not of this realm. A language from a distant place, so it seemed. One particular symbol was a horizontal line, slightly curved on top, which then took a right angle downward like the trunk of a tree, circled outward with the outer ring intersecting the straight trunk line, two thirds up from its base, and continued spiraling inward with three more smaller rotations, each intersecting the trunk line before jogging downward towards infinity, opposite the top curved line. It was mesmerizingly beautiful to Medicine Girl as she studied it for a long moment.

Noticing Medicine Girl's fascination, Omeday explained its meaning, "It is an ancient Starr People symbol," she said. "It means to open, to increase the power of intention. When you have a pure, heartfelt intention or something you wish to manifest, place this symbol over or above your vision in your mind. It will instantly increase the power of your thought vision many times and project it into the stars to a place among the stars. Your vision will be materialized back to you. When we do this together, with all of us of the same mind, along with the tone vibrations of these instruments, it lifts us to a place where our ancestors dwell and raises vibration in every direction! All things are lighter, connected, including thoughts, visions, and intentions."

Omeday looked around at the others, "I believe it is now time to show you this teaching."

26 Living Earth Speaks

Mahiliekut, who was the fourth Abenaki women in the group, tied a braided tether to the two ends of a four-foot-long log. She then proceeded to pull it along the fire grass making a large "crop circle" in the very same design as the symbol on the wooden instrument, complete with its spiral end large enough for all four women to sit comfortably at the vortex of the inner spiral.

She then asked Medicine Girl if she would like the large teetering boulders to be rearranged to form a truer circle than their natural arrangement. Medicine Girl blinked her eyes, questioning the idea. After some thought and observation, she noticed that only one boulder was out of place, "I — uhm — I suppose if that one," she pointed to it, "if it could be moved over to here," she took a few paces and pointed to the spot, "it would complete a more symmetrical circle and spacing equal to the others."

"So be it," the women replied, as they motioned for her to sit in the center of the grass vortex spiral.

What occurred next was something no Nehantucket has ever had the opportunity to experience and henceforth only a select few ever would. It was nothing short of an ancient birth right and teaching derived from none other than the very ancient original Starr People from a distant planetary cluster. This teaching, if not for the select few, may very well be lost or intentionally hidden from subsequent tribes and current human cultures if its use of energy is in any way misused. It is meant to be protected in this way until a time of mass spiritual human evolution.

They sat in the center, facing inward toward each other. These five women each possessed a very special ability to connect with higher energies. Omeday spoke softly as they set the stone crystalline bowl in place and unwrapped the long hollow flute instrument. "This day we call forth great ancestral star-spirit ones to join us in this work and teaching as we welcome this one, Mahkiwasie, who we have found to be open and ready. We welcome her to join this realm."

They sat and entered into a meditative state. Within a few moments there was a simple quietness that overcame even the natural sounds of the woods. Only the warm sunshine seemed to exist in the quiet. Medicine Girl's palms became very warm as they did when she performed healing on others. Then, she felt her body become lighter as the low mild musical tone began to fill her essence. Slowly and gently, it became louder. As Medicine Girl opened her eyes, Ninigret was plying the mallet, circling the outer rim of the crystal bowl. The lower the mallet went toward the middle of the bowl, the more intense and louder the vibrational tone became. The sound's pure vibration filled and penetrated every cell of her body. Next, Ninikiji began her strokes of the mallet atop the short log. It began emitting the low earthy tone again from its core that harmonized together with the crystal bowl's vibration.

Now, another low monotone sound emitted from the long tube flute. Omeday was humming into it by using her breath, causing the vibrational tone by passing air through her lips. The tone emerging from the lower end of the tube at her feet was lower than the bowl's tone but in complete and perfect harmony. The vibrational tones filled and penetrated everything. Mahkiwasie, not feeling any sense of gravity, felt as if she would float!

Mahiliekut, with only her voice, began to emit a singing chant at a higher octave than the other instruments, another fourth harmony, with a tone of such perfection that the four tones together created a vibrational frequency that reverberated through and into everything. Medicine Girl instantly knew this vibration was of earth herself. It was Mother Earth's voice, always present, omniscient, and connected within all things of the earth from her core to the heavens.

Still singing her harmonic tone, Omeday rose from her seated position and took Medicine Girl's hand, leading her toward the boulder. It was if they floated over to it. She gestured to Mahkiwasie to lift it with the palm of her hand. Twice she made the gesture for Medicine Girl to lift the massive boulder and move it into place at the new location. Hesitant at first, Medicine Girl touched it lightly and it moved just slightly, like a feather. She bent herself down and, with both hands just under its massive shape, it lifted effortlessly. She looked at Omeday and then, at the others for approval. They nodded, smiling. She slowly walked it over to the new spot and set it down as it seemed to teeter once again on the moss-covered ledge foundation. It now completed a perfect symmetrical circle of eight large boulders within the fire grass spiral symbol.

They adjourned back to the sitting positions as the harmonics continued to reverberate, each of them now elevated vibrationally. Medicine girl opened her eyes again as ancient elders appeared and materialized within their circle. They were of many different cultures and tribes, all dressed in their individual adornments. They were all overjoyed with Mahkiwasie's presence in this realm. The ancients were speaking without audible sound. The message was, "Call upon us anytime, we hear you and we are here to help and guide you! Your work is important for the future of the Nehantucket people. Know then, that you will now have all hidden tools that you need in your work and all that you can manifest out of love and purity, of thought energy! Dear One, we hear you!"

As the entities faded, the women slowly brought the sound frequencies down. First, Mahiliekut quieted her vocal tones, Ninikiji slowed her strokes. Then, Omeday softly quieted her flute, and then Ninigret slowed her rhythmic mallet circling around the crystal bowl as it now rang quieter, still in vibration. Then she tapped the top of its rim for one final ringtone ending the session. All was quiet as it was when they began.

It was important that all instruments slowed in the same sequence in which they were introduced as for the closure of the session.

Tears of joy flowed from Medicine Girl's eyes! She just kept looking to each of the Abenaki women, over and over! Overwhelmed and speechless, her emotion glowed from her eyes!

The four Abenaki women, each smiling with joy, moved closer and put hands on Mahkiwasie as she lay now in a fetal position. Her first session of this magnitude had caused her to collapse in absolute exhaustion as she reentered back into her physical body and the lower dimensional vibration of the earth. Medicine Girl slept deeply over the next hour, while her mind and body healed and adjusted to the attunement.

27 Canoe Craft

Lone Wolf wandered along the shore of the Nehantucket river, all the while hoping to find Medicine Girl. At first, he pretended to be interested in the fishing men and women, stopping here and there, watching the women who wove the nets and the ones who would make and tie the stone net weights, then those who worked the sharply pointed bone hooks.

Down shore, two men were working on the carcass of a ten-foot long blue fin shark, its flanks already harvested for the filleted meat that were set upon racks for drying. What caught his attention and impressed him were the large, serrated shark's teeth the two men were harvesting by using a long narrow stone chisel with a rounded heavy stone as a hammer. Many of the dark colored teeth were lying in a wooden bowl. These shark teeth were razor sharp and uniform in size. The two men would place them at the split-end of an ash-wood shaft handle, normally to be used as excellent knife blades or as the lethal points for atlatl shafts. Now that the Abenaki had introduced the bow and arrow, these two Nantucket entrepreneurs decided to use these shark teeth as a more effective arrowhead point. These would not require any of the long steps in the tedious task of chiseling and shaping stone or quartz shards. Lone Wolf inquired about this massive and dangerous shark that far too many have not survived encounters with!

These two were respectful; they had heard tales of Tibamahgan's legacy with his timber wolf companion. Now, here he was, impressed with their craft. Excited in their talking and, finishing each other's sentences, they were eager to tell the tale both speaking at the same time! It was explained how the shark became entangled in one of the nets after being attracted by the bait fish. The two young men who fished every day for the tribe fought with this shark for the better part of a day out in the bay. They were finally It did not go to its end without causing wounds to the men as well, they proudly displayed their cuts and gashes to Lone Wolf who admired the razor-sharp tooth he held, testing its sharpness across his thumb slightly, quickly drawing blood from the cut.

Something else had also caught Tibamahgan's eye, after he had made plans with the two young men to make him several of the new arrow shafts with the shark points, for which he would provide the shafts and the bird feathers. The deal was that he would exclusively introduce them to the Abenaki shaman scouts to discuss these improved arrow points and other ideas they may have. They were honored and elated to be included!

What caught Lone Wolf's eye was the very different canoe partially covered with reeds alongside the fishermen's hovel. This was not the typical hollowed dug out log style canoe that the Nehantucket had been building and had perfected for so many generations over the years. Confident that no one else was watching, they pulled it out. No, this canoe was of a much different design! In the older style a large log would be chopped, chiseled, and carved by placing hot coals into the cavity burning the wood then chiseling it out to achieve its length and depth to the required proportions to hold two or three men and to float in a stable way, requiring balance and skill. Later they adapted this design with a wooden pontoon for better stabilization in the bay's surf and more distant coastal expeditions.

Now here lay a much different and unique canoe design, also built by these two young fishermen. They were very nonchalant about it, for they had had it for quite some time now! It had a framework of birch, ribs bent approximately one foot apart and each lashed to the heavier rails that ran along its length. Four at the bottom, two at mid sides and one larger round stock for its top rails. All came to a point front and rear to form a bow and stern with a spine piece at the bottoms center that served as a keel of sorts.

Lone Wolf was mesmerized and intrigued as ran his hand along the smooth outer sides and bottom trying to understand the nature of it.

Seals, they explained, were very abundant out at the small islands and stony outcrop reefs. Large animals, quick and agile in the water, seals were slow and cumbersome on land. Herds of them were to be found along the Nantucket Bay, unafraid of humans who could walk amongst them unmolested. The dark thick skin of the seals was pliable and water resistant with its oily smoothness. With hides of the seal sewn together and glued with pine sap at the seams, they found this sealskin wrapping to be far more watertight, lighter and more durable in all types of surf and waves. This canoe was also far faster due to its lightness compared to the heavier dugout canoes! These two were truly entrepreneurs!

"When we were young, our great grandfather gifted us both a drawing etched into a very old birch bark parchment." From a woven satchel they retrieved and carefully unwrapped an inner rabbit skin pouch. The two took great care in the unwrapping of this article. With one man holding it with his palms upward, the other unfolded the rabbit pouch, unfolding its folds five times. Finally, the contents of the rolled birch etched design was revealed. Carefully unrolling it on the flat stone table, it depicted a hieroglyphic styled sketch of seals on a rocky ledge outcrop and then of skins hanging on a rack. Next, the staves of the birch tree structure of the canoe were laid out in a sketch showing the sides and bottom in its dimensions, followed by a drawing of the joints and lashings depicting the best method of construction. There was a detail of hides being stitched together with sinew. Finally, the stretching procedure was depicted, showing the steps required to fasten the skins to the outside of the frame, first soaking and wetting the hides and then the type of stitching needed to keep them taut at the top rails. Most likely this etching was derived and handed down throughout many generations, originating from an earlier design of ancient ancestral kayak origin.

This prototype just recently completed by the two Nehantucket fishermen was yet to be revealed to any other clans along the coast or the river. They had tested it a few times, made some adjustments and slight improvements. They found it to be a very worthy craft for light fishing and coastal shoreline travel. When not in use, they kept it for the most part covered, hidden from prying eyes!

This is what they explained, one of them holding his finger to his lips indicating that Lone Wolf keep their secret too. Lone Wolf nodded in agreement, smiling. They wanted to enjoy their fishing success for just a while longer before revealing it to the elders and be the ones to receive status. They were both truly visionary entrepreneurs. Their secret would keep well with Lone Wolf. Remembering his council meeting he bid them farewell.

28 Nordic

From the small clan village at Pauquatuket, he ran the trail westward, only stopping along the way wherever the trail took him close to a stream or clan hovels to hydrate himself. He was the designated runner, carrying important news and messages. This urgent message was not just verbal, this news included a rolled birch parchment drawing. His destination was the chief council elder at Nantucket or Crescent Beach as it is known today. Starting out at just before daybreak, his trek would take him half the day to complete. Crossing the wider sections of rivers we know today as the Mystic and Thames rivers would be the only delays. For these he would commandeer a dugout canoe; they kept one at the trail head that meets the water for this very purpose.

His name was Kijibashie, "One Who Runs," because of his swiftness, even while navigating the rough trail and terrain. His job was to run messages of importance between clan villages in his area. But this was an important message that needed an expedited currier directly to the council of elders. The clan's lookout had spotted the eerie scene on the beachhead in the early afternoon the day before. Kijibashie was the only chosen runner for this task.

Normally and routinely, he would deliver just between the local clan villages on the eastern side of the rivers up to the Thames, as it is known today. Correspondence between shamans, or elder leaders of the tribal clans, usually included news of a death, herd movement, or the best location of fishing grounds in offshore waters and inland streams, especially when the salmon runs, or the seat trout runs began. Sometimes he delivered the shamans' predictions of severe weather, such as storms, messages important for the clan communities to heed and hunker down. Thanks to Tibamahgan, there was essential news of the best winter camp locations. Kijibashie would run and deliver these messages.

He was agile, gifted as a runner, able to navigate the trail terrain nimbly and light footed. His secret, most times, was to run alongside the beaten pathway in the softer forest carpet of leaves. He wore a type of heavy padded moccasin made from the very durable thick sealskin with a double layer at the sole designed to protect from sharp rocks and jagged ledge on the beaten path. The off-trail paths were much easier on the feet, legs, and body overall, cushioning each step and providing a better bounce to maintain an even stride. His keen eye and focus of vision directed each landing of foot upon which the toes and balls of his feet were the only ground contact.

Kijibashie arrived at the chief elder's large wigwam long house. He had to slow himself down before presenting himself. To do this he would jog in a circle for a few minutes, then just walk around at a fast pace before coming to a full stop. He did this to bring his body's metabolism down from the full speed running pace he had kept over the last couple miles, once he had crossed the Nantucket River at the Narrows, near Mago point.

The women attending chores outside Migiwishkanj's lodge now knew that Kijibashie was the bearer of important news simply because he did not linger with them, tasting the morsels they offered. Instead, he went directly to the entrance and stood there with the pouch in his hand indicating the urgency to see Eagle Claw in private. One of the women entered the longhouse to inform the sachem of the runner's arrival. She reappeared, motioning for him to enter. She then reluctantly remained outside, returning to the inquisition of the other women. All were eager to find out what news Kijibashie brought.

Still breathing deeply and now sweating from the run, Kijibashie knelt in front of Eagle Claw and his main women. Nodinosi, "Spirit Woman," smiled at "One Who Runs," knowing that he had just endured many hours on the trail from the clan village of Pauquatuket so many miles to the east. She offered him the wooden bowl of fresh water that she had ladled from the larger watertight basket.

Eagle Claw embraced him by extending both hands and grasping his shoulders with a firm shake and an affirming nod of his head. Sitting back, he spoke, "What news do you bring this day my friend?" Wordlessly, Kijibashie unveiled the rolled scroll of birch bark parchment from his pouch and carefully unrolled it to face Eagle Claw with its script.

The pictured etchings unfolded the scene and tale of visitors. Eagle Claw looked at One Who Runs inquisitively, asking "This is where?" Kijibashie answered, "It is at Pauquatuket. They camp on the sands just inside the gut," meaning the inlet sand bar. "The canoe," he continued, pointing to the picture etching of the large ship, "is many times larger than our dugouts." Holding up eight fingers, Kijibashie explained, "This many dugout canoes can fit inside this vessel, end to end." Another sketch of the strange men revealed them as tall and bearded. "Fire hair," he said, as he pointed to the picture of the figures.

"They are many men of this count," holding both hands up with fingers extended, closing and opening them twice, "another six of them who appeared to be female with long flame red hair as well. They dressed in dirty white fury skins and brandished large, rounded, disk shaped spheres strapped to their backs. The bow of the canoe," pointing to the sketch again, "comes upward into the shape of a serpents head!" and he formed it with his hands to emphasize the size and shape, not well depicted on the parchment. The sketched etching had been drawn hastily and could not depict its full description. Kijibashie's verbal emphasis was needed to further describe the event. He had seen these visitors with his own eyes!

Eagle Claw sat back deep in thought, contemplating this event. Closing his eyes briefly to go within for a moment trying to feel any sensation of danger for his people. With no intuition of that he opened his eyes, looking at "Nodinosi" for her sense and intuition on this news. She spoke softly at first.

"I would like to ask Kijibashie, have any of your clan elders sat with these strangers to know of whence they come?"

"Not the elders," he replied. "Only two of our fishermen ventured close. They speak not our tongue, they gestured for fresh water and the fishermen gave them a flagon. They asked where to fill their water pouches and our men pointed out the direction to a freshwater stream. That is when they ran back to the village to report the arrival of the strangers. Some of us returned to see them from a distance. By then the strangers had set up camp on the sand. We did not approach."

Nodinosi reflected on this for a silent moment, also closing her eyes. Then, opening her eyes and turning to Eagle Claw, she began to speak, "My sense of this is the same as that of the visitors from the Abenaki, who have come to us from a great distance seeking knowledge of our ways. Respectfully asking to join us for a time and present knowledge of their ways. I feel that these strangers are also from a place of even greater distance. Yet, all the same, until we can know them, we must remain suspicious of their intent. There may be much to learn from them if they wish to share in their ways. We must remain a distance from them, we must show them only kindness for now."

Eagle Claw summoned one of the women outside to message the neighboring clan elders and all shaman to his council this early afternoon and ask the Abenaki men to attend as well. He believed news such as this needed to be discussed with input and insights from all perspectives.

He handed out the rattles for the younger boy runners, including Bird, who would find Lone Wolf and the Abenaki, Nashkid. The boys would run the summon rattles to the clans at the east side of the Nehantucket River, on to the western villages along the beach and shoreline now known as "Black Point" and "Giants Neck," in today's Old Lyme; traveling as far west as the "Konnectakutuket River." Quinnehtukqut

Eagle Claw then instructed Kijibashie to remain for the council meeting to share his firsthand account and perspective on these visitors and to answer any questions that would certainly arise. He then invited One Who Runs outside to enjoy some food and rest with the company of the women attendants.

Kijibashie always enjoyed their attention whenever he was at the Nehantucket village, including the opportunity to see a very pretty, younger maiden, about his age. She was often with them as she was in apprenticeship with these older women.

They in turn, of course, always loved to gossip about any new news he might bear. They immediately began to pry systematically and cunningly, coyly bribing the info from him with sweet meats and salted dried fish morsels. He let them stew for a while until they brought the young woman of his eye to the fire. They baited him with her, but he knew their scheme. So, when they had the girl sit next to him for the informal introduction, he finally revealed a very brief description of the visitors' arrival at Pauquatuket.

He knew the word was soon to spread anyway. Smiling, he felt as though this was a mutual win! The young woman smiled at him, also liking to be in his presence. She became mesmerized with the firsthand news and honored to be one of the first to be informed by One Who Runs. Kijibashie spoke his tale directly to the young woman, as if he was sharing it only with her. Meanwhile, the older biddies listened in, straining to eavesdrop on every syllable of his words.

This women's network has always proven to be very efficient in communicating messages far faster than any runner ever could. The word spread rapidly throughout the local clan villages by the buzzing women's network.

Council members, shamans, elders, and scouts of the local clan villages arrived, including the men of the Abenaki. They organized and took places at the inner circle. It was late afternoon now with an air of urgency hovering over the circle, with everybody wondering at the purpose of this summoning.

Most of them knew Kijibashie. If he was present, it meant something of importance had happened. It could mean danger from shark attacks for the fishermen, a massive pod of walrus, or the large long-toothed cats were prowling near the village. Perhaps even the huge and dangerous short-faced bear, with a taste for human flesh, had been seen.

These speculations were whispered amongst them. As Lone Wolf looked around the circle, his wolf companion again just off in the tree line, the question formed in his savvy mind, "Why just men?" He looked again and saw Bird, or Mammototh Scout. For some reason, he could not remember to call him that; "Bird" was stuck in his brain. The boy looked much older, and his demeanor was more manlike. He seemed to have grown in physique and had a more focused seriousness about him. His eyes met Lone Wolf's with an acknowledging nod.

The Abenaki men sat alongside Lone Wolf. Mammototh Scout took his place a few seats down amid the most senior Nehantucket hunters and fishermen on the opposite side of Lone Wolf. The other tribal clan leaders and elders, with their contingents, formed the remaining circle.

Eagle Claw entered the circle holding both of his arms high above his head. Turning in rotation, he faced each of the "fours points." Beginning by facing in the easterly direction, he then turned clockwise to the southerly, westerly, and northerly directions, and then back to the east to complete the tribute. As he completed the ceremony the sound of a rattle was heard. It penetrated the air and all chatter ended. Only the popping of an ember in the fire pit could be heard.

Eagle Claw began his speech, "You have all been summoned to know of the presence of a strange and foreign people unlike our own. They have arrived at our clan village shore at Pauquatuket. They came from the great water, within a canoe of vast size that bears the head, body, and tail of the great serpent. We here know not of the land or place whence they came."

"These visitors are few in number," he continued, "with hair of fire red. The men are tall with hair that comes out of their faces. We know not of their intent or why they have come." Eagle Claw motioned for Kijibashie to come and stand next to him at the center of the circle. Somewhat apprehensively, Kijibashie joined Eagle Claw. Touching his shoulder, Eagle Claw continued, "One Who Runs has been to their camp on the sand. He has seen their large canoe and he has heard them speak a tongue unlike ours. He now brings this news to us firsthand!"

Holding up the scrolled birch parchment with the etchings depicting the stranger's boat, stature, hair, and implements, Eagle Claw passed it to the member to his right to pass around the circle for all to view. He asked Kijibashie to speak of his encounter with these visitors, as the parchment was passed from one member to the next. All were eager to study the parchment.

Kijibashie answered questions from whoever asked while standing in front of the individual member.

Each question and Kijibashie's response were the only verbal voices heard while the rest of the members remained in perfect attentive silence. Most questions were about the "canoe," its size, width and length, and its effigy of the serpent head on the bow and tail on the stern.

When the parchment reached Mammototh Scout, Bird, he studied it thoroughly. Since all obvious questions were already answered he had none of pertinence. Just before passing the parchment off to the next member, he hesitated, standing up with Kijibashie waiting. Bird cocked his head, looking around at the members, then said hesitantly, "There is no image of these visitors' women here." Holding out the parchment he said, "You mentioned that there were six females." Kijibashie said, "Yes," holding up six fingers for all to see. Bird felt the smooth skin on his face and chin.

Among the Nehantucket people, men do not bear facial hair. This trait is one that no one in the tribes ever had knowledge of or had thought about. The drawing of these visitors depicted red facial hair as a long, shaped beard hanging down to mid chest. Bird pointed to the image showing it to Kijibashie. Then he again felt his own face and chin. "My question is this, One Who Runs," began Bird, "these six females, do they bear the 'fire hair' on their faces also?"

It was a very good question according to the other members, who all began to murmur amongst themselves about it. Then some laughter broke out among a few of them at the very prospect of it!

Kijibashie even chuckled a bit as the mood in the circle lightened and dispelled the tension that these strangers were dangerous. He answered, still surprised at the question and smiling a bit, "No, they do not have hair on their faces! No, none that I could notice, although I was not all that close while observing them. With all the other things to try to remember I did not have the time to look closely."

With that, Bird nodded thankfully, proud that he was able to come up with a different question. Resuming his sitting position within the circle, he handed the parchment off to the next member to his right. Some members just studied the parchment handing it off, others had pertinent questions one of which was about the weapons and the purpose of the round wooden disks.

When the parchment finally came to Nashkid of the Abenaki, at his first glance he stood up immediately, somewhat flushed. He looked at the parchment again, then he looked straight at Lone Wolf, and then directly at Eagle

Claw, looking past Kijibashie, who was standing in front of him. There was an air of urgency in his body's demeanor, with a sharpness in his eye.

He walked past One Who Runs to the center of the circle, holding both hands up above his head and turned to Eagle Claw, who was now sitting next to the only woman in the circle, Nodinosi, Spirit Woman. "I am Nashkid of the Abenaki from the mountains far to the north," he said, for the benefit of those in the circle who had not yet made his acquaintance. "I ask not a question, but for permission to speak, for we Abenaki know of these strangers to your shore! He did this, all the while looking at Eagle Claw for permission before continuing, knowing it would be granted.

Eagle Claw, surprised by the statement, rose to his feet. Nodinosi also stood and whispered something into the sachem's ear, then looked at Nashkid just to give her own support of acknowledgment to Nashkid. With a nod and a gesture of his hands, Eagle Claw allowed the Abenaki to continue.

Nashkid looked around at the members, all of whom were eager to hear his words. He made eye contact with all of them, stopping to focus on Lone Wolf.

"I have seen these same red hair men," began Nashkid, "they come from a land very far to the north, a land across the great water. They arrived in the same canoes from our great lake water and lived amongst our Abenaki people for some time."

"The first arrival was not much different from these here at your Pauquatuket! They asked only for a place to shelter and hunt for the winter moons. They were few then as well and they remained hospitable, accepting gifts of stone tools and food from our people who were inquisitive of their tongue and appearance. Eager, like you, to learn of their ways and craft, our people from my clan began to trust them as we would our own. Then one mid spring, just after the great equinox moon, another of the serpent canoes appeared. Many more of these Norse stayed and their camp grew. They did not move on as the days became warmer and longer. They did not share their bounty, or gift any knowledge or crafts back, as is our custom and yours."

"Winter came upon us again and they encamped in their long house dwelling. Game became scarce as our forest was over hunted. These Norse did not prepare for the long winter with dried meats and fish, they did not grow any crop except for a strange round yellow brown orb that was shown to us but never shared."

"It was to be a cold and deep snow winter. The time came when most of our village would travel four days south to winter camp. Only ten of our men would remain for another moon. It was then that these Nordic began to "take" what was not given. Stored food went missing from our winter cache. Then one of our own hunters went missing!"

"We found him after many days," said Nashkid, as he held up his five fingers. "He had been slashed three times by axe wounds, two in his back and one at his neck. His right arm had been broken here," continued Nashkid, as he pointed to a spot on his own forearm.

"Parts of the deer he had harvested for our camp were nearby. Our good friend, Tataohan, a brave and skilled hunter, was killed by these red-haired Norse for the meat that he would have shared or traded. We gathered all our men and went to their camp. We watched them from a distance for some time. Then we went to their fire circle. We tried to speak with them but could not."

"One of our men saw inside their hovel the bow and quiver of arrows belonging to Tataohan, said Nashkid. "He reached in and grabbed the weapons; they clearly had the mark of our tribe. They had stolen his prized heirlooms! We held them up to show them they was our friend's and that we know how they came to possess them! The stolen deer's bones were still lying at the edge of the fire pit!"

"There was much anger and hard words from some of them, wanting a fight with us, raising their axes and round shields. We drew our arrows at the ready, should they charge us! Then, one stood and shouted loudly, and the angry ones retreated. He was one of the very first to arrive, a chieftain or sachem of power. They had many words amongst themselves. There would have been blood that day on the snow had it not been for this one."

"We then went back to our village. With stone we buried Tataohan with proper ceremony, with his tools, pouch, and bow. We gathered our winter stores and traveled the five days to the southern winter camp. We left the Nordic with nothing more of ours to take. When our people returned in late spring the Nordic were gone. There was no large canoe, no sign of them, only the long hovel remained."

"Like you here now," Nashkid said, as he pointed around the circle to include all the Nehantucket with his gesture, "we Abenaki had never known these visitors existed until they arrived. We had never seen nor heard any tales of them before. We had no reasons not to trust them and so, as is our nature, and also the Nehantucket's, we welcomed them and allowed them to live near our village and to share in our ways. I speak this truth to you now, our spirit people and guides warned us of these Nordics. It went wrong-headed because of our curiosity of them. We should have turned them away. These Nordic should not be trusted. There is no 'honor' with them, as we know it. They did not respect our ways. I believe they will not respect the Nehantucket ways." Nashkid, before resuming his seat, looked back around the council circle making final eye contacts. First his gaze met Spirit Woman's eye, Nodinosi; next was Eagle Claw, Migiwishkanj, and last, was Lone Wolf, Tibamahgan. No words were necessary during these long intense gazes; it was with pure intuition that he sensed deep within each of them that they knew which decision to make.

29 Sachem Contemplation

The council members were silent for a few moments, glancing at each other for confirmation, then the chatter began. The circle members were buzzing with speculations, intrigued with these strange visitors. Where had they come from, what is this big canoe, the facial hair, the woolly skins they wore, and the most prevalent question was, "why are they here?"

As they dealt with all threats, to the tribal camps or villages alike, when large carnivores, packs of wolves, or the big cats that prowl with a taste for human flesh are near, the tribal community would band together and form a strategy to suppress the threats. The entire community, acting as one, would focus upon each goal to completion.

The Nehantucket would never have considered other tribal people or different cultural visitors as threatening in the same way as carnivores. Never had they encountered alien people such as these "Norse." With only the insight of a dreamed warning of an old sage woman to guide them, they would have been vulnerable without the warning from the Abenaki.

A few months earlier, the sage woman had predicted this event, with a warning that was now whispered to Eagle Claw by Nodinosi, reminding the sachem of the sage's vision. Along with the experience of the Abenaki with these Norsemen, the combined information provided much more clarity and sealed the tribal sachem "Eagle Claw" in his decision.

These visitors, these "Norse men", would be kept at distance from the tribal clans as the vision of the elderly shaman medicine woman had foreseen a few months earlier. She was an oracle who predicted the arrival of these aliens in their large serpent canoe. She said, "They will bring intrigue and curiosity with their ways and tools, but they will not respect the Nehantucket ways of spirit, earth mother, and star knowledge. They will remain for a time, inland, far from our villages."

Eagle Claw stepped back into the circle center with both hands above his head, the chatter died down, and he spoke with a strength of voice.

"You have all heard Nashkid of the Abenaki speak of encounters with these "Nordic" visitors who are now upon our shore. It is with great thought and deep insight that we, as head council have come to an understanding that it is not the Nehantucket way to turn away others in need. We do not know if these Nordic are of the same as Nashkid has described. It is only upon learning more of them and knowing from whence they came can we decide. Only upon our understanding of all these things, and their willingness to share their intentions and trade with us, can we make a change of mind. Until this time, all Nehantucket will remain at distance from them. You will pass this word to all Nehantucket villages!

"Kijibashie will go back to Pawtucket village. One Who Runs will be the one from the Nehantucket who will speak our message to the Norse. He will bear food, water and supplies for them and ask them to return to their serpent canoe back to the great water."

"We will ask Nashkid, and some of his men, to stand with Kijibashie so that they can witness if these Nordic are of the same that they encountered in the north mountains. At this time, they will not be welcome on our shore to live amongst our people. If they show anger in this, we will know their nature. We will show them our numbers with many hunters holding weapons, as Nashkid and the Abenaki men had done in the mountain village. They will stand from a distance in full view to show our strength, as we do with the predators. Our hospitality will only be by the provisions gifted for them to continue their water journey. No other Nehantucket will speak with these Norse."

"It is with great compassion that this decision can be taken back only if these Nordic visitors show and display no hostile intent. If they show a willingness to share knowledge and trade, we will only then allow them to remain a distance inland, far outside any of the Nehantucket village areas," Eagle Claw finished.

With this final statement, Eagle Claw raised his hand once again above his head, as he turned full circle, acknowledging all within it. He gazed at Nodinosi, nodding his head slightly, then at Lone Wolf, Nashkid, and finally Kijibashie. His final words reverberated through the silence, "So be it!"

Kijibashie would stay the night; in the company of the young maiden he met earlier, he hoped. He would depart in the early daylight hours ahead of Nashkid and his contingent of Abenaki and Nehantucket men who would guide Nashkid to the Pauquatuket village. Kijibashie would relay the council meeting discussions and final decision of Eagle Claw to the Pauquatuket elders and wait for Nashkid and his members to arrive before any approach to the Nordic. The women resumed their briberies on Kijibashie, council meeting details soon to spread through clan villages like wildfire. The maiden made his night memorable, and his morning fatigued!

30 Message of No Words

Kijibashie departed at first light. He ran his course for the most part of the day at the same pace and agility as he had two days prior, although not at first. He thought to himself of how he would get to rest in the next day or so, being still fatigued and not quite finding his pace in the first leg of his course. It wasn't until he reached the crossing at the narrow gut of the Nehantucket river that he regained his stride after a short break sitting in the dugout canoe.

It would take a better part of the that day to reach Pauquatuket village. It was early evening when he arrived. It may very well have been one of the faster runs he had ever done between the two points, driven by the importance of his message.

After he had walked off his adrenalin and wound down his muscles by walking in small circles at the central village hovels, the womenfolk brought him a wooden bowl of fresh mixed strawberry and blueberry and hickory nut, a rabbit skin flagon of fresh spring water and dried venison jerky to help him rehydrate and rebuild protein.

Word spread rapidly of his return, almost immediately it reached the chief sachem and his five-member council of two women and three elder men. All six arrived at the small hovel where Kijibashie was still winding down along with the prominent medicine women and clan shamans.

The Nordics were still encamped down at the beach-front inlet, upland a bit, just into the dunes. A contingent of them had ventured to the outskirts of the clan's village hovels, seemingly studying their surroundings, remaining reluctant to mingle with their hosts. Every movement of the Nordics was observed and reported as instructed by "Magwagonk," the leading clan elder.

Magwagonk had instructed his people not to attempt to speak to or contact any of these strangers until Kijibashie returned. This was a very hard and difficult task with such curiosity welling up inside everybody within and outside the small village. So, over the two days villagers had positioned themselves at the higher knolls to stare down at the Nordics in wonderment.

The testament and directive message from Eagle Claw and the Nehantucket council was relayed in detail formally, along with its parchments, to Magwagonk and his council members by Kijibashie, including the instruction to wait for the contingent of Abenaki and selected Nehantuckets to arrive before approaching the Nordics.

Magwagonk, with better understanding of the potential danger that these Nordics could bring to his clan village, was in full agreement with the Nehantucket council mandate. He and his local council had already, by the insights of the shaman's vision, decided to keep distance from these visitors.

Nashkid's contingent with the Nehantucket guides was soon to follow, as they had left a few hours later than Kijibashie. Walking the distance at a much slower pace, it would take them that day and half the following day, even though they traveled well into the moonlit night.

During the time it took for Nashkid to arrive Kijibashie had a chance to rest a bit in his own wigwam hovel. It seems that, besides being quite handsome to the women, he held a fair amount of prominence amongst members of the Pauquatuket Nehantucket clan. His speed and agility navigating the trails with messages of importance had become legendary among the young and old alike, especially among the young women who would vie for his attention.

There was a gaggle of women who tended to him as soon as he returned. When he retreated to his hovel a very pretty, young woman called "Ikwea" came and insisted on rubbing sage oil on his feet to help him sleep soundly. She was sitting outside his entrance when he arose three hours later. He had gone completely out of body during this deep nap, arising totally refreshed. He thanked Ikwea as he caressed her hair brushing the side of her face and neck down to her shoulder, as she cooed with its sensation. "I must go now; we have many important tasks to attend to this day. When these tasks are done, you will return with your oil?" he asked. She smiled brightly with acceptance. No words were needed.

Here at his home village, he would be in attendance at all council meetings and discussions. His opinion on certain topics was heard with open ears, many times expressing an alternate perspective or solution.

At this meeting, just after Nashkid and the Nehantics arrived, Kijibashie joined just in time to do the formal introductions. Nashkid and his two Abenaki comrades were encouraged to rest, eat and get acquainted in a manner with such attendance and such a welcoming hospitality that one of his Abenaki partners smiled, saying, "We should like to visit here once again very soon!"

It was agreed. Arising from the small council's meeting, Magwagonk spoke his directives to the support women, who ran to gather the gift baskets and spread the word. The men began the half-mile trek down to the beach head. Although they would not approach until all was in place. This was to be the very first organized encounter with the Norse.

The strategy was set. Nashkid and Kijibashie would be the front men to approach first and speak directly to the Norsemen chieftain. Magwagonk and his contingent of medicine shamans and all adult hunters would remain fifty paces behind them, including the other Abenaki and western Nehantucket men.

Other curious young men women and children would remain farther away at the tree line. The two would first offer gifts of dried venison, fish, sweet berries, and herbs in the woven baskets, a gesture of peace.

31 The First Contact

The selected people gathered at their prescribed locations. The gifts were placed at Kijibashie and Nashkid's feet. Meanwhile they spoke quietly with one another, further planning how they would begin this approach. They identified the one Nordic who appeared to be the chieftain or leader. They agreed to start by simple introduction and displaying a parchment sketch of the clan village and other villages and people with a figure taller than the others representing Eagle Claw as head sachem.

Nashkid, gazing down upon the Nordics from a distance, looked at Kijibashie, nodding his head while he spoke, "These Nordics look to be the same who came to our northern mountain village. They wear the same skins and bear the same fire hair on their face." Pointing, he said, "See the round shields and the axes? Yes! These are the same!"

Kijibashie swallowed hard, then looked at Nashkid and, raising his eyebrows wide, holding his hands open with a shrugged shoulder, said "Yes." Unsure, he added "This is a good plan? This should work, yes?" Nashkid replied, "Well my friend, they can only try to kill us with those big axes if it does not work!"

Taking a deep breath and gathering courage, Kijibashie turned to look back at his so-called reinforcements one last time. He squinted once or twice, not quite making out in the distance a silhouette. He took another double look, then looked back at Nashkid and pointed. Nashkid turned and squinted as well, standing between him and the group was a familiar sight.

There stood Tibamahgan and his tamed timber wolf, raising his hand to them he walked straight down the slope. He commanded the wolf to stay on his heal. Shaking hands was not in any way a Nantucket custom. Rather, a man would reach out and grab one firmly by a shoulder with a slight shake as a custom of reuniting comradery. Tibamahgan did this first with Nashkid and then Kijibashie.

Lone Wolf had decided to make the trek to Pauquatuket at the last moment. He left a few hours or so after Nashkid's contingent left. He felt as though he should be there in support and as an additional representative toward the cause. He also was very intrigued by the Nordics and just wanted to see them for himself.

To begin his trek he had gone back down to the beach front to find his two fishermen friends and commissioned them to transport him and the wolf in their sealskin canoe over to the east side river inlet of what we now know as "Thames." Putting a hood over the wolf's head they were able to keep the reluctant canine calm, being over water and in a canoe for the first time. Lone Wolf had to keep a constant reassuring hand on the wolf most of the trip.

The canoe travel cut many hours of walking off the trip by trail and brought Lone Wolf there just in time for the encounter, very much to the satisfaction of Kijibashie and Nashkid. The entire Pauquatuket clan village was also in awe of Tibamahgan.

They approached the Norsemen's makeshift camp. They halted just a short distance away standing in quiet alertness. The four Norse, two of which were women, did not at first hear or notice the three Nehantuckets approach. They stood in silence holding the baskets with their adornments and implements belted or strapped to shoulder and waist. The two males were younger than expected. It seemed that they had been tasked with chopping poles and bringing them back to the large serpent canoe. There was an obvious foot path now worn into the sand from the short trek through the sandy dunes back and forth to large serpent canoe.

Some knocking on wood could be heard in the distance coming from the boat. The older Norsemen were attempting some type of repair, chiseling and shaping a large log of driftwood beached near the boat just above the high tide water line.

Kijibashie, staring in silence at the Nordic women, spoke softly without turning his gaze, "I was very much wanting to see hair coming from their face!" With the myth finally debunked, a chuckle came from both Nashkid and Lone Wolf, who glanced at each askance, perhaps thinking "Of all the things to be observed and the tension around what they were about to do with this first contact, this is what Kijibashie notices?" It did lighten the tension a bit for the three of them.

Nordic women did not have facial hair, but all the Nordic men did: long reddish beards that hung down onto the chest, stained and discolored around the mouth area.

They stood there in silence. Staying still for many moments, until finally one of the women looked up and noticed them. Startled, she gave out a slight shriek and retreated backward a few steps, gaining the attention of the other three.

One of the males reached for his axe, then gathered in front of the two women speaking some words of directive. The other male ran hastily to his side. One of the women ran toward the serpent canoe some fifty paces away on the beach. What occurred next was just a silent staring contest with the three Nordics under a tense spell.

Unbeknownst to the Nehantuckets was the fact that their adornments and dress, common to them, was quite intimidating to the Nordics. Together, the feathering hanging downward from their hair, the leather strip upper arm bands with wampum shell trinkets, the belted stone axes, adorned bow and arrow quivers, spears, deerskin leggings painted with hieroglyphic symbols, bronzed chest skin recently painted with red okra and blue berry paste in patterns meant for protection made a formidable sight. Except for the protection paints, which were added in preparation by the medicine shamans that morning, this was the normal daily dress and personal implements each of them would wear and carry highlighting their individual personalities, taste, and stature.

The eight Nordic men arrived and took up position in front of the women at the makeshift camp. Other than the very first encounter a few days prior on the beach with Kijibashie, these Nordic had not had any direct contact with the Pauquatuket Nehantuckets, other than the gift of fresh water and one basket of dried fish which was placed on the sand that day.

The Norsemen, with axes and shields in hand, were also in awe and somewhat intimidated by the colorful garb. They perceived the spears as weapons of war but, most of all, it was Tibamahgan's massive wolf standing alongside the three silent natives that shook fear and intimidation into these Norsemen causing them to take an immediate stance of defense. After another very long tense moment of staring in silence, the body language of the Nordics finally relaxed. The one who was presumably their head chieftain spoke a few words to his fellow kinsmen with a slight nod to either side. Then, they stood down a bit!

Kijibashie glanced at Nashkid and Lone Wolf standing on either side of him, then bent down and lifted the two baskets of offerings. Holding them outward, he stepped forward a few paces, knelt on one knee, and placed them just in front of the Nordic chieftain. He then stood and stepped back into position with Lone Wolf and Nashkid.

Kijibashie was the only familiar face the Nordics remembered from a couple days ago when they had first landed. Kijibashie made a hand gesture, holding his open palms up toward the chieftain. He brought them back to his chest. Then he turned and put his palm on Nashkid's chest, next towards Lone Wolf, and then towards the chieftain, to indicate that they all should try to speak.

In the next moment, it was the Nordic who implied with a hand gesture and a nod of understanding, that they should continue, all the while steadily eyeing the very large timber wolf of Tibamahgan's, standing there with a primal intensity. The wolf slightly bared its white teeth, as its frontal lips curled back instinctively, his nostrils filling with the scent of these Nordics.

Noticing the reluctance, Kijibashie turned to point at the group of elders and hunters standing at a distance at the elevated ground near the tree line behind him. Again, he gestured with his open hand from his chest toward the chieftain, to indicate that they three were here to speak on behalf of the council in the distance behind them.

Nashkid noted that the Nehantuckets had the upper hand. To avoid any fear-based reactions, he spoke softly to Kijibashie and Lone Wolf, careful of his tone of voice as he said, "We should now just sit down in this sand facing them. Let the basket offerings speak now of our intent." Lone Wolf and Kijibashie simultaneously raised eyebrows, glancing at Nashkid in surprise! Lone Wolf, not taking his eyes off the chieftain muttered, "Do you really think that is wise?"

Nashkid said in response, also holding his gaze on the Nordics, "If they were going to kill us, they would have done so by now! If we sit, it will show we mean them no harm". Lone Wolf responded, "I think you should sit first!" It was Nashkid's eyebrows that now were raised! He nodded slightly and let out a groan. Then he abruptly plopped himself down into seated position, crossing his legs in the sand, and nodding his head for the rest to follow. Lone Wolf, after Kijibashie sat, motioned to his wolf to stay put at which the wolf crouched down. Satisfied, Lone Wolf surveyed the Nordics for a moment and not sensing any negative body language from them, he sat as well. Then he glanced at Nashkid, rolling his eyes in reluctance of the idea.

The Norsemen were all in awe of the control Tibamahgan had over his fierce and intimidating timber wolf as it obeyed the command. The power behind that simple action, without words being spoken, was impressive enough for the Norsemen's chief to realize that any aggression would not end well.

32 An Arduous Journey

Kijibashie put out his hands with palms up toward the Norsemen, and then pushed the baskets more forward, inviting the Norse to also sit. And so, within a few moments, the Norse sat in the sand. Tensions were now relaxed and the awkward process of establishing a dialog began. The chieftain tasted a few of the blueberries and delighted in the flavor!

He kept a watchful eye on the timber wolf, just yards behind the three natives. He was careful not to make any sudden actions that could cause Tibamahgan to want to react. There was, he noticed, a powerful aura and essence surrounding Lone Wolf in comparison with the other two. It was a quiet, yet unintimidated, fearless energy that demanded his respect.

The Norse chieftain subconsciously sensed now the hospitality as genuine and, that if they were to acquire access to supplies on this foreign soil which they desperately needed, it would only be by the outcome and favor of this encounter with these three here in the sand.

Seeing the gifts baskets were chockfull, he could tell there was abundance here on this shore. So far, an atmosphere of peaceful, yet cautious hospitality existed. However, he was aware it could rapidly turn defensive in very short order. He turned to his members behind him, speaking a directive for them not to show any form of hostility or provocation. He had come to realize that they were the guests here on this particular shore.

These natives were in fact displaying a hospitality so far unlike any of the many previous encounters the Norsemen had had since their journey began so many months ago. On one of their landings much farther north after a long three weeks of open ocean travel by sail living from iceberg to iceberg on nothing but seal meat and fish, they made landfall finally along the southern shore of what is now known as Nova Scotia.

Replenishment of fresh water, greens and berry was their only priority. After barely doing so and within only two and a half days, they were immediately deemed trespassers by the local inhabitants known as the "Mi'kmaq," in today's terminology. Those natives were very warlike in their ways, fiercely defending their own hunting and fishing territories. The Norse were immediately perceived as intruders when they took some game birds without the customary permission.

No dialog was established before conflict broke out between three young Mi'kmaq and two of the Norse, who barely made it back to the longboat, one of whom was severely wounded by an atlatl spear tip of shark tooth that pierced his side. The Norsemen had to hastily take to the water with barely enough supplies that rationed them for only five days. The Mi'kmaq, for days, tracked them along the coastal beaches and shore for many miles taunting the Norse longboat. No landing was possible.

It was only after the five-day sail southward keeping distance from the shore by a mile or so were they able, on the sixth day, to land on a beach area somewhere about the mid coast of Maine, as we know it today.

Here they made landfall! By the time they were finally able to replenish water and meats of rabbit and fowl the wounded comrade was in a very bad way. His wound had begun to fester. Their limited herbs and poultices of mosses and lichens were not effective, they had no knowledge of this region's natural pharmacy. Within just a few days all supplies were restored. They set to harvesting roots, drying meats, filling kegs with fresh sweet spring water, filling baskets with berries of the season, and loading dry wood on board. Their land camp provided peace and comfort unencumbered by natives.

It was in peace and warmth by the fire that the wounded Norseman died during the fourth night in the silent comfort of his sleep. He had seemed to be on the road to recovery as he smiled at the taste of herbal root tea just before his slumber. A simple stone pedestal was placed as his marker after the traditional ceremonial burial.

Hugging close to the shoreline for another two months of travel, they continued southward hitting landfall along the way only after surveying the shorelines for sign of indigenous inhabitants, now to be avoided if possible. A day or two at most, to collect fresh water and replenish fresh meats left little tell of their brief stops along the New England coast, although a more permanent place to land and settle was their ultimate goal.

This very small band of Norsemen, brave and adventurous as they were, brings wonderment to us today as to what reasoning warranted them to venture so far from their clansmen and homeland? Could it have been clan rivalries, shifting glacial ice melts, storm surges at sea, a seeking of warmer climate, or just a quest to explore the next horizon? Whatever it was that drove them, they had come many leagues, finding a much gentler climate and abundance of game, fish, and fowl wherever their landings found them.

Then a sudden storm moved in fast and fierce. Two miles offshore, its winds of hurricane proportions circled with intensity in a southwesterly direction. The Norse had no to time to navigate landfall. Neither to the small islands on the southeast, known today as Block Island or the mainland beaches at Rhode Island. The winds took them closer towards the tip at Montauk. Still fiercer winds blew them toward the tip of Fishers Island, but despite staying hard on the tiller for hour, the intense wind shifted and drove them to the mainland again.

Battered by wind and surf of over twenty feet, two Norsemen lashed themselves to the tiller just to navigate the waves. The others just hunkered down into the hull, bailing water as fast as possible trying to keep up with it as it poured in with each wave. Nighttime fell upon them as the surge of storm's gloom hindered any view of land. Now, it was only through instinctive navigation that they were able to steer the tiller toward the mainland. The wave surges pounded the small craft. Its design was ingenious for its time. Handed down through generations of original Norsemen living along the North Sea, its built-in design endured the sea's moods. If it was not for this durable craft our Norsemen, who have endured many storms in open ocean, would have never survived their lengthy journey.

Exhausted, battered, and blind in the gloom of a moonless black clouded night, they remained at the mercy of their gods to face whatever fate had in store for them. Being bashed upon a rocky reef and splintering the craft to shards was possible. They tilled the vessel to stay just off where they estimated the shore to be, merely guessing as to where they were in the gloom. It was the thud of the boats keel upon the sand bar that woke them.

33 A Meeting in the Sand

It had been five days and nights now since the offshore storm fatefully landed these strangers, these "Norse", upon the sandy point at the Nantucket village of Pauquatuket. It was only out sheer fortune that the craft hit the three-quarter mile long sliver of sand bar, isolated between ledges and lethal jagged rock face cliffs which jutted out into the surf at both eastern and western points. In between, the land sloped gently down, allowing the Pauquatuket village the benefits of its sandy shore.

With tensions and apprehensions finally eased, the language of body, hands, picture sketches drawn in the sand, and etchings of parchment continued through the better part of the day. The Norse were able to describe their endurance of the storm and the distant direction from which they traveled upon the coastal ocean.

They were also able to sketch out drawings of their shelter styles such as narrow long houses with sod roofing. Then so did the Nehantuckets, showing their village's rounder, bark covered style wigwams.

Among the Nehantucket, there was no concept of possession. To them, earth mother gifted its bounty to the Nehantucket people. Thus, these Norse could live where they chose upon it, just as any other creature. There were no boundaries of land between Nehantucket villages, no sense of "land ownership" or territory. The only concept was that of acknowledgment, certain natural harvests foraged by a certain individual or groups such as berries, herbs, roots, reeds for baskets, and even bark from trees for the hovels. Individuals or groups would "own" that area for the duration of such harvests until their needs were met.

Areas cleared, tilled, planted, and cultivated by the women's labors were owned by the individual groups until the plot or soil used up its nutrients. Meanwhile, no others would interfere with the plot, or even dream of taking from it. These harvests were always shared throughout the clan or village community.

It was the same concept for the men who hunted the smaller game or deer and moose. Those men who fished the shore waters and inland stream waterfall areas for spawning sea bass and trout would "possess" that location while their nets were in place. Smaller game such as rabbit, grouse waterfowl and beaver caught by individuals or groups setting their snares would "own" these locations or territory, so that they could make their rounds every few days to check the traps and harvest the catch.

The larger migratory creatures, as we mentioned earlier, such as woodland bison, elk and caribou, would require a larger group effort of ten men or more in a small hunting party, and upwards of one hundred entailing the entire village including women and children to drive or separate the larger herd into the ravines for harvest. Other clans would respect these hunting territories by not interfering unless invited.

This concept was finally conveyed by Kijibashie. It was only after the drawings showed each prospective Nantucket village with a large scale "territorial" area surrounding them, then a potential Norse village with a very long distance between the territories. This was demonstrated by Kijibashie. He drew the Nehantucket hovels in the sand showing an appropriate distance apart by pacing more than five long, exaggerated steps away, then drawing the Norse style dwellings.

This seemed to make the point. The three Nehantucket believed the Norse chieftain understood.

Then there were the territorial boundaries. This concept was a bit harder to convey, the more complexity of the various territories of hunting game, fishing, village areas and sacred ceremonial places. These were off limits to these strangers as the Nehantucket sachems directed.

It took quite a while for Kijibashie to try and describe this meaning. The confusion grew worse, the Norse not understanding, as the hospitable gestures at the start of the session had seemed to welcome the strangers to stay.

After an even longer while, everyone had moved to speaking amongst themselves, loudly and all at once. Finally, Lone Wolf had had enough! He stood up abruptly, which summoned their attention. He spoke softly and deliberately, with a tone of authority and command.

He pointed to all the Norse, then picked up the basket of berries and thrust it forward. He then pointed at the sun and held up four fingers on one hand, an indication of four days. Next, he drew the Norse boat with the serpent head at the bow in the sand. With two fingers, after pointing at the Norsemen again, walked his fingers to the boat and pointed at the blue ocean then he waved his hand twice, flat and sideways, to indicate they should sail away!

Now the Norse chieftain had no more confusion. He understood the message clearly. He looked Lone Wolf straight in the eye, whose gaze never wavered. The Norse chieftain nodded twice. One of his men began to speak, at which point, everyone stood up. The chieftain held up his hand without turning around, motioning his companions to be silent.

Again, without turning around and lifting his gaze to Lone Wolf, he spoke words in his tongue to his kindred telling them that they had four days to gather supplies, then they would leave this beach. They would show gratitude for the gift of this temporary hospitality and not wear out the welcome of these people.

His gaze first met the eyes of the tall native Tibamahgan, who commanded the timber wolf still standing just to the side, then the eyes of the quieter one, Nashkid, who stood, holding his bow, and finally the younger talkative one who remained sitting. He nodded to each acknowledging the final directive.

"You see," said Nashkid, with a serious expression, "still, they offer no trade or gifts!" He mumbled it scornfully under his breath as if the Norse could understand. Kijibashie, who then finally stood up to indicate that this meeting was concluded, looked at his comrades. Speaking quietly, he said, "They do look hungry!" Lone Wolf spoke softly again, never flinching his gaze, "Well, we did not get chopped by those big axes yet! Perhaps that is gift enough," forming a half-crooked smile and jesting his comrades! Then, Kijibashie spoke more somber words, closer to the truth, "It could be they have nothing to give!"

The Norse chieftain commanded one of his men, saying something in their tongue and pointing toward their vessel sitting at low tide on the sand. The man made a beeline toward their boat, half running. Within a few minutes he trotted back with something wrapped in a type of sheep skin tied at both ends.

The three Nehantuckets had just prepared to leave the circle and started to walk back up the dunes where the villagers had remained lined up at the crest of the hill in observation. It was then when the chieftain loudly spoke out, "Tibamahgan!" barely pronouncing it with his Norse accent. The three turned as the Norse runner handed the package to the chieftain. Then he, in turn, walked forward and with both hands forward presented it to Lone Wolf.

Cocking his head slightly, bewildered, Tibamahgan undid the wrapping revealing a beautiful stone double edged axe with exquisite, engraved etchings upon both sides of the handle bearing an oblong hole at its haft end. It fit the hand perfectly. It was honed sharp on both blades of the axe, one blade being broader in width than the other. The stone it was made from was of a very hard ore of unknown origin, not found along the Nehantucket shore.

After examination, he handed it to Nashkid stating, "believe we were wrong!" Nashkid examined it and nodded approvingly, as he handed it to Kijibashie who also admired its heft and style. He nodded in approval as he handed it back to Tibamahgan. Careful not to show any emotion, all three nodded to the Norse chieftain again in approval and acceptance. The meeting was now formally concluded.

34 Monolithic Axe

There was an immediate sensation while holding the gift of this beautiful stone axe, holding it as briefly as they did, feeling its texture against the fingers and hand, each of the three Nehantuckets felt some form of soothing power emitting from it. The hand section formed to the palm of the hand. It felt as if it were a living extension of the hand.

Its weight was in perfect balance and proportion. Its etchings were of magnificent design, with effigies of birds upon its handle and the head and beak of a large eagle-sized bird forming its topmost point.

Its most outstanding feature was that it was monolithic, formed of one continuous slab of stone. Monoliths, of any size, were considered to hold special energetic properties. Lone Wolf felt the power from it immediately, but determined to suppress his surprise due to the intensity of the meeting in the sand and the message they were sent to convey. He felt reluctant to hand it off to Nashkid.

Nashkid felt it too; a lightness overwhelmed him, a sense of complete centering. For him, the texture of the stone from which it was made was flawlessly smooth. He was also reluctant to pass it to Kijibashie. As he did so he could only glance at Lone Wolf to see if the energy was shared in the same way. He decided he would ask later in private.

Kijibashie, overwhelmed at first once he took it in his hands, just stared at it laying across both his palms. He was lifted even more as he held the haft in his hand. It was as if the bird effigies sent his inner spirit to a place of flight above himself. Consciousness of body funneled him back to the physical world and he wrapped the artifact back up in its pouch and handed it back to Tibamahgan.

Made from a special ore, a mineral of black tourmaline, found only in a few parts of the coastline of what is now referred to as Greenland, it can only be assumed that this axe was made long ago and handed down through ancestral Nordic heritage. It must have held a powerful spiritual meaning to these Nordic who have traveled so far.

It was truly an exquisite gift, far beyond what any of them expected to receive from these Norsemen. The Norse chieftain knew exactly what they sensed while holding and feeling the energy of the artifact. All three Nehantucket men, now knew that for these Norse to share this powerful gift, was indeed a demonstration of appreciation for their hospitality.

Lone Wolf thought to himself that perhaps they were a bit harsh with the directives. Just before returning to the Pauquatuket sachem, the three convened for a discussion amongst themselves in which it was decided to allow select tribal members to provide dried meats, jerkies, dried fish, and fresh herbs; plus succotash, berries, and staples to be presented to the Norse for their continued journey.

A map etching on birch bark parchment would be presented depicting some deep river inlets just to the south along the mainland shore with potential sites distant from the river edges and well inland far from any Nehantucket clan village's territorial boundary. A place where these Norse could build their winter longhouse and live so as not to interfere with the Nehantucket. One such river was what we refer to today as the Thames River and another, the Stonington River. The Quinnehtukqut, or "long river" was much further southwest along the shore.

A site of what appears to be "Celtic" ceremonial stone henges situated a few miles up the Thames and a few miles inland on the eastern woodland shore, in a place known as Gungywamp is a place the exists today where these ancient Nordics may have landed and lived for many years for generations, prospering in the bounty of the land.

The heirloom artifact, this monolithic axe, was in fact handed down through generations of Nehantucket. Due to its mystical properties it was kept and used by the Nehantucket medicine healers, shamans and spiritual leaders, one of which was Mahkiwasie, the Medicine Girl, who became the first keeper to use it in her healing work.

After presenting the map and the goods to the Norsemen the three original Nehantuckets and just a handful of the village men and women, along with the Pauquatuket sachem, watched the Norse longboat launch into the surf at high tide and raise its sail of patched sheep skin. It sailed off toward the south, tacking with the winds. They watched as it became only a dot on the horizon. The villagers lined the high points along the shore to see this spectacle, some would even run along the shoreline for a few miles to try to keep them in sight. Folklore amongst the Nehantics, for quite some time, spoke of how the Norsemen visited the islands known today as Block, Fishers and Gardiners. Local lore described how they also visited the tip of

Montauk, as it is known today, before making it back up the River Thames.

This would not be the last time Lone Wolf would encounter these same Norsemen.

35 Power of the Stones

Preparing their individual satchel's and implements, Lone Wolf and Nashkid would soon depart on their trip back to the main village on the Nehantucket shore. With them they would bear the monolithic axe, the gift from the Norsemen visitors, to be presented to the Nehantucket head sachem Eagle Claw and his woman Nodinosi.

The details of the encounter at Pauquatuket would be explained in depth to the two leaders of the Nehantucket nation. Nashkid and Lone Wolf knew that the power qualities of the stone axe must be experienced firsthand to understand the full meaning of change that could affect the tribal cultures of not only the Nehantuckets but of all other neighboring tribes to the north, south, east, and west.

The very knowledge of the existence of another type of people, foreign to the established lifestyle of their harmonious living and their belief system, along with a culture of alien beings with a new technology and the ability to travel a great distance from an unknown land was inevitably disconcerting. It was exactly what the toothless old sage woman had envisioned!

Nashkid and Long Wolf would depart two days prior to Kijibashie making his run. That would give the travelers a head start at their slower pace to cover the distance back to the Nehantucket with an overnight camp to rest along the trail somewhere midway near the eastern side of the Thames River, as we call it today.

The sachem at Pauquatuket was at council on the evening of the Nordic departure and brought up fully with all interpretations by participants of the meeting in the sand. He then, on birch parchment, depicted his overview and offered council to be presented to Eagle Claw, along with words to be relayed personally by Kijibashie whom he directed to run the trail as well to be there in person since he was directly part of the Nordic negotiation.

Council elders, sachems, shaman and spiritual leaders, men and women alike, did not have the luxury of "living in the moment" and going about their daily tasks with great leisure, as did the general tribal men and women.

These leaders would have to use foresight beyond the moments of daily life and pleasures to plan for seasonal movements of village camps, severity of storm surges, and spiritual events such as solstice and equinoxes that represented their spiritual life. The latter warranted ceremony and giving thanks for the shifting of seasons and bounties of the earth that they were part of.

Nehantuckets lived very richly, having little in the way of wants or complaints. They understood and taught the concept to children at a young age that "to live in wanting," you must produce "much," while to live in "richness," you must "desire little," and to live in leisure, you must live in the moment.

The tribal leaders must have, at times, been torn in these teachings for the best benefit of the whole tribe, torn between wanting and being in the moment on a community level and scale at the same time. They often had to overcome inner personal burdens in order to make heavy decisions or voice counsel.

Lone Wolf and Nashkid had walked the first leg of the day after departing Pauquatuket. They kept an enduring pace, a little out of their nature of being leisurely in their daily tasks and endeavors. The four other Nehantucket men had left half a day earlier, eager to get back to their loved ones with the exiting news of the Nordics!

So Nashkid and Tibamahgan set camp on the trail for the evening. They would cross the large river we now call the Thames the following morning by dugout canoe.

Nibbling the dinner morsels from their pouches with the warmth of the fire, they reminisced about the Nordics. "Can I ask you, Tibamahgan, your sense about the gift of stone axe?" Nashkid asked in a subtle and apprehensive manner. He could not get the sensations he had felt from the relic, when it was handed to him on the beach, out of his head. He was curious if his friend Lone Wolf would reveal or share any similar experience of it, so he chose his words carefully.

To start the conversation, Nashkid reached into his possibles pouch and retrieved his quartz crystal, a bear tooth, necklace of cat claw, and some stones of various minerals that brought him personal power and held deep meaning. He laid his trinkets out on a flat stone at their fire's edge. "Tibamahgan! Have you tried your crystal and felt its power of thought yet?" he asked as he now held his own crystal in the palm of his hand.

Lone Wolf responded, with an affirming nod. Remembering his morning in his hovel dreaming of Mahkiwasie, and the out of body sensation he experienced with her. "My sensations have been as real as I am speaking here with you now. A 'very precious gift,' much thanks for it to you!" he said in appreciation.

Nashkid spoke again. Feeling a little more comfortable, he said, "I have not had any opportunity to bring this one out of its pouch these past few days. Being away from my woman, Ninikiji, for so long, thoughts of her are now coming in here," as he pointed to his head. "This night I shall finally use my crystal to think of being next to her, and she will know and feel my thoughts. We will slip off to some quiet place when we can after I return, and we will lay together in secret again as we used to do in the mountains."

Lone Wolf was enchanted, he immediately thought of Medicine Girl, picturing her beautiful face and long hair draping scantly over her breasts and flowing softly to her thighs. He flashed a thought of being with her as well, in a secret place he had already chosen far away from the village, a remote place with soft moss upon the smooth ledges and a cliff-like overhang shielding the fire. It would be bedded with fine pine boughs and grasses. He would drape a large hide over the entrance in case of rain and to keep the fire embers' heat in at night.

His hand reached into his own pouch and immediately found the crystal amongst the other trinkets, its length and smoothness unmistakable to the touch in the pouch. He withdrew it and placed it on a flat stone in front of himself. Then he poured out the other heirlooms onto the stone.

"Yes, my friend!" he said in a very low tone, "I like to think of Mahkiwasie in the same way. I have yet to find a way to be with her in secret, away from prying eyes, but I have planned for that! I'm sure she will like it very much!" He held the crystal in his palm, then squeezed it tight for a moment. Nashkid spoke again, "Then perhaps it is time to bring the Nordic axe from its wrapping too! Did you not feel its power when it touched your hands, Tibamahgan?"

Lone Wolf thought to himself of the sensation he felt from the artifact when he first unwrapped it from its folds, how the handle had formed to his hand and the air-headed lightness that overtook his being. He then remembered how he had to struggle to suppress it for the sake and importance of the meeting with the Norsemen.

But now sitting here with just his trusted friend, he could talk of it openly and take it out of its folds. He reached into the pouch and produced the deer skin bound and tied with sinew at each end. He placed it on the flat stone between his own crystal and Nashkid's. Before unwrapping it, his eyes met Nashkid's with intensity.

It was a very long silent moment with both taking a deep breath. Simultaneously they untied each end of its binding and unfolded the soft skin hide to reveal the article there in the firelight.

Nashkid leaned back sighing in a bit of relief as he was half expecting some sensation again from its power. Lone Wolf relaxed a bit as well. It was then that Tibamahgan's timber wolf rose from its laying position near the fire circle and approached, settling into sitting position just between the two men two feet from the artifact and the fires edge.

The wolf stared intensely at the stone axe; never before had the animal behaved this way.

36 Shifts of Time and Sand

What happened next was nothing short of eerie and intriguing at the same time. There was a sort of vibrational tone, subtle at first, that seemed to begin with a high frequency deep in the ear, then abruptly shifted noticeably to a lower more soothing natural tone, a tone that comes from the earth itself. It was a harmonic that is sensed by animals much sooner than humans, but sensed by humans at a very subconscious, at least by most, and consciously when focused upon by those few who choose to understand and explore it.

It turns out this evening that the monolithic axe exposed from its wrappings and placed next to the personal crystals was acting as an antenna that projected and amplified the earth's life frequency.

Its properties were dramatically enhanced by the quartz crystals on either side of it in some way! None of this was totally understood by the two men, only that they knew and felt the power of this artifact when it touched their hands, and now again next to the crystals. Even the timber wolf found himself attracted to it.

They both looked at each other, each feeling compelled to hold their individual crystals; simultaneously they each took and held a deep breath. With the deep vibrational tone still in their heads, Lone Wolf was the first to reach down, snatch his crystal, and hold it tightly in his fist. Nashkid did the same.

Lone Wolf's eyes were wide open, while he had a vivid vision of Mahkawasie standing next to him reaching for his hand, as they walked the obscure trail. Her touch was soothing to him. The trail led to a secret and secluded place; an outcrop of ledge hollowed out underneath by the ancient glacial river flow now long since dried for a few thousand years.

In his vision, the lean-to shelter he had made over the cave's entrance was intact. Here they lay with each other for days and nights at a time as lovers do. The days found them foraging the special herbs she was passionate about, ginseng root and *usnea* lichens that grow on apple, birch, and other trees. They collected elderberry, sassafras, sage grass, wild strawberries, licorice root, and birch root.

Evenings found them watching a herd of woodland bison grazing grasses down in a small open valley from a high cliff-like precipice, until the sun set below the horizon.

Every sense of him knew she was his woman body and spirit, his soulmate.

Next the vision went forward in time, where they lived together openly in the village, each holding positions of power and responsibility for the tribe. Close friends and other members of the tribe who were important to him like Bird and the fishing brothers, matured and grew older as grayness streaked their hair. It was a life vision of the near future.

It did not stop there. He felt and saw his essence suddenly thrust into a newer generation or many generations forward in time, while he remained as shamans with his people through these lifetimes, guiding them to retain the Starr People knowledge and the Mother Earth's power of things.

Visions flashed in his mind of the people working together building large stone mounds as they were guided to do. These were created in purposeful patterns to mimic star clusters like the seven sisters of Pleiades, Alfa Centauri, and Andromeda. These mounds would number in the tens and twenties at certain sites. Nearby, stone offering chambers and ceremonial circle sites were constructed and meant to pay tribute to the ancient ones from the stars, and to retain the teachings of great spirit knowledge. Also, on personal vision quests, stone structures were built effigies of animals, tortoise, eagle and hawk, copper-toned and black serpents of fertility; all cast in stone works of precision for eternity, along with small personal offering chambers.

In his vision, Lone Wolf helped to create the belted beads and hieroglyphic pictorial belts and straps to help remember and tell the tales of the Starr People, and to pass ancient knowledge and tales of escapades of ancestral people of power from the beginning times of the Nehantuckets. These were the first early forms of their written language to be retold for generations by the story tellers.

Next, journeying even further forward in time, he saw strange vessels vast in size, larger still than the Norsemen's ship. Dark turbulent charcoal and purple clouds surrounded the vessels. Then the sands of the once tranquil beaches shifted violently and moved like stormy ocean waves, as if to swallow whole the quiet, peaceful Nehantucket village.

It was disturbing to a high degree, provoking a surge of helpless anxiety in his core. Lone Wolf knew it was a vision far in the future; still its intensity jolted him back to his physical being.

Lone Wolf found his breath to be at a hyperventilating pace. Still, he felt that he was safe viewing this future event from a much higher vibrational place, as an observer. He could not determine when it was to take place, but his sense was that it was a dire change of things to come for the Nehantucket people in a very distant timeline. He sensed his people were safe from it, as prior to this storm vision most would have already raised their vibrational frequency and moved to a higher dimensional place, but it angered him none the less.

Lone Wolf jolted back to reality, breathing heavily. Regaining his awareness, he thrust the quartz crystal into his pouch. It took him a while to regain his full equilibrium.

Nashkid was still in his own state of trance standing there holding his quartz crystal. He was speaking in soft low indistinguishable tones; the words were in a tongue of some ancient language. He seemed to be in a cold sweat. Then he suddenly began to smile as he held the crystal in both hands to his solarplex center. Lone Wolf knew not to disturb.

Nashkid too eventually awoke from his own visionary journey; his also started with a sense of being with his soulmate in this life, due to his first and foremost impassioned thoughts of her. He found himself openly walking hand in hand and living happily within the Nehantucket community just on the outskirts of the village.

He became an important teacher, and sage of the tribe in his graying days of peace and harmony. His vision took him back to the green mountains of Vermont, as we refer to it today, and his birth tribe of the Abenaki. There his ancestors had already constructed massive stone ceremonial mounds paying tribute to the same Starr People and the constellations from which they came.

He visited this site twice during his younger days, attending the ceremonies and learning how over hundreds of years they were built. He learned about the knowledge contained within the massive formations with a large quartz crystal boulder placed at each center, drawing the celestial power frequencies to amplify the vibrations for his people to harness the power.

This site contained over one hundred mounds of processional placed stone; the construction masonry would prove to last for hundreds if not thousands of years. Nashkid's vision clearly depicted another race of human living in the same area at the base of the large precipitous mountain with vertical cliff faces in all directions.

In his vision, he knew that some of the older first largest mounds existed well before the Abenaki came to inhabit the region. In fact, the very early stories and lore of the ancestral Abenaki described a different human culture, a culture of extremely large beings much taller in stature and physic than the Abenaki.

These beings had double rows of teeth and massive strength capable of lifting boulders and slabs of stone that would take ten Abenaki men to move. Pictorial glyphs and etchings of these people could be found within the stone walls of caves and on mammoth stone pedestals. They were in these pictures twice and half again the stature of an Abenaki man.

Many stone markers were warnings for the early Abenakis not to enter certain areas at the base of this mountain. Lore told of those who entered on hunting excursions to never return.

Nashkid's vision continued more forward in time where he too was as a spirit in observance of the place before his life time, a long ago time when an earthly upheaval shifted the bedrock of the mountains and the narrow gorge that diked back the great lake waters, the very shore on which their village would later evolve with its Abenaki wigwams and huts at the base of Mount Horrid's lower slopes and gentle valley. The vast fresh lake waters receded very rapidly at first, over a short period of time of perhaps a few decades.

That pass was located miles to the north, at a place near the current town of Granville. The tumble glacial rock in this gulf held back the great inland sea waters, and to the south the great Vermont lake submerged today's lush valleys and lower sloping mountain grades.

Nashkid's vision showed how ages ago, the great water rapidly receded as a quake shifted and opened the rock dam at the gorge and how the torrents of water tore the gorge open, draining the inland lake completely and reducing its body to what is now Lake Champlain to the west.

His vision showed how more recently, the Abenaki people lived for thousands of years at the base of Mount Horrid, a sacred precipice for them, where they continued building the ceremonial mounds of stone.

It was here where Nashkid was born and grew and learned the ways of the land, nature, and celestial knowledge. Again, he became an observing entity as he was projected into the future, where his people prospered in the mountains for many, many years to come. The Abenaki would grow and expand to live throughout the Green Mountains, inhabiting its valleys and gentler slopes along its rivers and streams.

Lore and stories, knowledge, and rituals were passed from generation to generation, preserved and cited by the elder story keepers. As time moved forward again the versions became diluted. Starr People knowledge of energy, frequencies, power of the crystals, and vortex centers all began to diminish in their memory.

Future tribal people became overwhelmed with hardships of changing weather patterns, very harsh winters, deep snows, fierce winds and flooding rains. They would be forced to seek winter camps many miles to the south, taking weeks of travel. Yet they would return to the tranquil summers of the mountains.

In Nashkid's vision, there was a sudden appearance of an odd type of men adorned in skins of unknown fabric, with facial hair not unlike the Norse. They bore sticks that boomed and thrust fire. He saw his Abenaki folk lying in fever, moaning in illness unbeknown to them ever before.

The strangers brought great disrespect to the land, animals, earth and the tribal people. They brought senseless killing of women and children alike. Even more of these strangers came to the mountains, bringing disruption of all tranquility. These hordes of strangers adorned in colors of red and blues brought violence and war even amongst themselves.

Nashkid's vision left him with a feeling of upheaval, not unlike the great quake that shifted the earth and drained the inland Vermont sea; thus the cold sweat that Lone Wolf observed.

Even though Nashkid's strong inner power reminded him of this vision to be, thousands of seasons to the future, he was suddenly returned to his current moment in his physical time. His trance became more dreamlike, and subtle thoughts of being in the nurturing arms of his woman, Ninikiji, brought him back to conscious awareness. This was why he bore a peaceful smile. Opening his eyes, he too slowly put his crystal down exhaling in contemplation of it all.

Nashkid's and Lone Wolf's eyes met after the collection of themselves took place, no words needed to be spoken at first, with only facial expressions speaking for them, both with their mouths slightly agape. Even the timber wolf sat next to them, depleted in a way, emitting low moaning tones!

Both men simultaneously reached to re wrap the monolithic stone back into its layered pouches, eager to put it away as a way to shut its power off! Together they wrapped it up, Nashkid holding the final pouch open while Tibamahgan placed the bundled crystal inside with both hands and tied it off.

After a long while of silence they spoke of their individual visions. They had to share the intensity with each other in confidence, talking long into the night, to reach an understanding of the meaning of each vision and what now to do with artifact. They agreed its power should remain a protected secret.

37 Insights Shared

Both men slept well the rest of that night, mostly due to the intensity of the visionary experience, its energy not unlike any out-of-body realm of a higher vibration, followed by the returning to the lower vibration of physical earth and gravity.

Sunrise found them both asleep as the sun flickered through the leaves of the trees and danced its rays upon their faces. It was just enough to stir them from morning slumbers.

The wolf was actually first to awaken, letting out a wolfs yawning groan. Tibamahgan rose to his feet, scratched a few kinks out and relieved his bladder at the tree line away from the campfire's embers. Nashkid, now awake, pulled himself up to his knees, then stood, teetering just a bit. He too had to pee and chose a nearby tree trunk as well.

They gathered and strapped their gear, weapons, and possibles bags and headed back toward the Mystic River canoe crossing point; finally finding stride in the pace back by the early part of the morning. Ferrying that crossing, they reached the canoe point at the Thames River, as we call it today, by mid-afternoon. By early evening they reached the eastern embankment of the Nehantucket river, "living water," as they referred to it, at the narrows or "gut," which is located near the current mouth of the shallow river where it spills into the Nehantucket bay. Here they would make their final water crossing, home on familiar ground at last.

The entire Pauquatuket trip and events would require some final discussion as to what should be revealed regarding the "monolithic axe" and its power of revelation.

Both Lone Wolf and Nashkid decided to head straight to Lone Wolf's hovel for that night before reporting to Eagle Claw and his council. This would give them time to consider how to explain the stone axe, as well as the final agreement with the Nordics. It would also allow for Kijibashie to arrive so they could intercept him for a secret discussion amongst themselves about the stone axe.

Tibamahgan wanted to allow Mahkiwasie to feel the power of the axe as well, to get her sense of its healing abilities.

Tibamahgan and Nashkid too were in agreement of this plan to delay making a formal presentation to Chief Eagle Claw and the head council. It would be much better to meet with their full contingent first and with additional insights of the monolithic axe.

Sleep found them well enough again and daybreak found them both at the narrow crossing to await Kijibashie who appeared on the opposite embankment waving arms for the dugout canoe to take him across. The three held a quick conference there on the sand, and agreed to find Medicine Girl and Ninikiji. Kijibashie, Mahkiwasie, and Ninikiji would need to experience the relic's power.

Thus, the three men proceeded towards Mahkiwasie's clan village where the two medicine women could be expected to be found. There the women emerged from Medicine Girl's wigwam, surprised, to say the least, at the men's arrival.

Mahkiwasie was star struck by the arrival of Lone Wolf, whom she had been daydreaming about and somewhat worried, knowing of his trek to Pauquatuket to encounter the Nordics. She tried to hide her enthusiasm, but her mouth remained open in awe of it all. Ninikiji finally blurted the question "What of these Norsemen?" as she focused on Nashkid's face and took his hand, also missing her man.

There would not be time to reacquaint with the womenfolk just yet. "We must speak with you in quiet," Lone Wolf said, as he gestured toward the hut. All five of them retreated into Medicine Girl's hovel at the request of Lone Wolf, who spoke with some urgency in his voice.

Once inside, away from prying ears and with the entrance trap closed, the women were informed of the Nordic encounter, including the gift of the monolithic axe.

It was then that Lone Wolf and Nashkid began to finish each other's sentences with the axe's visionary powers. Kijibashie had only held the artifact briefly at the Nordic encounter, so Lone Wolf handed it to him after it was unwrapped and told him to hold it to his chest and to close his eyes. He did so and went immediately into a trance-like state. It lasted several minutes until he came out of the vision abruptly, placing the axe down on the floor and looking around to get his bearings. Sweat had beaded upon his forehead. Kijibashie also had traveled into a far future time, unsure of what any of it had meant. He tried to explain to the others what he had seen, but it made no sense to his understanding.

Next Lone Wolf handed it to Ninikiji. She immediately felt its energy. Unafraid, she held it to her breast, closed her eyes and began to sway from side to side. She chanted involuntarily. Then, smiling, she began breathing heavily as if running. Suddenly, she thrust both her hands out palms up while the axe fell to the floor at her lap. Slowly, she opened her eyes and focused on the physical reality of the hut. "Ohh," she sighed, as tears welled from her eyes. She could not speak. She just lunged into Nashkid's arms, sitting next to her!

It was Mahkiwasie's turn. Lone Wolf handed her the axe, but she was reluctant. Lone Wolf moved closer to her, and she took it, holding it at arm's length with both hands. He whispered to her that it would be alright and that he would be right there. "You need to have this experience, Mahkiwasie," he said. She looked at him deeply and slowly drew the artifact into her bosom.

What the four observers could interpret from Medicine Girl's facial expressions and body language was connected to what they had each encountered with their own visions while holding the artifact. They could only guess as to what she was seeing and where she was traveling or what timelines she would be taken to.

What they did not know yet was that this artifact held such vast teachings and universal knowledge that only a gifted chosen few would be allowed to use it as it was meant to be used. The Norsemen feared its power, they only used it in brief increments, by the select few that experienced its insights. Fear of it would not allow them the understanding of its potential.

Thus, they wrapped it up, protected it, and kept it hidden, believing it to be some kind of curse by some in their culture, and anything more by just a few. But they knew it was something not to be discarded. Opportunity through a series of synchronicities arose, and so it found its way on the Norsemen's sea voyage journey.

The artifact ultimately and spontaneously was "gifted" to the three powerful Nehantucket men on that sand bar in Pauquatuket that day. In a way the monolithic axe chose its keepers, its protectors; it was a synchronicity meant to be!

In the end, the Norsemen were only the couriers. True, they used it as a form of currency, and it served them well through their long journey, offering brief insights of very near future events for their small group. But the Nordic chieftain was the only one left of three that had held the axe, and never long enough to see any long-term future or obtain any understanding of universal knowledge from it. For them, it had served the Nordics one last time as a way to obtain safe passage in a new land, their final destination in a land of vast future potential.

The Nordics would finally settle in various places along the New England coastline, the first being established in the woodland area upriver of the current Thames, on the eastern shore near the area known today as Gungywamp. Here these same Norsemen would establish a small village, building henges of stone to uphold their cultural beliefs, interacting with the Nehantuckets, and periodically obeying the original mandate of the great Eagle Claw sachem of the Nehantucket people.

Within many of their hieroglyphics etched in stone, through legendary stories and tales passed down through the generations, it is said that an artifact of "great power and insight" guided and led them to this new land of gentle seasons, great bounty of fish and game, and prosperity of peaceful living. The monolithic axe depicted in much of the Norse etchings and lore became an iconic emblem and symbol of their culture and time.

When Medicine Girl awoke from her transcendental state, in the company of her closest friends in the secluded dim light within the hovel she found herself cradled in Lone Wolf's powerful arms. Tears streamed down her face, not of fear or sadness, but tears of joy. She took quite a few moments to collect herself. The others became concerned during Mahkiwasie's session because she was out of body for such a long time. Their own sessions were just a few minutes in real time, while Medicine Girl's trance was much longer, four and five times longer than those of Ninikiji and Kijibashie. They all became so concerned that they whispered to Lone Wolf to take the axe out of her hands. He instead cuddled into her from the side and held her petite body with his arms around her so that she could sense that he was there.

In partial consciousness she refocused in the dim light of the hovel, gently she set the axe back down onto its wrappings and folded one layer back over it; turning its energy off. She spoke very softly "We are the chosen!"

38 Living in the moment

Within this small hovel, with the five select few, an event took place that had not taken place in many hundreds of years. The monolithic axe had not been held by anyone for the durations that these five had held it nor had it been experienced with more than one or two at any given session.

In the circle, Mahkiwasie had not yet revealed her visions with the others, nor had Ninikiji or Kijibashie. But they all knew that each of the others had experienced something similar to themselves in a very profound way.

Tibamahgan spoke first breaking a long silence, "We shall sit here as our own council, we shall discuss revealing this artifact to any others. It has power that we cannot fathom; we must decide together if we should reveal this to any one person as keeper of it."

He turned to Kijibashie, "Would you share your vision with us now?" Kijibashie spoke softly, "I feel I must share it with you here! I just need to find words. It started with me in my body. I was older and had taken my wife, my children were grown, and I was sachem of the Pauquatuket. Then I was not in my body, but above it, and my people were prosperous for many generations until storm clouds came, dark and swirling."

"Out of the clouds came these men not like us, with no hair on the side of their heads. They were angry men and used their hunting tools to hurt my people. They took from the people and never gave back. They became many as the years went forward to a time of great unrest between us, the Nehantuckets; our friends, the Narragansetts to our east, and all of our neighboring tribes: Uncas, Hamonassett, and Mohican to the west and north."

"They would hold our sachems hostage to get tribute each season. They would take our women and kill any Nehantucket man who would stand against them or try to protect our supply cache's," continued Kijibashie.

"These invaders were not from this peaceful shore we call home. They and their kind, were not in harmony with the earth or the stars. Over the years after their arrival, these invaders, 'killer of men,' 'Pequot, split our tribal clan villages so that some clans remained here on this 'point of land' overlooking our bay, Nehantucket and the 'living river,' but the others to the east including the Pauquatuket were divided to the east and began to relate more with the Narragansett."

Kijibashie continued speaking with sadness. "Our strength in numbers was diminished. We could not fight against the Pequot invaders. The vision shifted again to another time when we were the great ancestors of our people. Observing from above I was of spirit. More storm clouds came swirling in, different men came to our sands from large canoes even bigger than the Nordics'. They came in small numbers first, then more and more. They lived amongst our people, and we showed them how to fish and hunt and grow the seed. These men were called "Englise."

"There became a great anger from them towards the invader tribe who we called Pequot, 'killer of men.' These strange new men had tools of great power and they went to the invaders' village of wooden logs and barricades. These new men attacked these Pequot with such violence and without mercy, even after the defeated gave to surrender. Still these foreigners continued the slaughter of them until there were no more."

"Our men and the Narragansett men and other tribal men who were there were appalled at the foreigners' brutality that wiped the Pequot away. None remained except for those that were out hunting or trading to the north. Some of them went to live among the Mohican and Uncas to the north in servitude, and some were taken in by the Nehantucket in servitude out of pity for the brutality of the Englise foreigners."

Looking up, Kijibashie finished, "I was in spirit form. I did not have my body. I was with other ancestors. We were the ancestors." He held his hands to his chest, "I began to weep from sadness over these changes. Our people were suffering and dying from illness unseen. I could not bear to watch anymore. I asked to be returned from this vision. I awoke back here."

The others consoled Kijibashie and reminded that these insights were not of this time, but truly from a far distant future; the people, the boats, the invaders, were all from a distant time.

All attention turned to Ninikiji, as they were eager to hear of her vision. Although each experience was very personal, they all knew that somehow all of their experiences were linked in some way.

Ninikiji tried to summon the words, struggling a bit at first. Then when Mahkiwasie touched and held her hand she was able to collect her thoughts, as she refrained from interpretations of any meaning. She explained how she first felt peace with openly being with Nashkid in their later years, serving as shaman elders here with the Nehantucket. It was a life of peace although she felt barren and void, without any children of her own.

Her power and knowledge of the vibrational frequencies and the ability to transcend dimensions was shown to her as just a mere beginning of how to use it. She was shown that she would only need to listen to the tones of the singing bowl in her mind's eye or ear in order to travel out of body to lift her own being to a higher place, and that for a healing she would be able to see the remedy the person required. Her vision journey took her forward into a moving picture of another life, whereby she was viewing her new body surrounded with many familiar entities, again as a native tribal member of stature with respect as well as the burdens a shaman healer must bear. It was plain to her that her knowledge would be retained deep within her soul and emerge from within her depths with each reincarnation.

Again, she was thrust forward in time, this time as an observer, witnessing the cultural changes her people would endure. She remained in spirit as an ancestral entity helping those in struggle who would call on ancestral help to understand changes and overcome struggles.

Then forward yet again, as invaders to her people implemented their perceptions, not in harmony with the earth, she was once again in a physical body using her inborn knowledge of vibration and frequency but this time it was meant for protection of her people from atrocities to come. She would teach her people in small groups to use these vibrations to ascend into a higher realm. She would do this in secret and quiet, only for those receptive to the teaching. She would help hundreds to ascend in this manner. She was once again in the green mountains with her heritage of Abenaki people in this work. She was then shown another future time, a time of disconnected closed-minded invaders. She knew not that they would be early Europeans, only that they would be invaders bent on exploitation of land, forest, animals, and her people.

It was a very emotional closing for Ninikiji, her tears were streaming down her face as it was for all five of this group. After some brief reflections with everyone in the hovel of Ninikiji's revelations, all eyes turned to Mahkiwasie. It was now her turn to describe her visual journey.

39 Birthrights

Mahkiwasie took a very deep breath. She then stood from her sitting position with a demeanor of confidence, like that of a teacher, and gazed deep into the eyes of each member of the group, touching their heads lightly. Her touch emitted a warmth, almost a hot sensation, accompanied by an invisible power that penetrated the soul.

Her touch was only momentary. She said nothing audibly; her gaze spoke for her. It was an attunement, a healing, a realignment and opening that centered each of them instantly.

Tibamahgan was last. With him her eyes held a special affection. With both hands she first held his handsome face, then she moved them to the top of his head. The power of the hot energy emitted from her hands and penetrated his entire being. It bound them and connected them as true soulmates not only in this current physical time but through many previous times and more to come in future timelines and dimensions.

In the few moments of her wordless touch with the palms of both hands upon the top of his head, her personal monolithic axe vision and journey and message was revealed to him. It shot through him with a clarity and precision both visual and audible. He saw them together as lovers, their bodies entangled in the throes of passion, at first in a secret place, then with the blessings of the elders as they lived together openly in the village.

In the vision, the couple was of high stature within the Nehantucket tribe, powerful shamans leaders, along with the other members of the group who now held the knowledge and power of the artifact, the "monolithic axe."

Her vision continued, to reveal that the artifact would be kept secret and protected, only to be revealed to Migiwishkanj, Eagle Claw, and his woman Nodinosi, Spirit Woman." It would always remain under the protection and possession of the five members, as sacred, until such a time when it would be handed to a select few for future generations.

Her vision continued to penetrate Lone Wolf's soul. It showed the five of them in private council, using the energy of the artifact and the singing crystal bowls and other instruments together, amplifying wonderful vibrational tones. They used these frequencies to manifest health, healings, protection, and prosperity of abundance for the entire Nehantucket tribe. The shared vision showed how the group and individuals would learn to use the power, the Starr People knowledge, in ways unfathomable to the common folk.

Her vision then revealed Mahkiwasie traveling into future times, into other dimensions and realms, communing with ancestral and astral beings, Starr People from constellations beyond the visual solar system, beings who held a great love and reverence for the jewel of the universe and the human children living upon the great Mother Earth.

Mahkiwasie would soon learn to travel to these dimensions at will without the aid of vibrational tones or the power of the "axe." She would soon become a master practitioner who would teach the others, Lone Wolf, Kijibashie, Nashkid, and Ninikiji, not how to *wish* for the ability to travel, but how to *feel* with an inner knowingness of intention, to raise the vibration and frequency of the inner spirit and soul that takes one out-of-body.

Mahkiwasie would lead the group during private sessions in their elder years, in which they would travel to astral dimensions as a group, each to experience the knowledge and teachings of universal law, including laws of intention, magnetism, manifestation, and earthly realms beyond physical things. Each would become teachers and masters within their birthright.

Mahkiwasie's vision did not preclude the atrocities coming for the Nehantucket people. The changes and shifts of the "sands of time," as the other members of the group foresaw, would prove to be real; but her view of it was one without the emotion of fear. She remained as an observer, with instructions from her guides.

Her vision, as Lone Wolf saw it, showed that the group would pass the teachings on to select Nehantucket healers and shamans. It showed how they would learn to use the power as well, for healing of an individual's body, and to manifest healing protection for the entire tribe. Visions of peace, harmony, and abundance through intention, manifested, including the sense that events can be changed or shifted to a parallel timeline and how an individual can choose his or her own experience. The vision revealed that we can manifest and choose to return to the earth experience whenever we wish. We can choose to vibrate our body into a different earthly dimension, ascend to places in the future without darkness and fear, to live only in harmony and abundance. This future was shown as a reality of choice.

Mahkiwasie's vision came with a message for her. It came from the universal source, the great creator, the Starr People teachers.

The message was clear and concise; and it was intended for all five of this small group. "You, Mahkiwasie, medicine woman of the Nehantucket, have been chosen along with your four brothers and sisters of special gifts and strengths to carefully teach, share, protect, and pass the truth of birthright for all Nehantucket, our seed, our children."

"We will guide and protect you and your chosen members forever in this endeavor. Know that you five are but a few of the chosen upon the Mother Earth's garden of life and love. We have put you five in place here as we have put others of like mind upon other realms of the Mother Earth."

"Know this: there will be future times, ages of ignorance, fear, and violence. These times will test the descendants of the Nehantucket. Only the sacred knowledge of all men and women of their 'birthright' will allow them to overcome dark times to come in the far future. You five will live in prosperity and abundance, with health and vitality of body. You will not perish with a withered body as your ancestors, but ascend to a higher vibration with the young, vibrant, mature body of your youth."

"You, Mahkiwasie, your soul mate, Tibamahgan, your brothers Nashkid and Kijibashie, and your sister Ninikiji, all will become guides for many generations of Nehantucket to come. You shall be the appointed keepers of the stone "axe" and its knowledge of universal truth. This is our gift!" Mahkiwasie lifted her hands from Lone Wolf's head, the session had only been just a few moments in real time, during which no audible words were spoken!

40   Skills of Living in the Moment

The group of five met with Eagle Claw and Nodinosi, Spirit Woman. They met with the two chieftain elders in a small, but not entirely private council. The three men imparted the entire encounter with the Nordics in full detail, each from their own perspective.

They spoke not of the monolithic axe; it was something that could not be disclosed in any public way. It would be presented to Eagle Claw and Nodinosi by the five of them in a private forum, as they had all agreed prior to the council gathering. For now the entire village and beyond was awaiting news of the Nordics. The whole village was abuzz with all types of speculation.

This semi-private council with Eagle Claw and Nodinosi lasted well over half a day. Nodinosi was instrumental in adding her perspective, especially with the allowance to let the Norse find a place close by to the Nehantuckets' territory, so long as they did not interfere with any clan village. Eagle Claw's ego was opposed to this and would have rather sent the Nordics off, possibly to their demise. Nodinosi stood her ground firmly and corrected him in her mild way.

At the conclusion, the chief elder sachem would send out the messengers to summon many more attendees to yet another council meeting, which would present the discussion of the encounter with the Nordics and the outcome to the public forum. This massive community event would bring all Nehantuckets into the fold about the Nordics, and alert them that they could encounter these Nordic some day in the future on the outskirts of their domain or possibly on one of the offshore islands.

The group of five, Tibamahgan, Mahkiwasie, Kijibashie, Ninikiji, and Nashkid, had discussed revealing the monolithic axe artifact gifted to them. They decided that it would be better first presented directly to Nodinosi, Spirit Woman, by Mahkiwasie, Medicine Girl, because of its power of prophecy and insight.

Not that it would not be presented to Eagle Claw. It would, but Nodinosi, they felt, would be initially more receptive to its power and to the steps needed to protect it from any misuse of its insights. Then she would be the instrument for its presentation to Eagle Claw and could help explain its secrets and importance.

They would select the proper time for this at a later time. At the conclusion of the Nordic private council, Lone Wolf was very eager just to get back into the secluded forest with just his timber wolf and his plan to steal away with Mahkiwasie.

All five were of the same mindset. Nashkid and Ninikiji retreated to their own newly built wigwam, while Kijibashie headed to the young Nehantucket maiden Ikwea's hovel. Mahkiwasie took Lone Wolf's hand when she thought no one was looking, as they walked back toward her hovel. At the fork in the worn path, he nudged her in the direction of his secluded hut. She hesitated for a moment, then surrendered with her deer-like eyes to her destiny with him. At that moment, keeping their mutual affection secret did not matter to them.

She halted suddenly, "I must get my personals bag from my hut! They scuttled back to her wigwam to gather these. Once they got back to his hut, Lone Wolf formulated a plan. He would gather his possibles, axe, and bow with quiver of arrows. They would trek to the north to a secluded place that he had sheltered in once before. They would be far from prying eyes, with fine soft mosses upon the flat ledge and a thick layer of soft white pine needles that make good bedding and fire starter.

Just down the ledge face was a deep indentation in the rock face, a cave of sorts with a large overhang from the ledge. It was all of eight feet deep into the ledge face and twice as wide with a perfectly flat bottom perfect for a soft bed of moss and pine needles and a fire pit. He wondered if his lean-to braces were still intact at the cave face from when he had sheltered there for two days a couple seasons ago while on his winter camp scouting trek.

Medicine girl had surrendered herself to him, feeling totally secure and safe. She reasoned that they were not in any violation of tribal law or protocol, at least not yet! It was not against any tradition to venture outbound with the shaman scout for the tribe to choose the location of winter camp. Moreover, as a shaman and lead medicine woman for the tribe she could use her gifts of insight and knowledge of the abundant herbs, plants, roots, and trees near where the camp would be located.

Initially Lone Wolf had a desire to have some private alone time with Mahkiwasie, and to fulfill the desire of affection that had begun with the fantasy vision from the clear crystal stone gifted from Nashkid. Now this vision could manifest into reality he thought.

It was a three to perhaps four-mile hike to this secluded spot during which Mahkiwasie stopped along the way, checking certain plants, hickory nuts under the trees, pine nuts, and roots, stuffing samples in her bag. Resuming the hike she tended to trail behind Lone Wolf, every so often to come skipping up to his side and openly hold his hand.

For the first time in her life she felt uninhibited by the open gestures of affection that were until this day only held secretly in her mind, fantasies. When Lone Wolf told her of this secret place, and his plan to camp at it for a couple days, she was in turn in agreement. A sensation welled up in her abdomen and loins then, and now, at the thought of it!

The timber wolf was their only other companion, always either just up ahead in the distance or as a silhouette off to one side or the other of the trail. On some occasions he would trail behind as if to check for carnivores trailing their scent. The Nehantucket people had learned from childhood to always remain ever vigilant while in the forest foraging, hunting, and fishing. They would most always work in groups for there were many creatures to cause danger and peril.

Lone Wolf was one of the few who could walk the dense forest in solitude, because of his keen senses. Large catamounts, feral timber wolves, black bear, flat-face bear, wild boar, and mountain lion roamed, just to name a few of the land-dwelling creatures, hooved or clawed. Then within the rock crevasses were the copper head serpents, rattlers, spiders, and other insect nuisances to be on alert for and circumnavigated at all cost!

On the coastal waters fishermen would have to be vigilant of sharks lurking near their nets or even getting tangled in them, other fish bearing spines, and urchins, even jelly fish with the poison tentacles draped down to sting their prey. One of the cures for jelly fish sting was to urinate or sponge urine on the lacerations of the victim which would neutralize the toxins of the sting with the ammonia in human urine. This would work well with the sea urchin spines, also so long as the barbed spine was removed. There was not much to be done for shark bite, except to avoid getting bitten! Most shark attack victims would not fare well and could easily meet demise immediately or suffer in agonizing pain for days afterward.

Yes, there were many perils in the forests and coastal areas, but the Nehantuckets were as much a part of the natural habitat and landscape as the woodland creatures, with whom they shared a mutual respect. Fire was one of the Nehantucket's great accomplishments. Fire, along with the spear, the axe, the long knife, and the atlatl, gave the Nehantuckets a large advantage in both hunting and defense over the other predators and prey alike. The newly introduced bow and arrow combination proved to be a huge tool of advancement for the Nehantucket. Even more advancements followed with the razor-sharp production of quartz arrow heads and other forms of points.

The techniques used in the making of these implements improved and specialization developed. Talented members of the tribe would custom process them to everyone's benefit. They would teach the techniques to young apprentices. With a careful eye, they would locate veins of quartz crystal and quarry the precious ore. Even today, one can note these ancient diggings in the forests.

Red okra was also mined from veins of ore and used to adorn the implements, or as body paints and as a way to create hieroglyphic records of events, effigies, legends and stories to be found today in chambers of offering, caves, and ceremonial sites.

41 Primeval Passions

Lone Wolf and Mahkiwasie finally arrived at Lone Wolf's special site. The lean-to braces were still very much intact. Lone Wolf pondered whether to cut some fir pine boughs to layer over the braces like shingles to shed water should it rain. The pine boughs were plentiful. Under the heavy pines was a soft bed of natural pine needles.

Lone Wolf took Mahkiwasie by her hand and showed her the lean-to shelter and the moss and lichen on the flat ledge that overlooked the small valley and a ponded body of water. Two large beavers were on the embankment gnawing upon the birch trees, eight inches around. The huge beavers, over twice the size of today's evolved species, startled by their presence and that of the timber wolf, dashed into the pond and slapped the water with their immense tails to sound an alarm.

The eerie splash-whopping warning broke the woodland silence as it echoed throughout the trees. It was a siren to others and their young of the presence of predators. The sound startled Mahkiwasie; she grasped Lone Wolf's arm. Pointing to the beaver structures at the outlet end of the pond, he whispered, "Beavers make good pelts. Put on top. Keep rain out of wigwam!" He smiled, half laughing at her innocence.

The huge dome-shaped beaver house protruded above the waterline, engineered to be impenetrable. The intricate dam structure built higher and wider each year would serve to enlarge the body of water by acres over the years, thus supporting fish life, turtles, and waterfowl. Lone Wolf explained to Medicine Girl how the beavers worked and how smart they were to build their own environment, so that they were vulnerable only when they were upon the shore.

After circumnavigating the one-hundred-foot round circle of this place, he purposely ended the tour at the thick pines, leading her underneath the four-foot-high boughs. "We will rest here for a bit," he said in a seductive manner. She smiled knowingly and was the first to lay down, pulling him down to her. It was the very first time for both of them to be in private intimacy, to embark on a whole new dimension of life, exploring each other's bodies and sensations under the heavy boughs of pine, on a soft bedding of pine needles and lush green mosses.

Entranced, he held the softness of her body as one with his. Her voice spoke no words, just the tones of cooing. Her long slender legs were like gentle vines wrapping around his own. Her breath felt warm upon his chest and neck; her long hair draped over his body, warming him even further against the cool air. Her back and long neck arched as her soft body quivered under his in heightened moments, only for her to surrender and melt back into his arms. Her breath became rapid each time his masculinity touched her. It was beyond anything she could have imagined, natural in every sense, primeval in its sensuality. It sealed his bond to her as his soulmate, a bond gifted from the great spirit, the earth, and the stars.

For Mahkiwasie, there were many firsts on this day. Other than trekking to winter camp each season, she had never been so deep into the wilderness before. To be alone, in seclusion, with the man she had fallen for at first sight, a man who stirred her innermost emotions every time she thought of him, was extraordinary. Here and now here she was with only Tibamahgan, embarking on a magical encounter, holding and absorbing him into her soul. The strength of his powerful arms could crush her against his chest but somehow he emitted a careful gentleness that made her feel protected. She relinquished her natural guard, instinctively melting into him, aware of every sensation and movement as they lay in the soft moss, trading and taking turns caressing each other. Her breasts seemed to swell as arousal tingled throughout her being. The slightest touch of his hardness sent her into a new physical realm of passion and she was oblivious to her surroundings. She became as one with him and then in the next moment felt only her own sensation of vibrating heat and wetness exploding from within her. It occurred multiple times while she continued to explore every inch of his masculinity.

Just his breath upon her neck drove her into a frenzy like a wave that vibrated down into her loins. She could not get enough of him; she did not think it would end until it did. She laid back, exhausted and spent, as did he, both sweating, with the cool air evaporating the sweat from their bodies.

It was a spiritual consummation for both; an unspoken bond and commitment as mates to each other, soulmates for life. They dozed off with the afternoon sun poking through the branches, warming their quiet napping moments. Lone Wolf arose quietly to leave her sleeping under the pine boughs. He cut some pine boughs and placed them over the lean-to braces to get ready for the night. He gathered kindling of dry pine needle and dead branches. Using his flint he quickly sparked the tinder to life under the ledge rock overhang where they would spend the pristine starry night. Again, by the warmth of the fire's embers, they would embrace in the throes of heated passion.

Tibamahgan's wolf would stay just outside the lean-to for the next few days as guardian and protector for them both. These intimate days included nature walks, whereby Lone Wolf would show Medicine Girl the wonders of the wilderness. It was a divine synchronicity for them to be finally mated in this way, for there would be much important work they would do as a team of powerful enlightened leaders guiding the future for the benefit of the Nehantucket tribal people and preserving the ancient Starr People knowledge.

42 Winter Village

Lone Wolf and Medicine Girl would day trek for hours in all directions from the lean-to cave. Lone Wolf took great pleasure in showing her the wonders of his world, which until now he had shared with no one except his wolf companion.

On one such trek, near a sacred spring where the fresh water bubbled from between the rocks, Medicine Girl saw a large rock off in the distance, downslope a bit; it seemed out of place. Tibamahgan was filling the water bladder from the spring when she called to him in a questioning voice. "Tibamahgan, Tibamahgan!!" She said it twice, pointing to the boulder. "Over there!" She pointed again as she gained his attention. She grabbed his arm. "Down there! That big stone! See it?" He looked and nodded, smiling. "It is moving!" Pointing again, she said, "See? It just moved again!"

It was perhaps three feet high and four feet around; all she could see was the large shape in silhouette off in the distance. No other rocks or boulders were nearby. Then it moved again and she pointed, excitedly grabbing his arm!

Tibamahgan took Mahkiwasie by the hand and led her closer to the 'rock.' He whispered "posikudo" and nodded smiling. "Poo sih kuh doo" he said again slowly, meaning "tortoise," more precisely "woodland tortoise." The smaller turtles, called "mikinak," usually found sunning themselves near a pond or body of water, were familiar to most Nehantuckets from childhood. But these immense and ancient tortoises, posikudo, were rare and known to be powerful, spiritual creatures of the forest, living for hundreds of years, protected from predators by their massive armor shell. They were held sacred by the Nehantucket, representing longevity and wisdom of the earth mother.

Leading her by the hand as they walked up to the tortoise, Lone Wolf introduced Medicine Girl to the posikudo. "This is Medicine Girl, Makahwasie. She too is one of great wisdom and power. She works in healing and like you knows the energy and vibration of the earth."

Medicine Girl had never before encountered a posikudo tortoise, never mind being introduced to one! She marveled as she reached out, touching his massive, armored shell! It was another first for her in Lone Wolf's world.

They moved on to another area of forest, walking quietly and slowly along moss and lichen covered ridges and small ravine valleys hosting woodland meadows of lush vegetation. It was in one of these areas that a pair of massive bull moose came alert to their presence, lifting their heads with massive antlered racks spanning over five feet in width, much wider than a man's arms held outward.

The moose were grazing the lush wetland grasses at the edge of the meadow when Medicine Girl and Lone Wolf emerged from the tree line. Lone Wolf grabbed Medicine Girl's arm and pulled her down to the crouching position. Bull moose in the early fall can become aggressive and territorial as Lone Wolf had already experienced once before! "Best to just keep a distance," he whispered, waving a hand gesture at his wolf to stay put. Medicine girl stared at the massive animals, having never before seen one this close in the wild.

After watching the two moose return to grazing for a while longer, they navigated around the wet meadow staying into the tree line to another section of forest. Lone Wolf was scouting the areas while also guiding Mahkiwasie through these places, abound with wildlife.

At another marsh location, with a beaver dam and open body of water, were about fifty woodland ducks, splashing and preening themselves. They danced in the water playing about, sometimes diving under and emerging ten feet away. The males were full of colored feathers with green headdresses and multicolored bodies, while the females were of camouflaged brown and grays. It was delightful to watch them, uninhibited by the human presence, unaware even of Tibamahgan's wolf standing alongside.

They were protected by the water itself from land born threats. The only type of predator would be the massive snapping turtles lurking in the depths below, "mikinak," another type of prehistoric turtle.

Just then the wolf came to alert mode, his keen senses detecting something at a distance in the wooded brush off to their right. The wolf's hair raised at the back of his neck. Lone Wolf pulled his bow from his shoulder and reached behind his head. In one smooth motion he drew an arrow from the quiver and affixed to the bow string. He positioned himself behind the wolf and in front of Mahkiwasie, who remained instinctively crouching and alert. She had learned to pay attention to the wolf's body language.

The distant brush rustled again, something large was thrashing about. As it drew closer still, the wolf began to growl a low tone, fangs bared, as his lips and nose crinkled upward.

Whatever it was, it was large and was heading straight toward them, when it suddenly emerged from the thicket into a small clearing, grubbing its nose into the ground, tearing the ground up in tufts of grass. Now alert to our wolf's growling presence, the wild boar, with its deadly six-inch tusks, jerked to attention not twenty feet from the three of them. Large and dangerous, these beasts can and will charge if challenged. For now, this one was just grubbing for forage including the moles, mice, and grubs that were the larger part of the daily menu.

Eyesight not so keen, the boar did not focus on the humans just behind the large timber wolf which was its main concern, a creature to be avoided by the boar at all costs. Finally its eyes saw the movement of Tibamahgan raising his bow to the ready. Having never encountered a human, the boar had no experience with them or the scent of them, but with the three silhouettes standing larger than itself, it decided to use precaution and retreated after a brief moment of indecisive action. With the wolf and Tibamahgan's razor sharp shark tooth arrow the boar may not have fared well with any assault. It may have pondered that, or just instinctively in its brief moments of undecidedness, decided to retreat back into the thicket. This did not mean it was gone, nor was the danger!

Tibamahagen knew full well that wild boar can circle back and charge in from a better vantage, so they all remained on full alert for another ten minutes or more. Finally Wolf relaxed from his alert stance. Mahkiwasie could hear her heart racing in her chest; it was truly another first for her. Her voice came out as a whisper, "Can we go back to our cave now? I think I like it there, with the warm fire!"

It had been a long and adventurous day so far. Lone Wolf nodded in agreement reasoning to himself that to make camp and fire would take some time, hopefully some coals would be glowing under the ash to bring the flame to life, then they would lay with each other's warmth until sleep overtook them.

When the sun went down, the Nehantuckets would by natural metabolism wind down. They would gaze at the glorious sunsets sinking into the western horizon and they would give homage and thanks for the day's events as the pastel painted sky lines of pinks, blues, and red hues spread across their world, as the moon rose, getting brighter, and as stars began to dominate the night, the aurora borealis or northern lights wafting in a soundless magnificence of dance.

43 A Discreet Return

Four nights of these pristine sunsets and star filled skies went by as if it was meant to be for them to have this time alone together. The days were clear and sunny with only a few puffs of lenticular clouds drifting by.

They would nibble lightly through out the day. Occasionally Mahkiwasie would reach down and pull some leak roots or wild carrots. At the evening fire they would lightly nibble parcels of dried venison and fish from the pouch that was brought along. Lone Wolf could have easily hunted small game or waterfowl for a meal, but he refrained, not really needing to quench serious hunger.

Nehantuckets were accustomed to going for a few days without a heavy meal; it was natural for them to partake in light portions for days at a time. Their metabolism would well extract all nutrients from every morsel taken in.

It proved to be a very healthy and natural part of daily life to eat only when hungry! Winter stores and supplies, such as corn or maze, were prepared, dried, and buried in the ground in water tight baskets. These and other grains grown or harvested from the forest could and would only last for a certain duration, as they were rationed amongst the winter camp people. During these times the Nehantuckets' metabolism would slow down a bit, adjusting to the scarce supply.

Winter camp villagers would share the bounty of fresh meat brought in from the hunting parties, ten to twelve men at a time out tracking and stalking game in the deep snows. Even then the meats were rationed and shared throughout the winter villagers, allowing just a bit more sustenance, providing proteins and nutrients. This should not be construed as hardship, but just a natural way and order of things as they would adapt to each of the seasons whole hardily.

On the fifth day Lone Wolf and Mahkawasie made the trek back to the summer village to resume their place of work and council. Over the last few days and nights at the wilderness lean-to cave, they had become intimately bonded to each other, not only with soft tender touches as young lovers do, but also through acclimating to each other's masterful abilities and knowledge of the woods.

Medicine girl, with her knowledge of plants, herbs, and sense of energy sources from the earth, pointed out to Lone Wolf power-full energies emitting from the pure spring water sources, how the water is the life blood of the earth and how she could feel it vibrate when she was near the spring location as well as certain rock formations and crystals within pockets of the flat ledges, within the veins of white and clear quartz. She pointed out pedestals of clear glass-like quartz with magnificent rivulets of pinks, reds, and greenish-blue minerals wafting through and deep within the cores. She explained that these pedestals were the antennas of the earth, drawing energy from the stars and the starr people.

Lone Wolf had his keen senses of the terrain and certain animals that inhabited areas within the different dells, ledges and bog's. His demonstrated his ability to read the tracks and hoof prints of both pawed and migratory animals and to accurately anticipate their movements and courses through the oncoming winter months.

His skills with spear, axe, bow and arrow, as well as the atalal, were unsurpassed for both provider and defensive actions. His inner sixth sense and knowingness of the presence of predatory and game animals was to him natural, but to her it was impressive. He somehow knew that animals would be drawn to these energy centers and invisible vortexes throughout the forest.

The two talked upon these subjects for hours throughout their days together and shared each other's deep understanding of knowledge, instinctively knowing it was all interactive.

On the way back to the summer village they took a less direct path on Lone Wolf's suggestion, just to procrastinate a bit. They both knew that they could not be lovers openly amongst the villagers' inquisitive eyes.

The trail way that Lone Wolf choose led them through an area that had previously been used by the tribe as a productive hunting ground. It encompassed about a two mile square area of pristine forest hard woods of oak, ash, hickory, and maple, along with abundant grandfather elms. The landscape at ground level of this area was very different from the other natural forested landscapes.

The Nehantuckets would purposely set the underbrush of vast areas afire to not only clear underbrush off for better visibility in hunting game but to also provide nutrients to the natural soil to allow lusher grasses and low edible vegetation for both the Nehantuckets and the wildlife. By so doing, they created a balance of growth in a method of ancient cultivation.

Mahkiwasie walked up to one of the massive hemlocks that stood over one hundred feet high, it's trunk well over eight feet around, where no two people could wrap their arms around and touch hands from opposite sides! She touched its dark blackened trunk curiously trying to fathom the discoloration that rose beyond her height before it faded to the natural hemlock bark. She vaguely remembered as a child seeing the tribal men burning controlled areas of the woods, but she did not comprehend it back then, only remembering the smell of smoke in the air.

Tibamahgan knew her question and explained without her saying a word, "the dark area comes from the fire's heat, it has charred the bottom of the trunk just a little; the tree grows stronger from this!" Medicine girl held both hands upon the trunk once again, this time spontaneously putting healing prana into the hemlock as she whispered thanks to it for its strength and stature. Smiling, satisfied with her sensation of it, she turned and took Lone Wolf's hand, surveying the distance of vision with just the strong tall forest trees unobscured by brush or briar. Off in the distance to one side of a rolling knoll stood six female deer unafraid of the human presence, just staring at them with curiosity. Wolf remained just next to Tibamahgan.

They walked upon the trail for another distance, still quite a few miles from the Nehantucket summer shoreline village. This was in the area we now know as Boston Post Road in Niantic, where both Scott Road and Bride Brook Road intersect. The old Boston Post Road actually was one of the original Nehantucket main travel trails leading easterly and westerly in those ancient times. It would soon branch off onto another main trail heading more southerly just near a large body of water now known as Pattagansett.

Off in the distance through the open hardwood, a silhouette of a man drifted through the trees, disappearing, and then reappearing. Wolf had sensed it first with a series of short gruffs. Lone Wolf recognized the wolf's tone, but wondered, after seeing the wispy silhouette himself, why Wolf would only gruff and not growl louder. Mahkiwasie had also learned to come to attention whenever Wolf would alert in this way. As the form of the man came closer, Wolf still just huffed a bit, remaining alert to the presence. Wolf seemed to be in recognition of the scent. The individual who came into closer view seemed to be stalking something. When he stopped, as stalkers do, to survey the landscape, his eyes rested upon Medicine Girl, Lone Wolf, and the large wolf, all three now standing there in plain view, with just a short distance between them.

Lone Wolf spoke out loud "Only a boy named Bird would be so unvigilant in the open forest!" Mammototh Scout, Bird's new title, adorned with his feathered hair, beaded wampum shell necklaces, with body and face paint of blue and green pigments in assorted designs of personal meaning, approached them smiling with open arms, surprised to find them together so far out from the village. It was only then when Bird noticed that they were both still holding hands! "Ahh," he said, eyes twinkling, as they broke hands in embarrassment! Bird smiled again, coming in for a three-way hug, in total happiness for his elite mentors and friends.

44 Sacred Places

While Lone Wolf found it odd to encounter Bird this far out and alone, Bird also questioned finding both Mahkiwasie and Tibamahgan together out here! A sit down discussion followed, in which it was revealed that Bird was out on a personal trek for solitude, only hoping to find signs of migratory game and to discover new areas for himself.

Ultimately, though, Bird, without words, indicating his question with only his eyes by glancing back and forth at Medicine Girl and Lone Wolf, answered a question in his head; it was an answer he already knew. Medicine Girl sensed it from the beginning. Thus she started slowly to verbalize that Tibamahgan wanted to show her wilderness things, like new plants and herbs. She burbled on about sighting a *posikudo* or woodland tortoise, and then the large beavers, and then a wild boar! She exclaimed as her excitement grew, describing her adventure of it to Bird. But Bird knew there was more to it than that, especially when he glanced back at Lone Wolf, who in turn squinted his eyes a bit with an "I know that you know" kind of look!

Soon they would depart company after Bird explained a bit more as to why he was so far out. Lone Wolf said to Bird, "it would be wise to continue," pointing toward the northwest, "signs of good track and herd sign there." But Bird had a different destination in mind this day.

To the north of this area on the northern side of the lake water and just to the northeast about a mile or so, a small trail led still northward up and over large tumbled boulders left behind from glacial melt, clustered into one area as if a lost spilled bag of giants marbles! This spot was considered a 'power place,' an energy vortex the Nehantuckets would visit upon their individual vision quests and in groups at equinox ceremony. Certain boulders bore crevasses and splits in them in perfect alignment for these events, beaming sunlight into the natural occurring internal chambers of the boulders, many of which now seem to be placed intentionally instead!

Again, just to the north of these formations, water bubbled up from pristine springs sourced from deep in the earth. The Nehantuckets knew it was the earth's life blood, the essences of all living things, sacred to them in many ways. The pure water would pond here in a place we now know as Powers Lake.

To the northeast of this water body and the bubbling springs, that were held sacred by the Nehantuckets, individuals and small groups would build their offering chambers and effigies of animals, tortoises, and birds. They would give thanks and tribute to all creatures that sustain them and shared the wonders of nature's earthen world. More importantly they would give tribute to the Starr People from whom they came, from whom they received a retained knowledge, universal knowledge.

To celebrate this, the Nehantuckets chose a high energy place, a vortex place, to build over twenty-two mounds of stone, six feet in height, ten feet or more in circumference, each mound situated upon a gentle slope above these sacred springs. Arrangements within a five hundred foot circular area mimicked the star clusters of the Pleiades, Alpha Centauri or Orion as we know them today. Each mound was within a distance of forty to fifty feet of each other. Above this cluster of mounds, upon the peak of the narrow stone ledge ridge we find again stone offering chambers, simple three-sided chambers with flat stone tops and a quartz pedestal resting and pointing to the heavens upon its top. In nearby strategic locations, stone pedestals in pyramidal shapes with a notch etched atop its peak were built in true alignment with sunrise and sunsets of each day and the winter and summer equinox.

With great ritual, each generation would contribute to this site, many times working together hauling the stone to build the mounds and personal offering chambers. Individuals would visit the site during their personal vision quests to absorb the power of the waters and the energy vortexes of this place.

Mammototh Scout, Bird, was on his way to this very place this day. His adornments and body paints were meant for a personal spiritual connective purpose. He would intentionally spend perhaps a few days to build a stone effigy of his own personal design and contribution.

His effigy as he intended would be one of the great woolly mammoth, designed after that which led to his adult name and status as a scout within the tribe. His ceremony would give thanks to the Mammototh beast and all the tribal members that helped to create the young man he has become and the knowledge he has so far acquired. But most important was to give back thanks for his inner spirit, physical existence, and earthly connection gifted to him from the universal order of things.

The boy in him, Bird, would always remain, while the man, Mammototh

Scout, would quest on into adulthood to follow a destined path, a path he would over these few days choose and clarify.

Mammototh Scout would give much thought and thanks to the people who he had come to know as family: Medicine Girl, Mahkiwasie, the tribe's skilled healer who possessed an aura of magnetic attraction that came from not only her beauty of face and smile but from some distant star galaxy; Nashkid, the Abenaki scout leader, a powerful, enlightened, and skilled shamans; his woman, Ninikiji, spirit shamans of the Abenaki, who vibrated with an essence of clairvoyant knowingness; and finally, Tibamahgan, Lone Wolf, one who walks with the wolf, a shamans scout of high status among the villages and the elders, one who possesses strength in body and character, skilled in woodsmanship with insights of Starr People knowledge and earth energies. Indeed, this was one who Mammototh Scout would emulate. He was proud to be Tibamahgan's protégée, honored to be his friend.

Bird would project his gratitude to the stars for these people, these friends, on his personal quest, for he knew deep within that this kinship was not of coincidence, but one of synchronicity.

45 In Ritual

Bird reached his destination, the location of the twenty-some-odd stone mounds. He prepped and set his overnight camp just under a ledge overhang some distance away. Then he visited each mound, noticing the quartz ornamental stones and the pedestals atop the center of each mound. Having the purpose of enhancing the magnetic earth energies, they faced due east and west to track sunrise and sunsets and represented the seasonal equinox events.

As the sun was setting, Bird sat on the ridge overlooking the mound site, his thoughts of thanks for the day's events. The synchronistic meeting of Lone Wolf and Mahkiwasie filled his mind. Little did he know, these friends, along with the few others in the elite Nehantucket group, would soon bring him, Bird, Mammototh Scout, into the folds of the small group and the confidential knowledge of the monolithic axe.

The most interesting boulder of the mounds stood just over five feet high or not quite as tall as Bird himself. It was half as wide and twice as long as the height, its natural shape slightly sloping downward on the elongated side, very much resembling a mammoth's body.

Bird would spend much of his second day at the site that was a quarter mile distance from the mound site. It was situated on a slight slope amongst a boulder field of glacial till, an area where the not so ancient glacial melt had deposited it dregs of boulder and stone, now eroded somewhat after a few thousand years in which torrents of melt waters tumbled and dragged the rocks, nestling them into place.

Some had piled atop others to create natural shallow caves and chambers. Some beliefs held that these till sites held a magnetic energy, an unseen vortex holding a doorway or causeway into other universal dimensions.

Bird's intention had drawn him to this place, not by coincidence, but by a magnetic attractive force. Upon his arrival, the Mammototh boulder stood out perfectly and synchronistically called for him to build his effigy of the woolly mammoth that sealed his manhood.

He envisioned the stones he would need to mimic the legs and how he would make the trunk out of stone and how he would stack them to withstand the test of time. Bird dove straight into his task and began to select properly shaped rock, some loose and some wedged amongst others, some close by and others that he would toil over the distance needed to haul them and set them into place. It was his quest and privilege to create the effigy; it had great meaning to him. It would be a three-day project.

Upon its completion to his satisfaction, Bird spent the next two days and nights meditating upon his accomplishment. He made his offerings of gratitude within the small chamber just upslope from the mammoth effigy, burning sage and placing powerful quartz stones atop and around the chamber.

During the chamber ritual he ate nothing, cleansing through a short three day fast; only partaking of the pure spring water that bubbled out of the stone till downslope a ways from his effigies. It was as if the stone mammoth was guardian over the pure sacred spring waters.

Bird finalized his quest there at this high energy site. He gathered his possibles pouch, his hunting implements, and his personal medicine pouch. He then sat again in meditation, contemplating a different route to scout on the trek back to the village. The body and facial paints were now fading and slight hunger pangs had begun to creep in. Breaking his three day fast, in which he only drank of the pure spring waters, he partook of the last morsel of dried venison in his pouch, savoring every nibble of it. Dried venison had never tasted so good. To pay a final homage, he took in and absorbed the energies emitting from this place, resting amongst the nearby mounds in contemplation.

46 Nature Encounters

Bird had to collect himself from the few days of trance-like mind of spiritual meditation and bring himself back to physical awareness of body and alertness of mind. Nehantucket scouts, hunters, and even the women gathering herbs, roots and berries needed to remain ever vigilant of their surroundings and certain perils of the forest's prowling carnivorous creatures.

The sureness of foot at every step required almost all of the senses: eyes to focus the terrain and ground; balance to adapt the feet, toes, legs, and hips; ears to hear the distant sounds of the forest; and nose to catch the scent of nature's things. Even the use of intuitions, the inner sense, the gift all Nehantuckets retained, with the individual's knowledge of how to listen to it, honed the woodsman's skills.

Bird, through his teachings, had become a master in his adaptation of stealth in the forest. With the exception of his own scent, he could mostly walk the forest undetected and silent at every footstep. He would go so far as to even travel into an upwind direction as much as possible to avoid his scent from proceeding his path.

Suddenly, a covey of ten or twelve wood ducks took to flight from the pond water just a hundred yards downslope from the ledgy ridge Bird was traversing. He knew it was not own movement that spooked them to flight, his foot was silent upon the granite, his silhouette was distant and obscured by foliage. The soft breeze was from the opposite direction.

Woodland ducks and other water fowl would not likely take to flight unless a predator was in close proxy of the water's shore. Beaver were vegetarian and mostly nocturnal. A snapper turtle, *mikinak*, with its razor-sharp beak, would prowl from below but only along the brush lined shore. Water moccasin serpents would concentrate on frogs, mice, muskrats, and other rodents at the pond's edge. Catfish the size of a small dugout canoe were bottom feeders mostly, although they could seek prey from the depths upward, breaking the surface in a loud splashing manner. However, this did not happen, Bird knew, from his keen sense of hearing.

Bird crept cautiously forward to investigate further. Crouching, moving ever so slowly downslope, he closed the distance to a viewpoint overlooking the shore's edges. At his new position was a well-used game trail traversing the ledge rock, a mounded grassy knoll of reeds and cattail. He presumed a position on his belly to wait and watch.

47 Danger Close

There upwind to his left flank at the water's edge was a slight movement. As he squinted for better focus, the perfectly camouflaged silhouette of a large feline came into view. It verified the large paw print he had noticed on the game trail he had just crossed not ten yards from the knoll. It crouched down again in silent wait. Then with no reason other than impatience, the mammal stood on all fours in broadside view for Bird, as if to head along the game trail directly toward him.

Mountain lions, catamounts, lynx, and even saber-tooth tigers were prevalent during this period of our ancient Nehantuckets. Like the woolly mammoth, the saber-tooths were humongous in size. They were stealthy in the stalk, as well as fierce in strength and speed. Not to say that all the mountain cat species of the day were not as dangerous and swift in assault of their prey, because they were. However, the woodland saber-tooth was the largest and most powerful of all their cousin cats. Like the mammoths, the saber-tooth cats were then in decline in the shoreline region of Connecticut, also destined to extinction, but a few remained. Still, they were generally not to be bothered with hard-to-catch waterfowl.

This cat, though large in its stature, was not the fierce saber-tooth. It was in fact a mountain lion, a kindred relation, a sleeker more evolved version of the saber-tooth, inhabiting the rocky terrain of the ledges. In this case, it was prowling the water body edges of its territory, where woodland ducks venturing too close to the pond's edge in search of seedling minnows, would make a fine snack or evening meal back at its lair.

This mountain lion stood waist high to Bird. It would pose a dangerous threat to him if encountered. These cats could easily take down any hooved animal, deer, moose, elk, or caribou; its claws lethal with one or two powerful blows. They were one of the many carnivores to be avoided whenever possible. Not all that familiar or intimidated by human scent these cats would view a human as easy prey. Bird now had to use every trick he could to avoid detection by this cat, now heading in his direction.

Bird gathered his senses and resolved to retreat to an outcropping of tumbled boulder till just downwind of the cat's worn pathway and up slope from it, with a clear view and high ground advantage. To run now would only prove to give away his position and goad the cat from stalk into chase.

Bird's intuition told him to stand his ground. He positioned himself in a cluster of large boulders, each taller than he himself stood. The gaps between them were very narrow except for one, into which he entered.

Bird somehow remained calm but vigilant. Surveying the boulder cluster that he was in the center of, a thought flashed that this natural feature could make a very nice shelter if it only had a roof of bark slabs or sod! He snapped back at the ready, sure the mountain lion would appear in broad view outside the narrow entrance, just downslope, following his scent. While he remained obscured from the cats view, Bird prepared his bow and quiver of arrows; arrows that bore the razor-sharp shark-tooth tips lashed into the hafts.

He readied his spear, an eight-foot hand-hewn rod of hard, straight-grain white ash. Its tip was of clear translucent quartz, in an elongated triangular shape, six inches in length, with razor sharp edges narrowed to a point. This weapon was in all respects lethal, whether held and thrust multiple times or launched. In flight its perfect balance could propel it effectively from forty feet to plunge into its target.

Bird surmised that this large cat, this lion, had not yet encountered a human being in its lifetime, that the human scent was most likely new, and that its approach would be reveal a cautious curiosity. Bird intuited that he had all the advantage of surprise over the cat, which was accustomed to stalk prey running in fear to escape its claws, escapes that were rarely realized.

This lion, though, must be hungry, hungry enough to try to catch woodland ducks in deep water, thought Bird. He stood at the ready, an arrow's notch fixed onto the gut bowstring, the spear leaned against the wall of stone at his right side. As Bird sensed the mountain lion's approach, he consciously suppressed all fear, staying calm and centered.

Although the outcome would ultimately be uncertain, Bird willed it to be only what he intended. He envisioned the cat retreating upon the surprise piercing of the first arrow from a creature it had never encountered, one displaying no sense of fear. It would retreat in pain, sharply wounded. The animal would hesitate to attack, not understanding what had just occurred.

Bird surmised that the cat's reaction would then be to launch a second attack approach at the same entrance as the first arrow, in which his second would be ready, or so he thought the scenario would unfold. He surveyed his position again in the walled granite, eying the tops of the high boulders.

Bird suppressed an emotion of fear that began to well up. He resolved himself into calmness and simply surrendered all emotion into the moment, focusing only on his intended outcome; a teaching Tibamahgan had privately schooled him on, now to be put to the test!

48 Hunter or Prey

Most creatures upon two or four legs, knowing it was being stalked, would not willingly retreat to a location where it could be boxed in, at least not an unfamiliar place with no rear outlet!

Bird however did just that—and he did it with intention. He felt as if the boulders were somehow placed there by some synchronistic force for this event which was about to unfold.

Bird stood at the ready, calm and centered. As expected the huge mountain lion came into view downslope upon the open ledge rock, winding the ground and the air and exhaling with deep gruffs from its throat.

The animal was massive, its back stood half as high as Bird stood, with paws the size of sun turtle shells. Its shoulder and hind quarter muscles rippled with the precise movements of its body. Unintimidated, the cat moved even closer to the cluster of boulders, crouching down, warily surveying the boulders from a distance of perhaps sixty feet. Bird needed to wait and let it approach closer still to insure an accurate arrow.

Bird, obstructed by the narrow opening, remained undetected as of yet. The lion resumed its stalk again upon all fours. Then it crouched again in silent threat; the cat knew the unfamiliar prey was close by. Bird watched it as it crept closer still. He agonized over the decision to loose his arrow, he would first need to step sideways into the narrow rock entrance to aim, draw, and release the projectile. This needed to be done swiftly and with accuracy, knowing the lion would be startled by his tall silhouette.

Nose to the air the lion crept closer by two body lengths. It was time. Bird drew back the bow insuring the arrow was secure on his fore finger and his right draw fingers firmly in sync with the gut string and the notched arrow end with turkey flight feathers unfrayed and uniform. He wanted to wait until the cat regained stance or began movement again, to take advantage of a larger taller target, although he knew that even if the lion made another crouching movement the element of surprise would be to his advantage.

Bird remained unseen. The cat had no knowledge of this prey it was stalking, having only Bird's scent to go by. With familiar prey the lion would know and anticipate how to attack and how the prey would react. He was a master of it!

The cat went slowly to a half-standing half-crouching posture, precisely what Bird wanted. Decisively, Bird side-stepped out into the opening, aimed, and let loose his arrow. The lion winced with the impact as the arrow pierced its chest at the right shoulder. For Bird the encounter unfolded in almost slow motion.

The lion did not understand. What was this creature now in its view? What was this sensation in its body? What is this shaft and this sharp pain? The cat twisted and contorted at the impact of the arrow, pawing at the half-protruding shaft. Out of pure adrenalin, the cat leapt off to one side, placing himself broadside to Bird's view and then charged the entrance, trying to pounce in through the narrow opening to strike at Bird.

In anticipation, Bird retreated a few steps backward, simultaneously notching a second arrow, drawing the bow, and loosing another shaft just as the lion struggled to fit through the narrow rock sliver. Again, the second arrow pierced the chest of the massive cat. Again it winced in pain, struggling to retreat from the opening, which it could penetrate in its hasty assault. Still not understanding, the cat needed to rethink its assault upon this prey, obviously cornered amongst the boulders. It pawed again at the arrow shafts.

The cat, changing tactics, decided to approach this prey from above, this time with just a bit more caution. Something was stinging in its body. It tried to shake off the pain like a cub caught up in a thistle patch, or like the one and only time when as a cub, it pounced upon a porcupine, the quills penetrating its paws. This was a different, deeper pain, but the adrenaline continued to flow and the cat clamored atop one of the large boulders.

49   Skill of Lure

Bird, vigilant of the entrance opening and the lion now not within sight, heard his heart pounding, as if he was outside his body, like the distant drums at ceremony in the village. He surveyed his space again: no possible way could the cat struggle through the two other crevasses to his rear sides. The front entrance had already proved that the immense cat could not struggle through without great effort. Then Bird looked up, his roof design flashed in his mind, intuition kicked in and he had a flash vision of the cat looking straight down at him from atop!

Without thinking it out, Bird grabbed his spear and lodged the base of its shaft between a rock and the rear boulder wall. He stood back against the wall, spear pointing up at an angle between his legs, both hands upon its haft. He scanned the opening crevasse and the boulder tops, sensing something about to happen at any moment. He knew this carnivore was not going to stop its pursuit just yet.

The bow lay at his left foot; he withdrew another two arrows from the quiver upon his back shoulder and stuck the points into the ground at his right. In his quiver remained his last two arrows.

It was a shadow silhouette he noticed first upon the ground and boulder wall to his right, through his eye's peripheral vision. Then the lion loomed into view atop the boulder to his left, two arrows still protruding from its chest.

The first arrow had penetrated the cat's left front shoulder, its point cutting sinew and tendon, its thrust halted as it lodged into shoulder bone. It was not to be a fatal shot. The second arrow had penetrated the very front chest area, slightly to the right side of the cat's breastbone. This arrow penetrated much deeper than the first, cutting tissue and cartilage as its sharpness punctured one lung. This was to be a fatal wound, but the lion in its adrenalin rush had not realized nor understood its pending fate.

Charged with energy, it instinctively continued the pursuit of Bird. Unlike any other creature in the cat's experience, this a coy and intelligent human emitted no vibration of fear. As their eyes briefly met, it was a sense or vibration of dominance, a challenge of wit and agility, that emitted from the human creature.

Again, out of instinct only, the mountain lion leaped downward with front clawed paws extended outward, mouth agape, its massive teeth ready for the final kill. The cat was expecting his full weight and claws to suppress the prey while in one motion its fangs would chomp down engulfing the head and throat. But this was not to be.

Thanks to the extremely high boulder tops and the massive weight of the lion's girth, its slight hesitation allowed Bird to crouch a little lower onto the spear shaft strengthening and re aiming its sharp crystalline point. Then, as in slow motion, the lion was in midair. Bird thought he would be overcome by the sheer weight of the beast.

Still, just before the leap when their eyes met, Bird had seen the blood frothing from the cat's nostrils and corners of its mouth. He reckoned with a flash of thought that they may both perish from their wounds from this encounter. He surrendered himself to it.

The lions full weight smashed Bird into the ground. He heard its growling roar shriek to a higher pitch with pain. After impact, instead of flashing claws and gnashing fangs, its body went limp, the sheer weight pinning Bird to the ground.

Regaining his senses, Bird was not sure if he was injured in a critical way. All he could hear was the gasping breaths of the lion, laying atop him. As Bird listened for many minutes, the breathing tones changed from exasperation to a whispered wheezing.

The warmth of blood dripped down onto Bird's skin and face; he wondered if it was his own. The rock in which the spear shaft was mounted provided just enough of a tiny gap that he was able, with some struggle, to wiggle out from the now limp lion's weight.

Finally free from it, he checked his body for gnashing wounds and broken limbs. It was not his own blood that covered his face and chest. As he took stock of his injuries, he sensed that his back shoulder and legs bones ached, his skin was scraped and bruised on his legs, forearms, back and abdomen. Basically his whole body was battered, but miraculously he had not suffered any claw or teeth wounds that could fester and become fatal.

As his adrenaline now began to wear off, he lay half down against the boulder wall with his bow in hand and stared up at puffy clouds whisking across a perfectly blue sky. He chuckled out loud, surprised to be still alive! He lay there within the stone cluster, exhausted, for quite a while, unaware of time or anything outside the boulder walls.

The arrows would have eventually been the demise of the mountain lion. The punctured lung would have ultimately been fatal, but it would have taken many hours before death occurred due to the sheer size and stamina of the beast.

By all accounts, Bird should have been the victim. He would have made a fine meal for the carnivore, perhaps giving it a new taste for humans, which it might then scent and stalk at their villages. It would have been a dire threat to the native Nehantuckets, along with the bears, wolves, and sharks in the surf of the bay. Not this day. It was the quick thinking and savvy of mounting the spear shaft that saved Bird from demise. As the lion launched its death delivering pounce, it had impaled itself upon the sturdy spear's point, its sheer weight penetrated its heart and spine, ceasing all motor functions as it severed the spinal nerves within the vertebrae.

It would take Bird another three days to return to the village; taking that night and the next day to rest and reflect upon the whole event. This time he returned to his people and friends with the full hide and head of the massive mountain lion. He also packed onto a drag sledge some of the tender loin and hind quarter meat. It was all he could do to drag the weight of it all, stopping at regular intervals to rest along the trail.

Bird also took time to stack small stone markers along the way back, only stopping once he intersected with the familiar and more beaten path. He did this so that he and perhaps others could locate the place where he definitively proved his skill and sealed his hunter status.

Not many Nehantucket hunters, even in the lore, stories, or legends, had ever taken down "the great lion of the forest" alone. Oh yes there were tales of Nehantucket men killing the great cats, but they were all mostly in coordinated group efforts. The mountain lions in those tales were mostly caught stalking near the villages or hunting bands of men and boys in a forest setting. The tales touted the bravery of the group protecting the band and the village clan folk.

Bird, Mammototh Scout, would be the first to take a lion cat down while alone. This event would earn him yet another merit of high status in the elite tribal circles.

Bird set the stone markers, wanting a direct route to return to the cluster of boulders. He envisioned building a roof of thatched reeds and shingled birch bark over the boulder enclosure to make it his own secret shelter place, a place where he might come to be in solitude or in meditation or even to just reflect upon meaningful things.

50 None the Hero

Bird remained humble upon his return to the village, despite the crowds of women, children, and fellow clansmen all in awe of his feat. But he was still in a state of exhaustion and hoarse of voice from repeating his tale of the event and answering multitudes of questions.

All he really wanted upon his return was to first meet and sit with Tibamahgan and Mahkiwasie in private! They were the last friends and peers he encountered just before his vision quest out there in the middle of the forest. He knew now that they were an integral and synchronistic part of the event and he wanted to speak to them of the deeper meanings of it.

He also wanted to present some of the back strap loin to them in person. This would now have to wait just a bit longer until the villagers' frenzy calmed down some.

There would also now by mandate have to be a council circle meeting with Eagle Claw, the elder chief, and other sachems and shamans. Loin and higher end cuts of the meats would be given as offerings to the elders. It was ritual to partake of the trophy animal in order to absorb its symbol of power and prowess from the animal kingdom and to share this ritual with the Nehantucket elders. At this council gathering. Bird or Mammototh Scout, as he had been dubbed recently as his manhood name, would now be renamed with an appropriate title by the council to mark and celebrate an elevated higher status amongst the tribe.

Many of the excited womenfolk lined up offering to work on tanning and curing the lion's hide. Among the final women selected according to their pecking order, was a slender, pretty girl named "Abanimie," meaning "light wind." She had caught bird's eye many times before; this was so noted by the older womenfolk who have their ways on these matters! The group would scrape the inside of the pelt to remove all flesh and fats, rub in salt and oils, and knead it to a softer texture. At the outer fringes they would sew in sinew to create a clean hem at all the pelt's edges. The paws would be deboned with only the claws on all fours intact. The long tail would remain as is.

The inside of the pelt would be carefully tattooed with a replicated drawing of bird poised fearless in a kneeling position with his spear cocked at angle against the boulder wall. He would be holding it strongly, with the lion fiercely exaggerated in a leaping position from atop the boulder. Paws, claws, and fangs would be extended outward in midair, the cat depicted pouncing downward upon Bird and his spear. The exquisite artwork was done by none other than Abanimie, as this work was her special gift and forté.

Bird rested for almost a full day and night; he had never slept so soundly, oblivious to the sounds of the villagers bustling about outside his small wigwam hovel. He did not leave it for almost twenty hours except to pee, dozing in and out of deep naps, sometimes half-awake with contemplations of how fortunate he had been to not be the lion's meal! He thought very hard on how he would now be perceived by the clan folk as well as the elders.

The sound of two sticks clapping together outside his entrance snapped him from his doze; it meant he had visitors. Rubbing his eyes and sitting up on his woven branch bunk, he acknowledged with a verbal tone that he was awake. He peered out the flap entrance, squinting a bit. Slowly he rose and focused on the silhouette of Lone Wolf, Medicine Girl, and the tame wolf who came up to him and put his cold nose on his leg, exhaling a deep growled huff.

"The great cat slayer now sleeps his day away," jested Lone Wolf, in a man's way of acknowledgment! Medicine Girl smiled and gave him a long hug, drawing her hands, now warm with healing energy, down both sides of his face. She and Lone Wolf knew that Bird could have perished, and they both were thankful for his safe return.

Mahkiwasie immediately turned Bird around by his arm, inspecting his wounds and bruises. She looked at Lone Wolf, while putting her hand upon not one but two deep, reddened claw marks, marks that barely broke his skin just a bit. Whispering "these wounds will need tending," she reached into her medicine bag. Withdrawing back into the hut, he surrendered to lay face down, on her direct order. She looked at Lone Wolf again, indicating the seriousness of the claw wounds.

Kneading a poultice mixed of lichen, birch gum sap, and water from a sacred spring in a wooden bowl, she formed it into a putty consistency. The rare light green lichens she had collected from the bark of deadwood branches and fallen logs. Its anti-fungal and anti-bacterial properties would work towards the cure of infection. She knew not of any science of it, only through gifted insight and experience did she know of its proven herbal medicinal uses.

Lone Wolf retrieved a wide deer hide strap, handing it to Mahkiwasie to use as a wrapping bandage to hold the poultice in place on Bird's back. "There now, it is good we caught that in time! You may now sit up," she said, smiling.

Lone Wolf then spoke, "We both have come to invite you to attend a small private council meeting with just us two, Nashkid, Ninikiji, and Kijibashie. It shall be after your council lion ceremony with the elders." Bird nodded. Unknowingly, he cocked his head inquisitively. Lone Wolf, in his deep directive voice said, "This will be a teaching of great importance. It is only to be shared by a special select few. We have selected you to be one of the few. We had chosen you for this even before your encounter with the lion cat!"

Bird was somewhat confused about the invitation and began to formulate questions. Then he remembered that he was wanting to speak with them both about the mountain lion experience anyway. "I am very thankful that you have both come here, as I was about to seek you out after my rest. I am in need to talk of my event after we met in the deep forest! I am in need of guidance to understand why this has occurred to me; what is the deeper meaning of it all?"

Mahkiwasie, glancing at Lone Wolf, said in her calm voice said, "Bird, it was not by chance that we met in the forest. It is not by chance that you fought the great lion. Power and spirit is now within you." Lone Wolf then spoke, almost completing her thought, "It could have been the other way around, that the lion would have your spirit within him!" "It was meant to be," he continued, "that you not only overcame your fear, but remained calm with teachings of release. That my friend was what the starrs had planned for you. You will now soon hold an even higher power; your lion soon will pass to legend and you will be elevated even higher yet!"

51   Sachems and Secrets

It was time to make way to the council meeting. Bird felt more anxious about what Lone Wolf and Medicine Girl had for in store for him than the hoopla of the honor ceremony.

There, at the circle gathering was a massive fire pit, over ten feet long and five or six feet wide. The flame of collected dried wood consisting only of deadwood limbs and fallen logs burned hot on top while the coals below emitted an intense heat.

The Nehantuckets would only gather dead wood limbs and logs for firewood and kindling, never to cut a living tree down for the purpose of fire wood. They would have to venture well beyond the outskirts of the village for this, usually hauling bundles of dried wood upon their backs or upon makeshift sledges. This work was performed routinely by young boys and girls with teamwork until they were of age; then their personal aptitudes were recognized and encouraged. The collection of seaweed washed upon the beach shore was also tasked to the youths.

That seaweed was also in use at the fire pit. Wrapped in layers of thick seaweed were clams, scallops, little neck steamers, and lobsters of over a foot in length. Flounder and sea bass, venison, duck, geese, and turkey were also cooking in the wet steaming seaweed upon the edges of the fire pit. Many other recipes were stewing in stone-hewn kettles. The aroma wafted through the circle, causing the people's mouths to water involuntarily.

Just the scents mixed with the mild smoke from the pit was inspiring enough as one approached! The entire local village was invited, each bringing something to share from their trade. They continued to arrive, placing food stuffs and wares near the pit. The elders remained within the sacred stone circle, just as before with the council meeting of the Nordics, while the village folk milled around at the circle's perimeters.

At the one end of the fire pit upon the flat cooking stones closest to the stone circle, designated women would prepare the special cuts of lion's meat for the elder chief sachem Eagle Claw and his woman, Nodinosi, head spirit woman. All of the important medicine women and all of the shaman scouts including the Abenaki's men and women would soon be in attendance.

It was to be a very big event for the entire Nehantucket village, a celebration in Bird's honor, of his feat in taking down the massive carnivore that could have wreaked havoc upon the villagers sooner or later. No one in all the stories and lore has ever accomplished such a feat of bravery, especially not alone and single handedly.

Stories and lore of carnivores attacking villagers or hunting humans had been handed down over the evening fires, describing how groups of skilled senior hunters, under well-planned and coordinated systems had entrapped such predators, often involving many villagers, all armed with atlatls and spears. Always the tails depicted encounters of close and dangerous contact.

At this event, singing voices accompanied by the rhythmic sounds of drums and flutes with different pitches in several octaves would be raised in celebration! The people were adorned in their most prized attire with colors of blues, reds, purples, greens, and yellows. Feathers, bone, and shells made up their jewelry of bracelets, necklaces, anklets, armbands, and leggings. Some wore specially-fringed deerskin clothing and head dress feathers. Face and body paints made adornments where other trinkets did not. It was an event for all to show off and interact socially.

It had begun even before Bird's arrival. More villagers were still arriving and claiming their seat as close to the inner circle as possible; some setting up their displays for trade and barter, with groups of folks milling about, chatting and admiring.

A hush ensued amongst them as Bird approached and entered the sacred circle. He approached the elders' area within the inner stones and benches. Not knowing exactly what to do next, he remained standing, taking in the surrounding people, many of whom were now just looking at him!

He was greeted by Nodinosi, Spirit Woman, who took him by the hand and led him over to the great sachem chief, Eagle Claw. Eagle Claw, in his stately, elderly way, arose to stand and greet Bird. Bird's heart pounded with pride at this gesture! It was as if to greet him as an equal signified his new-found status.

Eagle Claw then took him by the hand, gesturing for him to come sit next to him and the other prominent shaman leaders, some still arriving to claim their seats. Bird looked around at the group milling about, noticing that Lone Wolf and Mahkiwasie were not among them.

At the chief's gesture, Bird sat down cross-legged next to Eagle Claw; then Nodinosi sat to his left side. Not being used to any of this kind of attention,

Bird became a little nervous sitting in the presence of the great shaman leader and his woman! It was not long ago at the last council meeting when he was not allowed inside the stone circle at all! Just then Eagle Claw leaned into him, speaking softly, "I do so like these gatherings! Look at them all." He waved his hand, half pointing with his forefinger, "So much excitement! I once was young like you, and we took down a pijaki, a woodland bison. He was running straight at me! He wished to impale me with his horns and run over me with his weight! If I had not tripped over the rock boulder behind me he would have sent me to see the ancestors!"

The chieftain nudged Bird in the side with his elbow, trying to get him to relax a bit, to make him feel accepted into the inner circle. Bird, still a bit nervous, looked at Eagle Claw and then at Nodinosi. Feeling more comfortable with her, he said, staring out at all the people, "At this moment I think I would rather be up against the lion! I do not fare well with crowds gawking at me!"

Both Nodinosi and the chieftain burst out with some laughter, chuckling out loud at his humor. Nodinosi grabbed his arm as any friend would do and turning to look at him, still with laughter in her voice, said "The people need to have something to celebrate! Today it is you and the great feat you have done!" She stared at him with her sparkling eyes for a few moments longer. Speaking again she said, "All the village knows the great lion you have slain in battle would have made its way here to the village soon enough. It would have preyed upon our people until the best hunters could bring it down, not without great pain. Now you hold the lion spirit in here," she said, tapping her two fingers on his chest. "You are Lion Spirit Protector. Embrace this ceremony for the village."

Bird nodded his head to her and to Eagle Claw in acceptance of his new status. It was then that he looked across the inner stone circle and to his relief saw Lone Wolf, Mahkiwasie, Nashkid, Ninikiji, and even Kijibashie! They all were arriving at once, arranging and sitting themselves among the other tribal leaders.

He flashed in recollection of himself out on his vision quest and how it had started with just a simple trek through the forest north of the village. Most "rites of passage" vision quests by individuals in the tribe would be expected, even mandated, to last for an entire cycle of the moon.

Bird, already familiar with the ways of the forest and "other spiritual things," had thought this would be another simple excursion! He had to chuckle to himself as he looked beyond the sacred circle and the villagers at the outer edges in attendance, all trying to get a glance at him!

It was as if he was still on his vision quest! He was glad that his friends and peers had arrived; he was not to be alone on this adventure of being in ceremony.

He still did not like the attention and still would rather be in the quiet of his hovel or even back in the deep forest with its sounds and smells, the breeze, and the night stars.

52 Orientation

The celebration went full into the night: laughing, drumming, dancing, and eating the feast. The children ran and played and the older folk told tales of great adventures of their own as the evening wound down under the stars.

Bird sat among the elders, shamans, spirit workers, and medicine women chit-chatting and conversing with no need or want of attention or morsels of food. Permission was granted to some common folk to enter the circle to present small gifts of things made from the person's trade.

One of these presentations was the lion's pelt itself!! Cured and tanned to a soft texture with the fur and features combed and cleaned so the fur flowed freely in the slightest breeze. The artwork of the tattoo designs throughout the inner hide of the pelt was exquisite; portraying and depicting the entire story of Bird's feats starting with his vision quest through the conquest over the great lion beast.

It was the work of Abanimie, the pretty girl of Bird's eye. He had sat with her when she was working on the pelt with the other women. When he had some quiet time alone with her he told her the story in confidence and her awe swelled his pride. He did this because he fancied her. There was something about her persona, her subtle smile, the shape of her petite frame, and her pretty face that touched him in a way no other woman ever had. Now her artwork and sheer talent would be added to the list. Abanimie was of the five women granted permission to enter the inner circle in order to present the finished gift.

After its presentation, he motioned for her to join and sit with him, knowing she was not allowed. He motioned to her again as she stood there reluctantly. Then Bird looked at the chieftain and spirit woman, who nodded approval. Still Abanimie stood, glancing about unsure of herself. Then Nodinosi rose and walked over to her taking her by the hand and led her to Bird's side. Abanimie remained flustered in her shyness but took her seat next to Bird and remained with him throughout the evening, sharing morsels of food, a bit out of place with her subtle smile.

She joined him as he later walked out of the circle to walk and talk amongst the common villagers, showing off his lion robe and the girl of his choosing. It was not any type of custom to do this; it was just his own way to show them he was still a part of them, regardless of the prestige.

The people gathered around, each taking a turn to greet him one on one. men and women alike. Touching the robe or his hand would bring a bit of the lion power into them as well!

As the time of festivities faded, Bird was approached by Mahkiwasie, Tibamahgan, Nashkid, Ninikiji, and Kijibashie of the Nordic monolithic axe. They approached him as a group, to introduce themselves to Abanimie and to summon Bird to a special meeting in two suns Mahkiwasie's lodge.

53 Sacred Ecstasy

Bird and Abanimie managed to slip away from the celebration, under cover of darkness, just after the introduction with Lone Wolf, Medicine Girl, and the Abenaki contingent.

Unseen they emerged at a small grassy dune just above the sandy beach-like alcove overlooking the Nehantucket Bay. The stars were twinkling bright and the waves gently and rhythmically splashed the shore. They sat and talked of things, sharing personal dreams, things they each liked to do, and even the taste of foods each did not like!

While holding hands, a natural, simple silence fell upon them; Abanimie leaned in closer to Bird's masculinity and the strength of his arms. He in turn held her softness into his chest. She cooed into the safety of his strength and nuzzled her face into his shoulder and neck just under his ear, emitting sighs that expressed desire.

Bird's breathing became much heavier, as he felt a vibration from her that was new to him, like nothing he had encountered before in his life experiences. It was her pheromone, which, unbeknown to him, had caused his attraction to her all those weeks ago. The subtle scent emitting from him likewise created in her an undeniable inner desire so much so that she could not get her mind off him from the first moment they met. It was a mutual, natural attraction and bond.

All of his senses were filled with her vibration as they began to stimulate each other with caresses and a form of kissing by touching noses like Inuits, taking turns nudging each other's necks and lower ears. Their hands naturally explored each other's bodies. Her pert breasts, smooth thighs, and soft buttocks drew him even closer. He took great pleasure in holding her pretty face in both hands and caressing her closed eyes and forehead with his thumb and fore fingers.

She delighted in the massaging of his powerful arms and marveled at the tautness of his muscular torso and toned abdomen. Her fascination became much enhanced by his now swelled arousal, something that she had no experience of. Indeed, she had never experienced being this close with a male Nehantucket at all. She had heard whispers from other, older girls about this foreplay and the changes that occur with arousal.

Of course, she had seen the various mating rituals in the wildlife, but these usually lasted for only moments, without the nurturing foreplay she was having this night. She had never experienced this loss of control. She could not stop, nor did she want to, and neither could he. She was enchanted with his member that swelled from soft to stiff, doubling in size. With a little fumbling, he located her wetness. As his fingers explored this newfound nirvana, she was driven into some kind of quivering frenzy with every caress. Multiple times she would quiver and moan out loud all the while holding his splendid manhood. He lay back and let her have her way, only to resume exploring her womanhood. They took turns with each other many times, neither knowing of the additional pleasures of intercourse that await a man and woman.

Then, after another of her moments of ecstasy, when he lay back again with his arousal now straight up and throbbing, as she caressed it, enchanted, suddenly and without much warning, he exploded! She smiled in surprise as his deep moan turned into a bellow.

She could not understand his exhaustion as she was ready to continue, after they both laughed a bit in the enjoyment of it all with beaded sweat and heavy breath. She took his hand putting it upon her wetness, wetness that now had flowed completely down upon both thighs. She tried to coax him to massage her again, but his exhaustion was overwhelming. All he could do was to lay back and she finally succumbed to his hugging her in closer for a bit of rest. With the lion robe wrapped under and over them they both fell into a deep sleep upon the sandy knoll. They now were mated.

The sun had risen enough over the Nehantucket Bay's horizon to burn off the morning mist and slight fog. However, this went totally unnoticed by the two as they remained sleeping under the robe. They were still sleeping when the two fishermen brothers, who Lone Wolf had befriended and commissioned to make the shark teeth arrows, came upon the lion robe there at the base of the dune. They did not realize anyone was under it!

From a distance, the brothers first thought it was an animal carcass, as they were walking with their nets to a natural stone jetty near what we now know as Crescent Beach. One brother picked up the top half of the robe exposing the couple to the daylight. All four were startled and surprised! Bird jumped up to his feet, while Abanimie rubbed her eyes.

The two brothers were shocked by the encounter, especially because they had not gotten the chance to meet Bird at the ceremony the previous evening nor were they able to touch the lion robe when he came out to walk among the more common folk! Thus, they were caught completely off-guard! The two brothers began to stutter apologies as Bird held his hand out to stop them. Half laughing out of the slight embarrassment, he then just smiled his characteristic innocuous smile, acknowledging his predicament, which drew a chuckle from the fishermen. Then acknowledging the brothers, Bird put his two hands together, upright, with a slight bow to them, as if to remain in their honor.

Abanimie donned her loin wear and gathered her moccasins, tying them off about her waist and filtering out her hair with her fingers. She then raised the exquisite robe, shook out the sand, and moved to drape it over Bird's shoulders. He took the robe in his hands instead and held it out for the fishermen to admire up close. He opened it up to the inside pelt, uncovering the exquisitely tattooed artwork.

He held his palm open towards Abanimie, stating "This is Abanimie's craft work." He indicated they should all look closely, and they all knelt down as he displayed the open robe on the sand to full view, saying "I think she will now have many requests for her skill upon the bare skin of our villagers, do you agree?" With this a bond formed between the fishermen and Bird and Abanimie. The encounter evolved into an invite just down the beach a ways to view the new lightweight sealskin canoe that the fishermen brothers were proud to share, telling the story of how it came to be!

After some instruction from their newfound friends, Bird and Abanimie were able to take the craft just off the shore a bit for a paddle along the beach front, and to bait a line. To their surprise, they caught a nice big striped bass on the first drop. It proved to be another whole new experience, while on shore the brothers got to admire the robe in private, taking turns with it adorned on their shoulders!

54 Sleeping In

For Bird and Abanimie, the new fame (and elevated status of 'shaman scout' for Bird) had not been realized yet. But very soon, the entire village would learn through the gossip network that Abanimie was now Bird's woman-mate and he, her man. But it only came naturally well before his adventures began.

They stayed with the two fisherman brothers into the high sun of the day, enjoying some morsels of crab and lobster and baked striped sea bass at their fire, the same bass Bird had caught earlier. So much knowledge came from the brothers who were glad to teach of lines, hooks, nets, and baits. Their teaching even included the plants and blooms of flowers and trees that told the tale of what fish were running in the rivers and shallow salt waters and their seasons to spawn and feed. They told how and where mummies could be caught even in winter, with one scoop of a pole net in the brackish creek water, to be used as bait for lake trout, sea bass and any saltwater favorites.

When the shadbush flowers there is sure to be a shad run in the Nehantucket River. The roe of shad was considered a delicious and nutritious addition to soups or just alone. The women would use all the fish heads to fertilize most any crop in the tilled growing areas. The young fishermen knew that when the yellow dandelion flowers turn to white puffy wisps, it was time to hit the salt ponds, the coves, and the estuaries within the Nehantucket River for certain abundance of the striped bass arrival from the deeper bay waters. When the flocks of night herons stood watch on the shoreline, they knew the alewife and herring spawn run was underway.

Lilacs and dogwood blossoms along the shore indicated the post spawn feeding frenzy of walleyes and weakfish. Then the striped bass and blue gills laden with milt, and females with roe, would protect their sandy nursery nests from intrusion including the fisherman's bone hooked bait fish, making it an easy haul with sinew line and stone sinker.

When crab apples fall in October, the albacore migrate close to the shore and mouth of the rivers. Other signs of the albacore include the gulls and waterfowl, themselves fishing the rivers and coastal zones. Where there's bait fish frothing the surface, the larger predators follow!

The water temperatures were also important indicators as to how deep the brothers would send their nets and weighted lines, from the canoe. They could bait a bone hook with a stone sinker, drop it to bottom out, pull up three arm lengths, tie it off, set bait on another line drop it, go back to the first line and pull up a twenty-pound cod fish every time and return tired to shore with a haul filling the center of the canoe well before mid-morning!

Villagers would arrive daily to barter bone hooks, stone sinkers and weights, deer skins, and implements of all sorts. Every part of the fish was used for food, fertilizer, sewing needles, fishhooks, or jewelry. Even the intestines were used, braided into line or lashings!

The two brothers were in no need for want. Even in the inland winter camps they would ice fish the lakes or ponds, chopping holes in the twelve-inch-thick ice and setting a bent branch "pop up" to indicate a fish on, usually a large mouth bass or lake-locked trout. Pickerel were very bony but usable. These, as well as bluegills, northern pike, and monster bullheads were predominant in the larger ponds. All could be dried and stored for later consumption. These "land locked" fish were all very large, unlike even the trophies we catch today, and the brothers knew no lack of abundance. It was common to return with nets full every time out.

Their acquired and honed skills of reading the water, the plants, the blooms, the bugs, the currents, the birds, and temperatures all played a role in refining the young apprentices' abilities. These two brothers were not the only Nehantucket fishermen of the village; they were, however, known as the shamans of fishing. Each village along the Nehantucket shoreline had its own skilled men and women, sharing knowledge and techniques throughout the adjacent villages and down through generations.

It was soon time for Bird and Abanimie to depart the fishermen brothers. She, for one, would certainly need to present herself and update her status with her peers and the senior women, who would ordinarily scorn her actions in openly forgoing the tribal protocols of the matchmaking rituals, even worse - the permissions of the pecking order.

She knew reprimands would be in store for her, for not returning to her hovel the night before and for not joining the morning chores. Abanimie collected herself at the distant tree line outside her cluster of wigwams where she resided. She primped her disheveled hair and tried to brush the sand from her buttocks and arms the best she could before casually strolling in, as if nothing had happened the night before. Suppressing her enchantment, she arched her back, walking firmly, proud to be a known woman rather than the naive girl she was the day before.

To her surprise all her peers, even the most senior women, even the two staunchest, crabbiest wrinkled mother hens of the pecking order welcomed her with open arms. Bringing her into their hut and their circle, they began adorning her with beaded bracelets and necklaces. They washed her with spring water and adorned her hair with intricate braids and tiny shells! In their eyes, she was now elevated to a new status amongst their group, chosen by the lion shaman. They chattered and giggled and planned things for her as she was their prodigy. Little did she know what her future role amongst the whole tribe would become from this point on, from this life changing event!

Bird, quite exhausted, slipped quietly back to his hut, crawled in, hung his robe from the eves, and just fell into a deep sleep. But before dozing off completely, he remembered his appointment with Tibamahgan, Mahkiwasie, the Abenakis, and Kijibashie. He wondered about it a bit and why it was so important, he wondered why he was to come alone, he so much wanted Abanimie to attend with him. His mind reeled and flashed all the events over the last ten moons, fighting the lion, the gentle healing energy from Mahkiwasie, the strong camaraderie from Lone Wolf, the ceremony, and his sweet Abanimie. Trying to set his body clock to awake in time for the meeting the next day, he fell off to an out-of-body place of the deepest sleep!

The rattle outside the entrance flap of the hovel shook multiple times, seemingly distant at first as Bird was sucked back into the physical realm. Squinting his eyes he emerged from his hut and glanced around, but there was no one there. He went around his hovel, still no one there. Then the rattle sounded again, just as Bird went to step thru the entrance to go back inside. With a sixth sense he turned; not ten feet away in the open, there materialized a young boy, standing at attention, with the summon rattle for Tibamahgan's group meeting at this setting sun.

The boy stood mesmerized, almost petrified. He had not known he was to be delivering a summon message to the powerful lion shaman himself! This just added to the awe of being called upon to be the runner by the even more powerful shaman, Tibamahgan, who walks with the wolf! Bird, who remembered his first time nervously delivering a summon message to Lone Wolf, smiled at the boy and said, after rubbing his eyes of the sleep, "well, is it your tongue that is tangled?" Saying this, he watched to see what reaction he would get!

The boy, finding his courage, spoke softly at first, barely audible. Looking up and down at Bird, all disheveled, he stepped back just a bit and finally repeated what he had mumbled. "Am I not at the right hut?" Bird cocked his head, not expecting that response. Bird looked from side to side, then back at the boy, asking "Is this summon rattle for the lion slayer?" The boy said, "It is, it comes from the great Tibamahgan and Medicine Woman!" Bird replied, "Then how is it that you believe you are at the wrong hut?"

The boy looked Bird up and down again and shifted his eyes from side to side then to the ground. "Well, it's just that you seem like you could be a fisherman!" Bird cocked his head again, not taking his eyes off the boy, but continuing to stare with a bit of a glare, asking "And what is it that brings you to this belief?" The boy shuffled his feet a bit, then he stood up straight, gaining courage, and just spoke out the words, "I mean no offense, but the smell of fish comes from you, and there is much sand sticking to your skin!" Bird stared at him in disbelief. Then he smelled both his armpits quickly and shook out his hair a bit!

"All right then," remembering his long night on the beach and his new found fisher friends, "come inside" waving his hand for the boy to follow. The boy came into the hovel. As his eyes focused, he saw, there hanging on the rack the lion robe. Bird just jutted his hand out at it, "See," he said, "you have the right hut!" Shaking his head he touched the boys shoulder, "It has been a very long couple of days! Do I really smell like fish?" The boy spoke out loud, "Ohhh yes, yes you do! You should try to do something about that before you go to your meeting!"

Raising his brows a bit, Bird immediately took a liking to this boy: it was his candor that stood out. "Well then it's down to the river for me!" He looked back at the boy as he gathered his pouch, "What do they call you?"

"I am called Kimozika. I am good at sneaking and observing quietly!" Bird turned again at the hut entrance, saying "Hmm, yes you are. Well Kimozika, the stealthy one, are you coming to the river? ...or do you wish to sneak up on me down there?" He gestured with his open hand in invitation!

Kimozika pondered the invitation a bit, thinking to himself that he had not much else to do. This opportunity would be far better than going back to playing games with his friends or being put to chores digging clams or hauling fire wood by the older women. He shrugged his shoulders with a bit of a crooked smile, taking a couple steps towards the river.

Kimozika followed Bird, Lion Scout, down to the river, where Bird proceeded to cleanse and wash himself. He used the dried mint plants that hung inside his hovel, intended especially for such an occasion, rubbing the mint all over wherever the fish may have touched his person, arms, hands, legs, and torso. He then scrubbed his skin with a handful of clean white sand. Finally, he dove into the water to rinse. The river water was at the outflowing tide and infused mostly with the fresh water from the inflowing Latimer Brook, as we call it today.

They sat on the ledge rock as Bird dried off in the open air, chatting a bit, with Bird asking pointed questions of the boy, intrigued with his manner of stealth. After another hour or so, they returned to the hovel, where Bird donned his bow and arrows, his spear, his possibles pouch, his knife and hatchet belt, and his lion robe.

As Bird emerged from the hut, there stood Kimozika, hoping to accompany Bird to the meeting. "And where do you think you are going now?" asked Bird sarcastically. "Well," he said, "I thought I should come with you and keep an eye around the perimeters for you all." Bird looked him up and down, squinting his eyes, wondering what else the boy could dream up in order to tag along.

"That, my young friend, would be the task of Tibamahgan's wolf! As a warning system, you would not fare well if that timber wolf caught you lurking about the perimeters of our meeting place! I have seen "Wolf" perform his duties and he is by far stealthier than you my young friend!" "Oh, but I must return the summons rattle," Kimozika stuttered, quickly thinking of another excuse to come along!

Bird grabbed the rattle, stuffing it in his pouch, half smiling at the boy's attempt. "Run along now, home to your chores! You can stop by here tomorrow morning as I will have a task for you then."

At that Kimozika reluctantly departed, glancing back a few times. Bird departed on the path towards Tibamahgan's wigwam lodge. After a few hundred yards Bird stopped checking for movement to his rear and flanks.

55 Enlightenment

Bird arrived at Tibamahgan's lodge. Standing outside were also Nashkid, the Abenaki sage woman Ninikiji, the Nehantucket runner Kijibashie, and Tibamahgan. Bird, now known as Lion Shaman, sensed an air of seriousness as he approached. Bird was somewhat stunned, his thoughts whirling that he had been summoned to be welcomed into the circle of his powerful peers, all of whom were shamans, spirit and medicine leaders of the Nehantucket tribe. What he did not know was that his thought was only partially true; his new status within the tribe had already been acknowledged at the circle ceremony with much fanfare, but his new celebrity meant nothing to the members of this group.

What mattered to them was that Bird had now earned his place within their elite group, not because he was famous, but because he had overcome a power-spirit in the lion form and now could soon inherit a larger leadership position in the tribal hierarchy. For that reason alone they wanted him to see the future visions from the monolithic axe prophecy. For that reason they were bringing him into the fold of knowingness to serve the good of the tribal people during his generation.

Bird was embraced by each of the men with either a forearm shake or a man-hug-style shoulder grasp. Ninikiji gave him a deep hug as a women might do. During this embrace Mahkiwasie emerged from the lodge and embraced him as well with her enchanting smile.

The air of importance and mystery lingered; Bird still did not know why he was here. A question formed in his mind as to why his woman Abanimie could not attend. Thoughtfully, he took a look around behind him again to check if the boy Kimozika had snuck in. Then he looked at Lone Wolf and asked the whereabouts of his wolf.

Wolf is on stand out there, on my command to guard our gathering, Tibamahgan said, pointing in the general direction of the tree line. Sensing something about the way Bird kept looking back, Lone Wolf cocked his head with no words. Bird looked behind him again, then looked at Lone Wolf,

"It's that little rattle messenger boy. He likes to play sneek up. He wanted to come with me, saying he needed to return the rattle!: Bird pulled the summon rattle from his pouch, showing it to the group! Lone Wolf, rolling his eyes a bit, said "that reminds me of someone else not so long ago!" He looked at Bird from the corner of his eye.

Mahkiwasie gestured everyone into the lodge entrance with both hands and her beaming smile. Being the last to enter, Tibamahgan paused, cupped his hands, and let out a low vibrational tone by gently putting his breath through his thumbs. Wolf immediately appeared at attention at the tree line. Tibamahgan waved his hand in a straight across motion, then abruptly made a fist, closing it twice. By this the wolf knew he was to stand guard at the perimeter until summoned. Bird peered out the entrance in awe at the performance of this command.

There, in the lodge, the monolithic axe was ceremoniously laid out in the center of the room upon a wooden pedestal. Sage was burning in six wooden bowls around the perimeter of the sitting places, one sage bowl for each member.

Bird had a bewildered look on his face. not yet understanding the formality. Awkwardly, he took his place. After all were seated, Mahkiwasie welcomed Bird into the circle and thanked him for his bravery in coming to it, not knowing exactly why. She also thanked him for coming in solitude upon her and Lone Wolf's request. "We know you are in question of why we gather in this way, and why you only were invited. This will now be revealed to you." At that she passed the presentation to Nashkid, with an open palm.

Nashkid spoke with great power in his voice. "I speak to you as 'Bird,' the adventurous boy, as 'Mammototh Scout,' the stalker of the great beast, and now as 'Lion Spirit,' the powerful shaman scout. We here have all agreed to invite you into this fellowship, to bring you into a powerful teaching, a journey of vision and truths." He gestured toward the monolithic axe upon the pedestal, partially wrapped in its sacred hide scabbard before continuing. "It will be only upon your choice that you will venture into this journey. We here have all done this and we here will all be in attendance with you on this side of the veil. All you must do is to choose without fear or judgment."

Bird looked at the axe. He could not help but notice the exquisite engravings on the exposed part of the haft.

Kijibashie spoke next. Pointing to the easterly direction, he asked "Do you recall our encounter with the Nordics at the clan village beyond the three rivers?" He continued, "This was when we three, gesturing to Nashkid and

Tibamahgan, first encountered this stone axe. It was gifted to us by the Nordics in return for safe passage, food and a landing place to start their new home. This was at the commandment of the council of sachems. We each came to hold this artifact, feeling a taste of its power! Now we invite you to taste of its power briefly, so you can choose."

Kijibashie then gestured to Lone Wolf, who paused for a long quiet moment, contemplating the words he was about to utter. During the pause, his eyes met with all in the circle, saving Bird for last. Lone Wolf then nodded his head in approval.

"My young friend, I have watched you grow from the mischievous boy to the powerful, skillful man you are today. I had some reservation about setting you to embark upon this experience today. It is only because at times all I see is the boy in you; but you have proven to be much more. You have found the purpose of your being. As I and even we, as he gestured to the members, have guided you toward this day, this moment in time, we will guide you into the next realm of knowledge.

Ninikiji, having no words, although she knew Bird to be a close friend of the group, smiled lovingly at Bird when Lone Wolf handed her the smoldering sage bowl, indicating it was now her turn to make a personal presentation. She arose and circled wisps of sage smoke all around Bird's body, chanting a vibrational tune with the perfect tones of her voice. She then sat and began to harmoniously vibrate the quartz crystalline bowl with the wooden pestle.

Ninikiji's voice, combined with the ever louder singing bowl, now harmonized the deepest penetrating frequency that filled Bird's inner being, elevating his consciousness and connection to spirit in a way he had never experienced before. The vibrating frequency of the tones emanated through everyone, including Wolf at guard some distance off at the tree line. She slowly brought the tones to a mild close; the room was quiet for a moment. Then she whispered softly, "Now you are ready."

Mahkiwasie, being the last, held the honor of handling the sacred axe still wrapped in its soft skin scabbard. She lifted it slowly and carefully, holding it out in front of Bird in presentation. She spoke softly in her enchanting, deliberate voice, "It is time to take this artifact from its wrapping and hold it ever so briefly. You shall taste its vision power. You shall then set it down and release it from your grasp. Do this to contemplate if you choose to continue into the next part of the journey that it reveals."

Bird looked around at each member of the circle, who all slightly nodded approval that he should hold the axe. Somehow he knew they each had already done so and it was nothing to fear. Medicine girl held the axe outward toward him once again.

Bird reached out with both hands unveiling the axe from its wrapping, in awe of its exquisite engravings. He then hesitantly and carefully lifted it with both hands, positioning it in his palms, and simultaneously drawing it inward toward his chest. He glanced again at the group inquisitively, waiting for something to happen. Suddenly, Bird was thrust into a dreamlike vision.

In his vision, Tibamahgan and Mahkiwasie were sitting in the inner circle at the sachem lodge as head council, their hair completely grayed. He saw himself with Abanimie at his side, holding the sachem staff in the same inner circle. Then he was lifted into the spirit realm, looking down from above at his tribal people, in guidance. All ancestors were with him. Surging ahead, he saw the Nordics interacting with his people in the river. Then he flashed into some other future; the earth shifted, the water of the bay rose higher, eroding much of the shore away. Here, the Nehantuckets had grown in population. Others, not of the Nehantucket nation arrived. They acted out in violence, imposing pain and hardship. He saw conflict and Nehantucket blood flowing down the ledge rock into the living river waters. Bird, feeling anger and sadness at the same time, became aware of his heart pounding in his ears and was sucked back into his conscious body.

At that, Bird reactively released his grasp on the monolithic axe, thrusting it back upon its wrappings and scabbard. Tears welled in his eyes as he looked around at his friends, slowly remembering where he was.

The smell of sage filled his senses; Bird somehow knew that they all knew what he had just experienced. He uttered only a deep sigh and slumped backward a bit to collect himself, staring intensely at the axe.

His mind roiled with questions as to what the vision meant. The silence was broken when Mahkiwasie softly asked "Tell , Bird, what did the axe show? What was it that you have foreseen? We will help you to understand."

Bird realized his body was still vibrating. He heard her words but could not yet get his tongue to form words. It took him another moment to collect himself and slow his rapid breathing! Finally he began, "It was as if I were in this room with you all, but it was not here it was some dream of another time with you and Lone Wolf but you were in Eagle Claw's place! Then it was me in your place. Then there were others who came and brought anger to our people but it was not in this time! It was in many seasons from now, so many seasons!" As he began to tear up a bit, Mahkiwasie touched his shoulders with both her hands; heat emanated from them and it calmed him.

Ninikiji spoke, "Dear one, this was just a taste of the vision power of the artifact! We did it this way with you, to hold it just briefly for a few moments, as an attunement for your spirit and body to adjust to its vibrations. In a short while, we will have you take up the axe again for it to take you on yet another deeper journey into another time and dimension, whence you may see a vision with much more clarity and understanding of its teaching." Bird, now recovered a bit from the first episode, sat back, regaining his playful personality, "Hmm, this is like a flying bird in the sky looking down! I am Bird" They all chuckled out loud just a bit!

56   Portal Visions

The members inside the lodge now began to chat amongst themselves, each congratulating Bird on his choice to continue, in their own way. They took water and settled back in place. Mahkiwasie and Ninikiji began the meditation again for Bird to enter the next session with the monolithic axe.

Bird again prepared himself, only this time without the anxiety of not knowing what to expect, or if he would be able to return from the place it took him. He became better centered through the meditation. The tones and vibration of the singing bowl and Ninikiji's perfect voice, in harmony with the tones of the bowl, penetrated him deeper as the scent of the sage and oils filled his senses. He was this lifted higher yet again into an almost out-of-body state.

They knew he was now ready. As this time Lone Wolf handed the monolithic axe forward with his open palms under the wrappings, Bird, eyes closed, reached outward and grasped the artifact with both hands and brought it into his chest.

He was thrust suddenly into what felt like a tunnel of light as it wound through the stars, only he was observing himself from a distance traveling within the tunnel. It took him far into the stars and in a circular motion returned him back to the earth, as if he was looking at it from the moon.

He saw the globe of the earth with oceans and continents, unlike anything he could comprehend. He was suddenly sucked back into earth's realm from far above as if he was flying downward from the clouds. He saw the land mass of the continent, its shape and mountains and shores.

As he flew downward even more, his focus centered upon the area we now call New England. He saw the green mountains of Vermont with a massive great body of water in its middle. He watched as it receded before his eyes and became what we now know as Lake Champlain. Ceremonial stone mounds once upon the lake's shore were now situated upon a gentle slope. From the bird's eye view, they resemble the Pleiades star cluster, giving tribute with their quartz ornamental stone pedestals to the knowledge of the ancestral star people. The vast mounds were built by the early ancient Abenaki, or perhaps even their predecessors. Bird saw the great grandchildren of a hundred generations, descendants of his friends Nashkid and Ninikiji's future bloodline. He saw Nashkid and his Abenaki friends now as spirit ancestors guiding from turmoil.

Then flying again Bird came to be above the shore of the familiar coastline of the Nehantucket people. It stretched from the great western river known then as "Quonoktacut." The Nehantucket tribe occupied the coast as far east as the sandy beaches of Misquamicut.

There the people were in harmony, still hunting and fishing and growing their simple crops. Rotating their plots in the fertile soils, they would selectively burn the underbrush within the forest areas for better hunting and for wild berries, grasses and herbal vegetative growth, improving not only their own harvests but also enhancing the feed for all forms of wildlife.

As Bird flew closer yet upon the shore of Nehantucket bay, he sensed a change, something had occurred, an earth change, a slight shift of magnetic poles, perhaps a natural adjustment of the Mother Earth's lay lines. Weather, climate and seasons evolved, their patterns shifting subtly. The shoreline had receded inland by about one thousand feet in today's measurements. The salt water had come inland by that distance. Migratory creatures had become less abundant, shifting their routes further northward.

Intuitively he knew that he was now in a future time of perhaps one thousand summers from his waking life. Not only was the shoreline much different, but also there were many more Nehantucket people in the villages. The wigwams were many more, being situated out beyond the tree lines of his time. The people remained tuned with the Mother Earth's harmony. The shamans still taught the teachings of the Starr knowledge, although it had become slightly diminished. They still practiced the power of manifestation, but with some loss to their understanding of how to connect.

Again Bird was thrust into still another future, one depicting his people in amicable trade and interaction with neighboring tribes. Nehantuckets fashioned beautiful adornments, bracelets, and necklaces of the *cohog* shells. This wampum, with the light blue, purple, and pink hues of the shells interior, shaped, pierced, and strung, became sought after by the inland tribes and were well traded, bartered toward all valuable forms of goods, implements, furs, and tools, in exchange.

Time moved forward again for Bird. Now he saw the arrival of another breed of tribal people, with heads shaved on both sides, with fierce dark painted eyes and grim faces. They slowly took hold at the third river's shore, to the east at the "missi-tuk" inlet. In the early years of their arrival they were welcome, in the tradition of the Nehantucket, trading, hunting, fishing, and foraging, as the Nehantuckets taught them their ways. Winters were harsh in those years; the Nehantuckets and the inland tribes learned to provision and prepare, by caching dried fish, venison, elk, caribou, beans, corn, squash, and herbs. Cached in the caves up in the rocky ledges of the Oswegatchie hills. Other caches included the inland winter camp sites, within stone-covered caves and crevasses. Also they would bury corn maze and grains in deep compost pits. This system of caching would sustain the clans during the harsh winters of those times.

These new arrivals, the "Pequot Nameaugs," did not prepare caches. Bird was shown how they instead became overcome with greed and violence. In theft, an taboo act forbidden in the Nehantucket culture, these intruders would take Nehantucket caches when they could find them at the shore areas, without trade, using force with weapons upon the Nehantucket women and men in charge of protecting the stores.

When hunting parties were dispatched to take back the food stuff, they were met with embattlement. Bird was shown how eight Nehantucket young men were slaughtered by these newcomers during a skirmish, another act of treachery, never conceived historically by Nehantuckets.

These newcomers disregarded all traditional uses of territorial boundaries, fishing territories, hunting grounds, and even disrespected the growing mounds and plots. These newcomers resorted to stealing the fish from the Nehantucket's nets, the pelts from their racks and maize from the baskets.

These new intruders came to be called "Pequot," meaning "killer of men," in the Nehantucket Algonquin language. They were to be avoided and shunned. They did not abide by any universal law or harmony. In the seasons following, more and more outrageous acts of violence persisted. Nehantucket men and women were indentured and demands were made for annual tribute. The Nehantucket were forced to train their young men in the ways of war, to make battle clubs and use their hunting implements as weapons for defense against raiding Pequots. Most Nehantucket families finally chose submission over defense, for the sake of the preservation of their kind.

Never had the peaceful Nehantuckets, nor the neighboring tribes, such as the Uncas, the Narragansett, or the Hamonasett to the west, ever encountered such a violent breed of people. Even the Mahican's to the north, who were brutal themselves, did not tolerate these people who warred and conquered their way up the coast from Maryland, overcoming less populated tribes along the way for a thousand winters. These violent people were driven out by larger tribes along the way and finally forced to the shore at Pawcatuck, as we know it today. The most violent of the Pequot were known then as "Nameaugs." They took foothold along the Mystic River and continued their harassing expansion for over three hundred additional winters to the east and west. Bird was shown how the Nameaug Pequots, killer of men, divided and diminished the Nehantucket nation. Still in his overview he saw how the now divided eastern Nehantuckets merged with the Narragansetts to the east. Protected by higher numbers, the western Nehantuckets, Bird's people, inclined to band with the Uncas and Hamonasetts to the west, and even succumbed to indenture by the Mahicans to the north, while still bearing the brunt of the Pequot harassment.

57   A Distant Future

Bird was suddenly thrust into the light tunnel again, traveling into the stars and constellations, he saw the heavenly star clusters of Pleiades, Alpha Centauri, Hyades and Tucanae, places where the Starr knowledge of universal law originated, Starr worlds from where benevolent beings had come and visited the earth, seeding the Nehantucket. He was shown that it was beings from the Pleiades star cluster, the seven sisters, who had seeded the earth in their likeness and with their knowledge.

This knowledge, an inborn knowingness, was planted and passed within the soul, within the helix of DNA of each man and woman. It is truly the birth rights of frequency and vibration used and focused properly and consistently to manifests all abundance. Knowledge of magnetic attraction even in thought, becomes energy vibration that travels faster than light back to the universal source. Thought put forth with the power of intention is the gift of personal creation.

Thrust into yet another light vortex, Bird was shown another timeline, one he understood and could not only see but "feel." It depicted his tribal people of his past and present living in complete harmony and balance within the bounty of the earthly natural world, a world in which there was no need or want. All things needed to sustain Nehantucket life were bountiful, children were taught and encouraged to utilize their inborn aptitudes, helping them to excel in the clan-style tribal network.

Women were honored as vessels of creation, spiritual leaders. and shaman healers. Deep connections with the earth and the stars centered each individual's belief system, even into the journey beyond the physical realm. Men were honored for their honed skills as fishermen, hunters, stone workers, and craftsmen. Scouts were honed in the skills of woodland hunting grounds. Fishermen held knowledge of the seasons for fish migrations and of their feeding grounds along the living river, the Nehantucket bay and the inland waters. All things, tools, implements, food, shelters and clothing were obtained in abundance and crafted from the natural sources of the forest, streams, rivers and ocean shore.

The vision then thrust him into a different future, a culture of people living now upon the exact same points of land and territory as his now ancient villages, his pristine bay waters, his living river, his inland woodlands, and his sacred ancestral burial grounds. As he was shown, they appeared at first out of the mist from the bay in large canoe-like vessels with cloudlike presentations that billowed in the wind. They interacted with the people to trade for pelts. Over the seasons they became bent on harvesting many fur bearing creatures not for the meat but only the pelts. They exploited the forests for its trees, cleared vast areas of animal habitat, built fences of stone, claimed the ground as their own, and disrespected the Nehantucket way and belief system.

Bird then saw how they had brought an unseen horror to the people, he heard the words in his mind, "dis – ease." With this he saw his people writhing in pain, sweating in fever, and breaking out in sores and wounds upon their skin. They were dying in agony in groups; even the ruthless Pequots were affected. Game became scarce, fishing was over exploited, and the meager survivors were indentured. Finally, his people were no more a great people, merely a few dozen straggling survivors living amongst these invaders, attempting to adopt their ways for survival.

This new culture defaced and exploited everything. Bird could not comprehend what he was seeing in this vision. He was shown a hooved creature called the "horse," that was moose-like in stature. It was tamed to servitude and burden for these new invaders. Other strange animals were held in corrals of stone. Implements of steel and weapons of fire and smoke enhanced the exploitation of all things natural. These invaders brought war, killing neighboring tribesmen. As the exploitation continued, the unseen disease carried by these invaders spread wide across the vast coastlines and inland woodland tribes of all indigenous cultures.

They came in small numbers at first, but as their population exploded, they seized lands and territories previously occupied and used by the Nehantuckets. Bird was shown how the remaining surviving Nehantucket clans were forced to live only upon the small points of land at Black Point and Giants Neck, as we call these areas today. Even the sacred burial grounds at the hill overlooking the bay waters at what we renamed McCook Point Beach were desecrated and built upon with square wooden structures.

In this vision further into a distant future, all things were out of balance. It was an infestation. Nothing these alien invaders encountered was held sacred or honored. Nothing was in harmony with nature's rhythms. Nothing was symmetrical, as all things found in nature.

It was an unnatural disconnected world.

58   In the Present

Finally, with tears streaming down his face, Bird forced himself to drop the monolithic axe. Upon its release, he was sucked back into his conscious body. Upon opening his eyes, he saw all of his friends hovering over him. Each was touching him wherever they could get a grasp, trying to draw him back from the trance as his body was contorting and flailing upon the reed mats. He had held such a tight grip on the artifact they could not pry it from his hands.

Bird regained his senses, wiped the tears from his face, and refocused his eyes in the room, He took some water from the stone cup and sat back breathing heavy still. The group, relieved that he was back, settled back to their circle. Mahkiwasie began to perform her closure ritual with symbols drawn out by both her hands, chanting a bit to thank all the spirits and guides of the session.

As calmness returned, the group began to discuss Bird' vision experience, much of which he could not explain, as he valiantly described the strange crafts and dwellings of the alien people and how they depleted and changed the landscapes.

He was, however, able to describe his sense of the future timelines being many thousands of seasons and generations away. His overall perception of the entire vision and the journey of the Nehantucket nation was one to retain harmony with the earth and all things natural, to maintain and live by the universal laws of the Starr knowledge, including the power of the vibrational frequencies of thought and manifestation. This perception was to carry this guidance over into the afterlife of earthbound experience and continue as ancestors to teach the future generations to remember the use and knowledge.

Bird had been shown that even in distant times the Nehantucket remained peaceful, despite the many hardships. His final perception was that many of the Nehantuckets throughout the future timelines were able to retain the universal Starr knowledge, learning how to manifest protections and more importantly how to ascend to the next dimension in mass groups or as individual journeys, leaving behind only those who chose to remain in the earthbound experience. He felt full of hope of teaching the newcomers to the land the ancient truths of the original native humans. He had seen how the artifact, the monolithic axe, would be hidden and protected, handed down from generation to generation, and how its knowledge would be taught and shared. It would help many of the woodland tribes to unite and defend their way of life under a unified cause. Then through an age of human ignorance, a time far in the future when masses of closed minded people would engage in complete disharmony with the earth and the universal law's, the sacred artifact would be kept hidden by the Nehantucket guardians, for these aliens would misuse its power, teachings.

Bird explained his perception to his friends, how the artifact would once again be revealed during a transitional time of Mother Earth, a time when all people were being awakened to their inborn birthrights. He saw a massive cosmic energy shift in the future, that would affect not only Mother Earth, but also cause an enlightenment, a mass conscious awakening for the humans who chose to move forward into it. The Nehantucket teachings would be restored once again to universal law.

Lone Wolf, Nashkid, Kijibashie, Abanimie, and Mahkiwasie joined hands in the circle and rejoiced in knowingness. They now would be the council and protectors of the artifact. Within this simple wigwam shelter, Mahkiwasie's hovel, they formed their pact to teach the knowledge of these revelations. They agreed to guide the Nehantuckets into the future even from the after dimension, and finally, to devise a system to hide and protect the sacred artifact. They discussed whether to reveal it to the now aging sachem, Eagle Claw and his shaman spirit woman, Nodinosi. The decision was made to do so, for as the lead sachems of all Nehantucket peoples they should bear its knowledge to continue guidance as ancestral teachers as well.

59   Rights of Passage

There was a commotion outside of the hovel, Tibamahgan's wolf was growling loudly, now standing in front of the flap entrance and peering intensely out at the tree line.

Bird and Tibamahgan, both silently exited the rear of the hut. Without a word they went out in two directions, with only a hand motion of the flanking tactic to converge on the intruder. By wolf's body language, Tibamahgan knew it was another human and not a predator. There would be no need of weapons, although his knife and axe were at the ready, fastened to his shoulder strap if needed.

Tibamahgan located the perpetrator lurking behind the brush at the base of a large hickory tree. It was the crunching of the fallen nuts that first alarmed Wolf's keen ears, followed by the unfamiliar scent. Wolf knew lurking was not a natural tribal human trait, so he sounded his alarm.

Tibamahgan stealthily approached to within a few yards of the boy, from the opposite direction Bird approached as well. The boy was unaware. Bird recognized him at once and gestured to Tibamahgan with both hands open toward the boy that he knew him, then gesturing again with his two fingers that they both should now walk up upon the boy from both angles. It had now become a little game to play! To see who could get closer first! The boy continued his spying only to see the wolf still guarding the entrance. Nashkid and Kijibashie both exited the rear of the hut while the women remained inside. Seeing them the boy focused his attention on them, not checking his rear or side views.

Both Tibamahgan and Bird crept much closer. Bird reached down and picked up some hickory nuts. Smiling he tossed one, bouncing it off the boy's back! The youth looked up, thinking it fell from the tree above. Then came another toss. Still he looked up. The third nut beaned right off the boy's head, as Bird struggled not to chuckle! Now the boy finally looked toward Bird's position, scoping the landscape. Tibamahgan stealthily slipped to within a few feet of the boy, who continued to scope the opposite direction and upward at the tree limbs, confused as to where the nuts came from.

Tibamahgan gestured with his hand to Bird that he would reach out and grab the boy's deer skin tunic. Bird then stood and stepped out into plain site, the boy's jaw dropped, while simultaneously Tibamahgan grabbed his garment by the gruff of his neck from behind, lifting him off his feet!

Bird spoke first, "Tibamahgan! Let me introduce the new rattle messenger runner, Kimozika. He is the one who specializes in sneaking and observing before making his presence known!" Tibamahgan spoke softly next still holding the youth in his grip. "I know this boy as well. Mahkiwasie engaged him to deliver the summon rattle to you for our council and now I believe he must have another message to deliver to us. Is this not right, Kimozika? Or are you just curious this day?"

Both Tibamahgan and Bird, "Lion Slayer," bore unbearable grins, almost to the point of laughter, at the trick they played on the boy. Bird said "I believe I may have to give you a new title, Kimozika. I may now have to call you hickory nut! At that they both burst out in laughter! But it was not so funny for the boy, who with his own sense of savvy, pulled the summon rattle from his pouch. A bit miffed he spoke, "When you are through with your laughing," he said, "this is from the great sachem spirit woman, Nodinosi!

"She has sent me to deliver the summon message for all five of you to the great Eagle Claw's lodge at mid sun tomorrow. I am to present this to all of you shamans. This is why I have come to Mahkiwasie's lodge; I expected you all would be here, but I had to sneak in to be sure," said the boy with a long face.

Bird remarked, "Well, Hickory Nut, next time you should approach a little more directly. You could have been eaten as a snack by Tibamahgan's wolf!" He ruffled the boy's hair approvingly and looked at Tibamahgan, saying "This is why I like this one!" Lone Wolf said, "Perhaps you should take your summon rattle to the entire group properly then. At that they walked him back to the lodge. The wolf came up to Kimozika who stopped in his stride briefly, while Wolf sniffed his scent as introduction.

Bird laughed again, "Now I do not think Tibamahgan's wolf will eat you! At that they continued to Mahkiwasie's hovel, where Kimozika was more formally introduced to the prestigious group. He smiled to himself, as a crooked grin formed on his face and his eyes lit up just a bit. To be in the presence of this group of shamans, while performing as a chosen messenger, was an honor. This had been his desire ever since he first brought the summon rattle to the Lion Slayer's hut.

A look of concern formed on Tibamahgan's face, as he leaned into Mahkiwasie and whispered in her ear, "Why would Nodinosi, Eagle Claw's sachem woman, need to summon us all?" Medicine Girl looked into his eyes deeply, "my insights tell me it is of a personal matter."

Meanwhile, Bird saw this as an opportunity to include his newfound lover, Abanimie, to the summon session. He wanted nothing more than to bring her into the fold of this elite group. All he wanted to do now was to rush back to her and tell her of his visions and sleep in her arms. He would need permission from the group to do both. Torn, he knew he could not.

The group disbanded, set with the plan to reconvene early at mid sun for the summon session so they would arrive all together. They were all weary, as the intensity of the day's session, with the energy required, was emotionally and physically draining to the human body.

Nashkid and Ninikiji took hands and headed back to their own hovel. Rest was calling them.

Kijibashie decided to go be with the young maiden he was enchanted with during the Nordic council. She in turn was pleasantly surprised. She immediately took him in, for an unattached woman could choose to be with an unattached male if she wished; it was sovereign choice of the woman do so.

Bird headed straight back to Abanimie's, to gather her up and take her to his personal hut at the edge of the clan village. They again spent the night in each other's arms.

Tibamahgan only had to look at Mahkiwasie. In his strong stance, he reached out and took her hand. He cocked his head slightly motioning for her to come with him. Her eyes lit up, then she rushed back into the hovel to grab her pouch, before returning her hand to his. They began to head towards Tibamahgan's remote dwelling to spend the night. He motioned with his free hand for Wolf to follow. Once there they enjoyed a few morsels. Soon satisfied, the long day caught up with them and they fell off into a deep sleep almost simultaneously. Both were overwhelmed with intense dreams of the vision's scenarios, mostly of the immediate changes to come in the next few moons. They awoke in the middle of the night, to whisper and share their dreams. Then they fell into a passionate embrace that held them well into the early morn. This was proven to be the best way to regain connection to the earth-bound physical world.

60 Permissions Manifested

As the mid-day sun was approaching, Mahkiwasie and Tibamahgan, with adornments, medicine bags and possible's pouches, prepared for the trek to the sachem Eagle Claw's lodge. Tibamahgan also had, of course, his basic stone knife and axe strapped over his shoulder. The other four members of the elite monolithic axe group likewise prepared for the trek.

Together, they had decided to bring the artifact with them but to reveal it to the high sachem and spirit woman Nodinosi only should the opportunity and their energy to receive it be appropriate. Mahkiwasie and Ninikiji would intuit this decision in the proper moment. No one in the group had any idea why they had been summoned to the sachem lodge. In speculation it could have been time for the tribe to begin preparations to relocate to the winter inland woodland camps, or to discuss the best location of the camps near where the migrating woodland bison, elk and caribou were to be moving. It was after all early fall, time to gather and prepare the harvest of squash, beans, and corn, most of which was already in ground storage buried in the compost pits. The hickory, acorn, and hazel nuts would need to be gathered now, to be pounded and mixed with berry and venison grease into the cakes that hold the nutrients and proteins through the winter months.

The variety of dried berries, elder, blueberry, strawberry, raspberry, blackberry, cranberry, and grapes would be sun dried and stored in baskets for the winter, ready for travel. The smoke-dried fish would need to be placed on the transport racks, and the poles and skins for the winter shelters and lean-tos would be bundled for carrying or dragging on sledges.

The craftsmen would bring their tools and implements to continue to make the points and arrows and atlatls from their collection of quarried stone best suited for each. This included making bows from ash, hickory, or birch and the wooden knife sheaths and quivers from split sections of white cedar. The centers of the split cedar would be hollowed out to specific dimensions and the two halves would be lashed back together with moose gut to form the vessels.

The craft work never really ended, for even at the remote winter hunting camps, the group of men would sit around the evening campfires working on their projects. These temporary camps were further removed from the larger winter lodges where the women, children, and elders would remain while the men and young teen boys would track and stalk game for many days.

In the early winter months, November and December before the heavy snows, all members, women and able children would participate in the deer drives, whereby after locating a good herd, they would align themselves in a funnel formation using suitable terrain to herd and spook the deer from the wide part of the trap into, usually, a narrow ravine.

They would rattle, hoot, and yelp in an organized manner in an area of over a half mile wide, driving the deer into the narrowing human funnel. Over another half to three quarters of a mile, the trap gradually reduced its width. At the narrowest section, the spear, atlatl, and bow and arrow wielders would target the confused deer herd from above, along the steep rocky precipices on either side, while an even braver group stood abreast a ground level to form a human barricade. In the early winter, this technique would provide a bountiful winter venison harvest, although only to exhaust the nearby herd so that the hunting parties thereafter would need to venture much further out into the deeper woodland forest for longer durations.

At the high noontime sun, the elite monolithic axe group arrived at the head sachem Eagle Claw's lodge. At the ceremonial circle outside the lodge, a small fire smoldered in the center fire pit, while smoke wafted out the top flap of the lodge from inside. In silence, the group arranged themselves around the small fire, remaining outside the lodge, while Tibamahgan's wolf took up his post outside the stone circle, on watch and ever vigilant.

Kimozika, the messenger rattle boy, could not refrain from sneaking about at the outskirts of the wood line. Hoping to learn what the summons meeting was about, he gradually made his way closer by stealthily positioning himself at the outer stone circle. He thought that no one except Wolf, who now accepted his scent, knew he was there.

However, Wolf's body language revealed the intrusion to Tibamahgan, who in turn motioned with his eyes to Nashkid and Bird. They in turn shook their heads a bit, indicating their approval to let the boy have his secret. No one was ever to violate the rules of entering the ceremonial circle of the sachem's lodge without invitation. Upon doing so, severe consequences would be imposed. Kimozika knew the rule all too well, his thinking was to keep his ear open to conversations, thinking the meeting would be held outside within the circle.

It was not to be. Nodinosi, Spirit Woman, head sachem woman of all the Nehantucket tribal people, emerged from the lodge. She acknowledged the group with her hand gesture and taking Mahkiwasie and Ninikiji by their hands, led everyone back inside the lodge.

The lodge was not just a small wigwam style hovel. On the contrary, it was fifteen or more feet wider, by our measurements, and close to twenty-five feet longer than the typical wigwam. It was furnished with benches of saplings lashed together and elevated off the dirt floor by two feet. The benches used for sleeping were fitted with woven mats for comfortable sleeping. Two fire pits dug into the ground a bit, were located ten or so feet in from the ends of the lodge, radiating welcoming heat from the glowing hot coals, with stacks of dry wood just nearby. From the rafters hung dried herbs while tanned hides lashed together formed an insulated ceiling. Useful tools and implements, wooden bowls and spoons, hung close to the cooking fire pit. Dried fish and meats and jerkies were also hung nearby, ready for the stone stew pots.

Eagle Claw, "Migiwishkanj," chief elder sachem, kept his hunting implements hanging in one whole section of the lodge, including his first long spear, his atlatl, with the improved adjustable stone weight, his various stone axes and bone-handle mallets, his stone long knife with the bone handle encased in its wooden sheath, and his recently gifted ash longbow and wooden quiver of shark tooth, with its quartz-tipped arrows. Upon the side wall hung his cloak of the massive black bear he had slain when he first came into his own on his vision quest, elevating his status within the tribe to "Bear Shaman," much like how Tibamahgan had become Lone Wolf, who walks with the wolf, and how Bird had become Mammototh Scout, and now the Lion Shaman.

Eagle Claw lay horizontal on his comfortable cot when they arrived inside the lodge. He looked pale and tired despite trying to hide it by rising to a sitting position with his back straight, holding his head high. Nodinosi quickly tended to him, primping his appearance, and placing his pipe and tobacco pouch at his side. He gestured for the group to sit on the woven reed mats laid out near the fire pit.

Medicine Girl, glancing at Lone Wolf, immediately sensed Eagle Claw as being in ailment, as did Ninikiji. Each of the other members, Kijibashie, Nashkid, and Bird remained in quiet contemplation. Eagle Claw spoke softly, as he took Spirit Woman's hand, "I summoned you special six, you of the Norsemen council, you of the shaman powers, women of the medicine healers, women shamans of the Starr knowledge." His arms raised up toward the sky, as he continued, smiling, "It has come time to pass the pipe; an end to my earthbound time soon approaches."

"I will not travel to the winter camps this season, Spirit Woman and myself will remain here in the comfort of this lodge, with a warm fire tended by some of my faithful woman friends. That is only if my spirit guides allow me to stay that much longer," he said jokingly, bringing a nod and another smile!

"So," he continued, "it is with great honor that I pass on the task of insuring all the Nehantucket villagers' preparations for the winter village journey, and for you, pointing at Bird, Nashkid and Kijibashie, to lead them the way to the place best suited for this coming snow season. I know it has been scouted, and already chosen by Tibamahgan and by Mamatoth Scout. Our new friends of the Abenaki," pointing at Nashkid and Ninikiji, "now adopted as powerful shamans of the Nehantucket, will be in all affairs of the winter camps in all ways that the gifts of spirit ancestors bring within each of you. This endeavor, now upon our people, is at hand and within the next few weeks, you will lead them on the journey and oversee them to settle deeper into the woodland."

Eagle Claw motioned to spirit woman, Nodinosi, to pluck a fresh leaf of the prized tobacco hanging from the rafter. This he rubbed between his palms to gently crush it and roll it a bit, ready to place into the long stemmed soapstone pipe. The bowl of the pipe was skillfully engraved with an eagle's talon grasping a full tobacco leaf, its barrel of a hollow, drilled wooden section of hard ash wood extending from the soapstone. He stoked the pipe and lit the crushed tobacco with a long stick previously placed in the fire's embers.

Eagle Claw now mustered the strength to rise to a standing position, not without a little help from his wife and mate Nodinosi. "With this pipe I now wish to grant permission for Tibamahgan, my dear and close friend and my chosen adopted son, to take Mahkiwasie as his soul mate, his wife in marriage, if she so choses!" With these words he then handed the pipe to Lone Wolf!

Tibamahgan was astounded, thinking that his affair with Mahkiwasie was secret! She also blushed with embarrassment that their secret love was revealed. Eagle Claw leaned into Nodinosi, laughing a bit, "There is not much in this village that goes unnoticed by me and my woman! You both have our blessing in this bond as I release you from the forbidden law. It brings us pleasure for you both to accept my decree!" At this he handed the pipe first to Mahkiwasie, who in turn, looking starry-eyed at Lone Wolf, took a draw from it and passed it to her lover. He in his turn drew a pull from the sweet tobacco flavor. By this they sealed the bond between them in front of the great Nehantucket sachem.

Eagle Claw raised his hands again, quieting the room a bit, as he then turned to Lion Slayer, Bird. "Now it has come to my attention that you, young lion slayer, Mammototh Scout, now grown from the mischievous boy named Bird, have fallen for a talented and special young woman of the village called light dancer, Abanimie. I now grant you both permission to become as one." He handed the pipe to Bird to draw from it to accept the permission and bond with Abanimie, if she so chose. As Bird drew from the pipe, it was then that Nodinosi went to the lodge flap entrance; with a motion from her hand, Abanimie entered the lodge. Earlier, the boy Kimozika had been instructed to run the summon rattle to Abanimie's hut as soon as the group entered the lodge. The boy, now elated, stood outside within the ceremonial circle, well within ear shot of the goings on within!

Abanimie, quite intimidated, shyly approached quickly to Bird's side; he was the only one within that she was acquainted with. She knew of the others within the room, their reputations and power, but never had she been in such proximity with them. Nodinosi, Mahkiwasie, and Ninikiji each joyfully took her by her hands and pulled her into an embrace, as women do, whispering joyously to her, bringing her into their fold. After some primping, she was handed the pipe, explaining how the great Eagle Claw had granted permission for her and Bird to be as one if she was in acceptance of it. It was explained that if she drew tobacco from the pipe she would be committing to Bird. Abanimie looked at Bird lovingly and withdrew a deep draw. She smiled briefly and then grimaced at the smoke entering her lungs for the first time. She coughed a bit on it, as her tears welled up from the tobacco and from joy simultaneously! Eagle Claw, still standing, now turned to Nashkid and Ninikiji, and without the necessity of words, handed the pipe to first Ninikiji, who partook gratefully and then to Nashkid. This was to formally bond them in the Nehantucket way.

Finally, the pipe was handed to Kijibashie, the one who runs, the one who bears the news and messages between the tribal clans along the eastern waterfront villages; the one who brought revelation of the presence of the Nordic's first landing on their shores at the Pawtucket River inlet; and the one member who sat with them and helped to interpret and negotiate the terms for them to abide by. Unbeknownst to Eagle Claw and Nodinosi, he was now of the elite group, the protectors of the secret power of the monolithic axe.

Kijibashie's woman, too, had been summoned by the rattle boy, Kimozika, and escorted to the great sachems lodge. Her name was "Ikwea," meaning "warm river breeze." Although she was of no real prominence or background, she was a reed weaver of fine water tight baskets with elegant embroidered designs, some of which hung from the great sachems rafters. Thinking she was in trouble at first, she was presented into the fold of prestigious women who joyously explained why she was there: she was to be by Kijibashie's side under the formal act of permission, a bonding by the great elder sachem. She too partook of the pipe tobacco for the first time, just a puff of it really. Releasing the smoke softly from her lips, she enjoyed the flavor, smiling as she handed the pipe awkwardly back to Eagle Claw. He then handed the pipe to Kijibashie for him to acknowledge the bond. The elder reached down and pressed Ikwea's hand into Kijibashie's, sealing their union.

Eagle Claw and Nodinosi then puffed deeply from the pipe to complete the circle of bonding between all the couples in the room. Still standing but beginning to fatigue a bit, the elder sachem resumed his sitting position. After a moment of silence, he began to speak, just after he motioned for all to sit again.

"It is with great honor to us, gesturing to his woman Nodinosi, that you great and powerful shamans, great devoted medicine healers and great special spirit women, have united with each other here in this time of our people, for now you all will become the council leaders of the Nehantucket people. I do this now only because I have had many insights and visions guiding me in this matter, of which we have pondered for some time now. My vessel body is also not holding strength as it once did in the years of youth. My time upon this earth is soon coming to an end. So now with great pride and passion we, as he looked at Nodinosi, who took his hand, we pass this work on to all of you with your newer insights and wisdom."

61 Transitions of Season

Eagle Claw sat back again with satisfaction, relighting the tobacco in the pipe, with Nodinosi by his side. Everyone chatted happily amongst each other. Lone Wolf, Nashkid, Mahkiwasie, Kijibashie and Ninikiji briefly convened in a huddle, while Bird and the other women continued to chat.

The huddle was just a short discussion as whether to present the artifact to Eagle Claw and Nodinosi at this time, and whether to do it as a group or delegate the task to a select few. It was agreed that Lone Wolf and Medicine Girl would do so in private after this joyous occasion concluded. For now, they would wait, because the other women, Ikwea and Abanimie had no knowledge of it yet. They would be brought into the fold soon enough.

There was some commotion outside the lodge. Women were chattering and menfolk were in discussion within their small groups. People were arriving in numbers. Word had spread rapidly throughout the clans about this union of their most renowned shamans. They came from both sides of the Nehantucket river and the shore points. They came with small gifts of adornment. Kimozika now stood as instructed, smiling within the stone circle as the mated celebrities emerged from the lodge.

Festive singing broke out, while still others were arriving as the word had been sent just a few hours ago. They had begun gathering outside the ceremonial circle as the couples remained sequestered within. Now the singing brought the newlyweds out to the ceremonial circle, surprised and delighted. Two by two folks entered the circle to express their blessings or present small tokens and gifts.

The two fishermen brothers, smiling away, came into the circle together and embraced Lone Wolf and Bird in their man-hug way! They presented shark tooth pointed arrows to each of the men in the group of mated pairs and fine sealskin pouches for each of the wedded women. Many villagers gifted small crafts from within their personal trades and expertise.

The ceremony lasted through the day and into the evening, with Eagle Claw and Nodinosi emerging from the lodge, after he mustered his strength, to address the crowd with his and Spirit woman's formal blessings. They passed the pipe once again within the ceremonial circle for all to see, and he held it high above their heads with a bonding gesture over each of the paired couples standing in front of him.

After the fanfare, Eagle Claw and Nodinosi quietly slipped back into their lodge; he was again fatigued, needing to lay down and rest. By the end of the evening each couple, Lone Wolf and Medicine Girl, Bird and Abanimie, Nashkid and Ninikiji, and Kijibashie and Ikwea, began to slip out to their hovels. One by one they pretended to yawn and stretch as if tired.

It took a few days for the couples, especially Lone Wolf and Medicine Girl, to accustom to showing open affection. In some ways Lone Wolf missed the secret rendezvous, the planning and the seclusion with Medicine Girl in the deep forest.

The other couples had not needed to secret themselves away so much, being not of such high status, at least not until the Nordic arrival. Most common male tribal members would show affection toward a maiden of his eye by bringing her a token or carved stick. If she smiled and kept it, he was accepted; if she did not and tossed it back, he was rejected. Accepted, a suiter would still need to prove he was a good provider if not already holding rank or status, as Bird, Nashkid, and Kijibashie already had.

Women oversaw all things at and around the wigwam hovels, as their domain, while menfolk were either out providing fish or hunting game, fashioning tools or implements, and shaping atlatls, spears, points or the newly introduced bow and arrows. Young girls and boys would help gather wood, berries, reeds and saplings; while older girls were trained in the arts of basket weaving and making clothing, and older boys would learn to be proficient with their small bows and arrows and hunting implements or in the savvy art of fishing in both fresh and salt waters.

Many times in the Nehantucket society a male would take two wives in the family network, with the first wife being matriarch of the household routines. Two women in these tasks made the daily work much more efficient. It was a very accepted and efficient family system, as each Nehantucket woman was honored and regarded sacred in their abilities, especially in the gift of bearing children. The head man of the family usually did not mind the warmth of two wives on the chilly nights either!

Children were taught to never cry in tantrum, taught early to be quiet and silent in the laws and ways of the forest. They were never abused, hit or reprimanded physically. Instead they were instructed and nurtured in the proper ways according to their individual aptitudes, allowed to enhance their skills and praised for their accomplishments!

The celebrations of the newly joined couples continued. It would be two full days before tribal business resumed. The winter camp preparations to move inland to the deep forest were now underway. It would take another ten days to finalize preparations and two days of travel to set up at the chosen inland location. The tribal leaders, shamans, and officers would supervise, inspect, and pitch in where needed in the endeavors. After hundreds of years this ritual had become almost automatic.

Meanwhile, the artifact group convened and trekked to the sachem Eagle Claw's lodge once more a few days later. Unannounced, they brought the sacred monolithic axe artifact with intended purpose.

Just prior, early in the morning, the group had met in secret at Lone Wolf's hovel, this time to bring Abanimie and Ikwea into the artifact fold. After the women's vows to secrecy, this session was to give them a brief vision experience as an introduction to its power. The session for each of the young women lasted just a few minutes so they could understand its potential. For them a learning took place, a learning that to hold the axe with intention and focus upon a certain question, would reveal variations or outcomes to the answers for the holder to choose. They were each in awe of the initial experience and looking forward to a longer, more structured guided vision. This would happen soon enough, but for now there was some important special work to be done as a group.

Thus, with the two women Abanimie and Ikwea now inducted into the fold, the group arrived at the sachem's lodge, to enter the circle, and announce their presence. To enter the ceremonial circle, they passed through the archway of a seven-foot-high pergola of bent sapling bows lashed together with grape vine and woven throughout with bittersweet berry vine and wild sages. It was all of six feet wide at its base, and before entering one would stop for a moment, center, and clear oneself by either smudging the dark charcoal of the unlit hickory branch upon the skin of the breast and arms, or to cleanse oneself with the smoking bundle of sage, elderberry root, and tobacco. This was done to release all negativity, anger, and animosity; leaving it all outside the sacred circle, to only enter with open mind and a connection to the spiritual world, with pure harmonious intention.

As the group entered the circle, their senses were filled with a mixed aroma of wood fire smoke and wild sage and herbs, as it wafted through the top lodge flaps, from the fire pits within. It meant that the elders were in fact inside. Mahkiwasie clacked the two ash sticks together four times, like a door knocker to let the occupants know that visitors have arrived. Permission to enter must be granted before entry at even the humblest of any wigwam lodge. It was a sacrilege to enter a hovel if no one was inside.

It took quite a while before Nodinosi appeared, opening the skin-covered, woven-sapling doorway. Surprised, she forced a smile, clearly questioning why the group of eight had arrived. Lone Wolf spoke, "Spirit Mother, we bear a gift of very great power for Eagle Claw and you. It is an important teaching for all Nehantucket."

She motioned for them to enter. Eagle Claw was once again laying upon his cot. Drowsy, he pulled himself to a sitting position. After his focus of them all became clear, he smiled.

A long silence filled the room. Nodinosi gestured for them to sit with another motion of her hand. All sat but Tibamahgan and Mahkiwasie, who remained standing, Mahkiwasie holding the wrappings against her breast.

"So it has come that you all would like to smoke more of my tobacco," jested Eagle Claw. Lone Wolf spoke, "yes, it is true that we enjoyed the pipe, and we all wish to show gratitude for your great blessing of our bonds to each other."

"This is not why we come, for we bring something of much more importance, a gift of vision that this select group is bound to protect. We have all come as one to present to you and Spirit Woman something that when held, will take you to places beyond our world," continued Lone Wolf. As the artifact was revealed from its wrappings, Eagle Claw reached out curiously to hold it and to admire its craftsmanship. He immediately began to experience its power, even holding it in his open hands for just a very brief passage of time. It had been perhaps a few minutes at best, before Mahkiwasie sensed his tolerance of it was at his limit. She withdrew the stone axe from his grip, breaking his trance state. The elderly sachem leader, mouth agape, slumped back upon his cot. Nodinosi rushed to his side tending to his sweating brow and wondering what had overcome him.

The sachem collected himself and brushed Nodinosi's tending hands away from his face as he sat more upright, this time pretending to be composed. He had no words, instead he just glanced about the room landing his focus on Lone Wolf, then to Mahkiwasie.

She still held the artifact with the wrapping in her hands. Eagle Claw reached out and with both hands under those of Medicine Girl, drew it and her toward Nodinosi. He was handing the artifact through Mahkiwasie to Spirit Woman, for her to hold it as he did, for her to take the journey for herself.

Nodinosi's vision was short, as well, lasting only a few minutes. However, she remained centered and with her eyes open, she surrendered the artifact back to its wrappings held by Medicine Girl. Spirit Woman's vision journey was profound. Her guides came to her and showed her how she would come to be powerful and loving as an ancestral spirit elder, guiding future Nehantucket people through durations of hardship. She would be able to travel between the dimensions and guide them through their subconscious dream states. She would work with the women mostly, helping the healers and medicine workers with knowledge of herbal remedies and prana energy. Nodinosi was in total comfort with the power of the artifact. For her it was as if she had held it before in another time, in another place, or another dimension.

Eagle Claw was deeply shook by his experience at first. It not until he collected himself that he was able to comprehend his vision journey, however brief it had appeared to the members in the room. For himself, he saw his demise from the physical body. He hovered over it as it lay upon the pole platform with winter snows accumulating. It was placed there because he would transition in the dead of winter, as he knew he would. He saw his village return in the warm spring as he watched them place his weathered body in his burial pit with full ceremony.

From there his vision took him into a future unfamiliar. He was now an ancestral quide, but what he saw his people enduring was unfathomable, from the aggressive violence brought to them by the Pequots, to the plagues and disease brought by the alien early Europeans. He watched helplessly the systematic exploitation of game, fur-bearing creatures, and forests. The sacred burial grounds were desecrated. Whole territories were raped clean and converted to unnatural meadows, even the nutrients in the soil were depleted. His Nehantuckets were subjected to a servitude that forced an alien religious belief system upon them. The Starr knowledge became lost to them, with only just a select few holding the secrets of truth and birthright.

Atrocities were not limited to the Nehantuckets. Far worse was forced upon other peaceful tribal nations far to the south and west. He and other spirit ancestor guides had to work hard to prevent his Nehantuckets from succumbing to war, violence and retaliation during these future hardships. Mid-western nations endured far worse at the hands of these alien invaders, these extorters of all things peaceful and in natural harmony with the earth and stars.

Eagle Claw was shown how his essence was adopted into a much larger council of ancestral spiritual elders which guided many other native nations through the times of desecration. Through hundreds of years of atrocities, these spiritual elders worked through powerful chieftain leaders, medicine men and women, and shamans, eventually bringing them to a time in a far distant future where once again in peace and respect, their ways were honored.

Eagle Claw rose. With the simple act of removing the large scallop shell emblem from his hanging peg, he summoned his energy and feebly walked to Tibamahgan, who was now sitting next to Mahkiwasie. Eagle Claw draped the shell over his head and positioned the emblem neatly upon his own chest. It was as if he wanted to cherish his reign as sachem for just a few more moments. Then he removed it again, leaned over to Tibamahgan, and placed the medallion onto Lone Wolf's chest, tying it securely. Then releasing it with both hands, he held his hands just in front of his chest for a moment. Solemnly, he said to Tibamahgan, "It is now your honor to lead our Nehantucket clans, with your great strength, foresight and wisdom."

Astounded, both Mahkiwasie and Tibamahgan, still holding hands, were in complete awe. Out of character from his strong, staunch demeanor, Lone Wolf's mouth dropped open. Collecting himself, glancing about the room, he stood up abruptly to try to ponder the reality of what had just occurred. The others in the group were astounded as well. They could sense that Eagle Claw was ailing in his old age.

With no sons of his own to inherit the sachem position, it was proper to pass the position to the strongest and most accomplished shaman, scout, or hunter. Tibamahgan was all three and was renowned for raising and walking with one of the most feared and respected predators in the forest, the "dire timber wolf."

Eagle Claw regarded Tibamahgan as his adopted son. He respected Tibamahgan's quiet demeanor, as well as his ability to listen and hear all perspectives before voicing his own opinion. Lone Wolf's skills of woodsmanship and stealth were unsurpassed. It brought the sachem pleasure for Lone Wolf to be mated with the beautiful spirit healer and medicine women, Mahkiwasie.

Eagle Claw embraced Tibamahgan with a handshake of sorts, locking both arms to cement the transfer of leadership, but more to just embrace him as a proud father would a son. He then turned with no more ceremony, and sat back upon his cot, where he gathered his pipe and tobacco and quietly prepared it to smoke.

Nodinosi then approached Mahkiwasie, and with no words she removed the quartz pendulum necklace from her neck and placed it over Medicine Girl's head. It was the gemstone of earth, air, and water that only the highest spirit woman can possess. It held the power of all previous shaman priestesses, gifted forward across the centuries. The gemstone could be taken nor could it be inherited; it must be gifted only to one who has elevated her consciousness to ascend beyond the physical realm, one who selflessly gives her abilities for the highest good of all things and beings that need healing.

Still with no words spoken, Nodinosi took Mahkiwasie's hands in hers and cupped them around the sacred stone. Medicine Girl felt the surge of warmth it emitted, soon to generate a mild heat that began to surge into her body, filling her with a lightness. Spirit Woman smiled with a knowingness, as Mahkiwasie teared up with joy and let the tears freely stream down her face. Kimozika, the messenger boy, was again called upon to deliver the news to the clan village elders of this transition of head sachem and high spirit woman.

62 Seasons to Come

Winter snows began to flurry early this season just at harvest moon of late October, as we know it today. The Nehantuckets did not label the months with time tables. They knew the changing seasons through an instinctive internal clock as natural to them as were the creatures, and animals. The black bear would now complete his forage and at the accumulation of the first snows head to its den for the duration of the winter months. Frogs and turtles would burrow deep into the mud, while flocks of waterfowl and geese would fly in formation towards warmer southern marshes.

This season, as they huddled near the fires within their hovels at the inland winter villages, they would speak and murmur of a noticeable shift; it was as if there had been a seismic event or a slight change of Mother Earth's axis. It caused the colder air to come very early and the snows to accumulate deeper than usual for the new moon in November.

This proved to be good for the hunters, able to better track the winter game that did not migrate but remained in the woodlands. Moose, deer, and elk were some of the hooved animals, as well as the bison.

Tibamahgan and Bird had done well in scouting the location this season for winter camps, inland, just along either side of the stream we refer to today as Four Mile River. The larger clan hovels and lodges were located at the base of the steep ledges, while still other clans preferred to locate further to the northeast just between two lakes, just shy of an eighty-acre body of water in the "Upper Pattagansett" woodlands, north of the larger Lake Pattagansett. This area would provide good winter ice fishing and netting at the stream between the two lakes. The winter clan or family camps were never more than a half mile between each other; This was to provide better support and communication.

Clans located at the points along the eastern shore of the Nantucket River, "living water," would locate northward this season along the east side of what we now call Latimer Brook, to what we now call the "spur" area. Still other clans would inhabit the winters yet further north and to the east along and around a lake area known as Konomoc."

Hunting parties of young men and teenage boys would venture miles from the base clan camps for many days at a time. Nights were spent around these remote open fires, chipping the points and shaping the arrow implements, or shaping bone within the makeshift lean-to shelters. It was near the upper area of the Beaver Brook marsh and the Grassy Hills area where our scouts encountered the large tracks of a small pod of eight or so of mammototh! Just one of these wooly mammoths could feed the clans for the duration of the winter. And so, word was sent back to rally the clans. It would take a large group effort for this hunt to begin!

Track was one thing, locating the pod was altogether another matter. To be precise, locating them without spooking them into a run was the challenge. It required a downwind approach in the thick underbrush that was not yet burned to open the forest floor for better visibility.

These mammoths were, despite their size, resilient and agile creatures. With keen senses adapted over thousands of years of evolution, they were quick to evade the few predators to endanger them and they would hold tight in the pack herd and charge with deadly speed and piercing tusks if cornered or challenged. Steady, they would not run frantic to evade a smaller, lesser threat. Evolution taught that protection and strength was better utilized by remaining in tight cluster groups and standing ground.

Saber tooth tigers, their cousins the mountain lions, dire timber wolves, flat-faced and black bear would be the select few carnivores to pose a threat to the behemoths at this mid woodland period of time, here in the New England coastal forests. The successful few were occasionally the ones stalking in organized packs. Nehantucket humans could not pose a threat even in numbers to the mammototh, with only one exception, the projectiles that they wielded.

Lone Wolf, Tibamahgan, now the new head sachem quietly contemplated this hunt. His first observation was that venison was now in plenty. His second was that snows had already accumulated to just over a foot or so. Finally, the winter camps had just gotten settled in. To coordinate a mass organized hunt would require involving most of the male population from all of the local Nehantucket clans. It would be a huge undertaking and require much resources and time better spent hunting smaller game. After much meditation, he concluded simply that the tribal people themselves were not in any desperation for the meat!

Alone, he quietly held the artifact with intention while considering this pod of mammoth. The first vision scenario revealed a group of young scouts prematurely stalking in close to the herd. With only their atlatls and spears, seeking to gain great honor, they attempted to take one mature mammototh down on their own to no avail. In the vision, one massive animal charged them, killing one teen, and critically injuring two others. Their blood stained the deep snow and the herd moved off with great speed, much deeper into the forest cover. This thwarted the organized clan hunt with the older skilled men. The mammoths were gone, well beyond the Nehantucket territory.

The second vision was one of the mammoths themselves. This small pod, as he was shown, was in fact one of the last of its kind along the coast of the New England territory. The vision showed of their extinction, not too far into the future. Climate changes and now human predators adding to the list of hardships along with the lack of plant foods during the harsh winters brought their demise.

Lone Wolf commanded his final word on the excited clansmen's hunt. Summoning Bird, Lion Shaman, also known as Mammototh Scout, Tibamahgan first told him of the visions and the wisdom behind his decision. He then sent him to deliver the orders for the tribe to stand down. Lion Shaman was now the first officer of the tribe, and he arrived just in time at the outlying camp near the mammoth location, where he held conference with the younger teens and older hunters. He allowed them to stalk in, to view and witness the herd from a distance, so as not to disturb their seclusion. The hunters would be noted for their skill and honored for the "no kill" hunt for many years with great stories told of the event and passed down.

It was now the first moon after winter solstice, with snow an average of two or even three feet deep. Fires burned steadily within the winter hovels and small game hunting was still bountiful. On makeshift snowshoes, a messenger woman trekked from the shoreline summer camp. She was one of the maidens who remained at the chieftain lodge to help tend to the elderly leader's daily needs.

Six days prior to her trek, Eagle Claw choose to pass over to the other side; he died peaceful and content in his sleep upon his sapling cot. The three tending women and one boy worked to wrap his body and hood his head in the ceremonial skins. They then built a scaffold outside the stone circle and placed his body up high upon the staging so as to protect it from scavengers. It would remain there until the spring return of the clans, at which time they would intern his body, in a sitting position, into the thawed ground with all full ceremony and attendants from afar.

Eagle Claw would be placed within the ancient knoll burial ground like his ancestors before him, overlooking Nehantic Bay and the blue sound waters. He would be placed facing east at what we now call McCook's Park at Crescent Beach. Many personal effects and offerings would be placed alongside him, personal things he would need to bring him comfort in the spirit dimension, including his sacred pipe and full tobacco pouch. There would be no markers or engravings, only a small mound of stone and a staff with eagle feather and talons for the breeze to carry him aloft into the stars.

Many who passed before and after would be buried back into the earth in this way, some not with such ceremony, but interned into the ground either here at this sacred site or at a favorite lookout point or place that the individual had enjoyed in life. Some of these would be marked with stone mounds and still others with an offering chamber of stone nearby. One such site was located inland to the north where Bird had his vision quest.

To this day, over twenty-five small stone mounds remain intact, weathered stone in eight- and ten-foot round shapes, protruding four and five feet above the thousands of years of accumulated composted earth creeping upward on their side walls. This site is now considered ceremonial as the mound pattern resembles the star cluster Pleiades. Many offering chambers are still found, above on the ridge peak.

Nodinosi, Spirit Woman, would remain in mourning for many moons after Eagle Claw's burial ceremony. She cut her long grayish black hair short to her shoulders, symbolically relinquishing her power. She put bindings on her ankles and wrists with braided hide, each trailing long tethers to show her one bond to Eagle Claw so that he can grasp her tethers and pull her back to him when she passes into the unseen dimension. Spirit woman would live just a few more short seasons, being well taken care of and honored for her powerful silent role in guidance through many important tribal matters. At her peaceful end she also was buried with great honor and ceremony at the sacred knoll.

It proved to be a long winter at the inland camps. Finally, the warmth of spring and melting of snow filled the streams and brooks high upon their embankments. Sea-run trout and salmon were abundant and eager to reach their spawning grounds. Black bear emerged from the dens along the ledge faces and massive glacial-till boulders. Once their plugs were discharged, they would begin to forage to fill their empty bellies. Salmon and shellfish were first on the menu. Storm surges would wash lobsters abundant upon the beach sands. At low tides clams, scallops, and little necks would be burrowed, shallow, in the sand and mud. Plenty for all including the Nehantucket!

It would not take long to reoccupy the village areas and happily resume the tasks that spring and summer brought. Tibamahgan and Mahkiwasie stood just outside the great sachem long lodge. Wolf, also by their side, stared at it as they did. It was now time to assume their role, to inherit the lodge, and to occupy it as head sachem and lead medicine woman for the tribe.

All important matters would be governed by them. The one change in this work was that they and the secret artifact council would use the axe for insights before making any major decisions for the wellbeing of the tribal community. This included foreseeing major weather events to give the people time to prepare. It was only used if intuition sensed an unusual event. The sachem Tibamahgan would always first rely on his wisdom, experience and common sense, and weigh all officer counsel and opinions before final decisions were directed.

Lone Wolf and Medicine Girl stared in silence at the long lodge for quite some time, both reluctant a bit to be in this new role. It was as if once they entered over the threshold of the long house lodge, all solitude would be gone. Lone Wolf took her hand and with a wave motion to Wolf, they both took a deep breath and stepped inside.

Every so often Lone Wolf would slip out and off into the forest for a few days with only Wolf at his flank. He did this to be in his private solitude. He needed the quiet subtle sounds of the forest to recenter himself. His acclimation to the role of "chief sachem" was trying for him. After all his name, Lone Wolf, was symbolic of his nature.

Mahkiwasie would do the same, slipping away to her secret remote place where her women friends held the energy, vibration, and frequency ceremony. There she would chant and make the singing bowl vibrate its harmonious tones. This connected her to the power of the stars and the earth frequencies that allowed her to raise and restore her own vibrational power.

Moreover, every so often they both would stealthily and quietly retreat out to their secret rendezvous place at the pine moss ledges, to the lean-to where they first made passionate taboo love. It was to become their secret annual getaway, a much-needed retreat from the sachem work, from the hustle and bustle of village endeavors.

As it turned out Bird and Abanimie would do the same, slipping away to be in nature. At these times, they would always visit with the fishermen brothers and learn to master the sealskin kayak-style canoe.

Nashkid and Ninikiji also would regularly trek into the forest and occasionally accompany Kijibashie back to his clan village to the east across the three rivers to Pawtucket Point. There they would reminisce of the Nordic encounter. In the quiet sundry summer eves, Nashkid and Ninikiji would whisper of their Abenaki homeland in the lush green mountains of what is now known as Vermont. They dreamed out loud of liking to one day return; it was out of a natural homesickness only.

The other Abenaki members became well adapted to Nehantucket life and customs, each took mates and became prominent teachers within the Nehantucket society. Abenaki women would regularly convene together, hosting the vibrational, frequency sessions, always including the powerful priestess Mahkiwasie.

63 A Return

The runner, messenger boy Kimozika, arrived at the sachem lodge. Out of breath he hastily smudged himself at the pergola entrance of the sacred circle and clacked the sticks together rapidly to gain permission to enter.

He called out impatiently, "Tibamahgan! Tibamahgan!" The flap entrance opened and Kimozika rushed in, still out of breath and sweating from the run. He had come all the way from the ancient "Pine Tree Grove" area of the "Living River Waters."

Very early that morning, when the sun had just risen over the bay, Kimozika had arisen from his corner of his family hovel. He was getting ready to make his rounds as a messenger when voices of the early rising Nehantucket women began shouting as they scurried to-and-fro near their wigwams. Upon the northern embankment of the small cove inlet, in the morning mist, appeared an apparition very foreign to the women villagers.

Lone Wolf commanded his wolf to sit back down as Kimozika entered. He told the boy to calm himself, handing him a ladle of spring water. Kimozika drank in deep gulps, breathing for air in between. Lone Wolf cocked his head to one side, curious as to what the urgency was. "Speak to me," he said calmly, as he put his hand on the boy's shoulder.

"It is a large canoe! It is at the cove at the pine clan village! It came in the night! There are men there on the sand point! They are not like us! They have hair that comes out of their faces," clamored the boy.

Lone Wolf instructed the boy to run to summon Nashkid, Bird, and Kijibashie, who were all still local. He felt sure he knew who these foreign visitors might be. The question he had formulated was whether they were the same group from the first encounter in Pauquatuket, or yet another group, perhaps more of their kindred kind? The message he gave the boy, as he grabbed his arm, before he scrambled out the doorway was simple, "Kimozika," Lone Wolf said softly, "Speak only these words, 'They have returned!' "

Further instruction was that officers were to rendezvous at the Pine Clan's village. No Nehantucket common folk or adult men were to approach. They must remain in formation at a distance. Only the original contingent with Tibamahgan and his wolf at the lead would interact with the foreigners.

The boy messenger departed almost at full run halfway out the entrance. His first stop would be Nashkid's hovel, next down to the beach area, to get word to Lion Slayer, as they now called Bird. Kijibashie was next in line on the way toward the Pine Clan village. Each immediately gathered their weapons and ran with the boy in the lead toward the pines on the worn pathway trail.

Lone Wolf belted his knife, axe, and spear and shouldered the bow and quiver. Mahkiwasie reached for his hanging sachem medallion so there would be no question of his status. She grabbed his hand and spoke, "I shall follow you to the pines and calm the people." He acknowledged her with a slight hand motion, as Wolf followed him out of the lodge.

The great sachem remained vigilant and open-minded in his thoughts, while pacing his journey to the gathering place, a mile or so away. He somehow arrived slightly before his contingent, who arrived within ten minutes with the messenger boy Kimozika.

It was an eerie sight for the Norse visitors looking across the shallow narrow cove. There on the embankment were four adorned and armed men and one huge timber wolf. Behind them stood a vast line of armed men, women, and children seemingly filling the entire embankment of the opposite shoreline as far as the eye could see. All stood motionless at Tibamahgan's command.

Surveying the visitors from the pine grove embankment, Nashkid stepped up beside Lone Wolf, as did Kijibashie. Simultaneously they both uttered the one name, the name Lone Wolf had already surmised, "Nordics!"

The Nordics had sustained heavy seas two nights prior. Their large boat had been damaged upon the reef outcropping some two miles out, across Nehantucket Bay. They had tried to make landfall at the narrow long island we now know as Fishers Island but managed only to reach a much smaller roundish island that the natives called "Tauabakon" or "Little Hill." After floundering a full day, they were encouraged to find that the island produced enough driftwood to enable them to finally regain the crippled steerage. Darkness came upon them again as they set out to reach the longer Fisher Island shore. The island seemed the closest destination, but with a full moon lit night, the currents and tide brought them closer to the mainland shore, which was their original intent. Trying to avoid the rockier shoreline, a sandy beach led the craft to a very narrow inlet at the "gut." At the time, it seemed a safe inlet haven to make landfall and proper repair. The midnight moon lit the way into the unfamiliar river; the incoming tide almost forced them through the narrows. They reasoned it would be a good shelter should another storm brew up.

Dawn's mist began to lift, revealing the clan camp across the small cove amongst massive pines. Now the smell of smoke began to rise from the fires from the clan camps over the knoll to the north at "Saunders Point," on a breeze blowing gently from the north. They realized their landing placed them straight in the middle of a native village. Hearing the frantic women from the southern hovels amidst the huge pines, they knew it would not be long before an encounter.

Soon enough villagers were lined up across the shallow cove, and behind them a formation began upon the knoll as well. Out in the forefront across the cove, four fully armed native men stood staunchly, staring directly at them. The tallest, strongest looking one stood out more than the rest because of the massive timber wolf at his side.

In his Nordic tongue, the leader commanded his small group of ten not to show any aggression, not even in defensive posture. What seemed like a hundred natives lined up across the cove with another forty upon the knoll behind. Without question, the Nordics knew they should remain passive, show no aggression. The leader squinted, looking closely at the four natives and the wolf; something seemed familiar about them. A thought crossed his mind, "Could this be the same men that they encountered now over two years ago in the sand dunes with baskets of food and the birch bark map, the ones he gifted the artifact to?"

Tibamahgan and his contingent took to the pathway around the cove and descended the slope to the craft upon the stony beach, approaching the foreigners but keeping a good distance. It was clear to the Nordics that Tibamahgan was the native head chieftain, not only by his powerful stature and demeanor, but also due to the wolf that stood at his side awaiting any hand command. Of the other four natives only three seemed familiar. Just then another walked up to join the group. It was "Kajagen," the Abenaki scout who was a witness of the first Nordic encounter at Pauquatuket. He had been standing on the ridge line with the Pauquatuket clan people.

Nashkid glanced at him in subtle surprise, then glanced at Tibamahgan for an approval of sorts. Bird looked surprised too, as did Kijibashie, all glancing at each other! Kajagen's bravery prevailed and with a slight shrug Nashkid approved.

The Norse chieftain and his group stood in silence. Two of the group were women, one of which was wrapped in skins and hunkered behind the others. After a long awkward pause, the Nordic chieftain smiled, recognizing Tibamahgan, Nashkid, and Kijibashie. He held out his two hands with palms up in greeting. Tibamahgan held out his two hands, nodding slightly, still with an obvious question upon his face, as he pulled his hands in and opened his palms wider, cocking his head slightly. He in turn recognized the Nordic leader as well as a couple of the men behind him.

It would take yet another long session of sign language and stick drawing in the patch of sand to understand why the Nordics had come here. Drawing the Norse settlement village at the upriver location at what we still refer to today as Gungywamp, the lines showed how they boated down to the river mouth to the Groton Long Point area. There they met with other friendly Nehantucket clan natives. The Nordics asked for help, through sign and showing them the ailing women in need of medicinal help. These natives indicated that they could not help the woman, but referred the Nordics to a "great medicine" woman healer, who was located at a small river further down the southern shore.

With an etched map showing the Nehantucket bay and the gut entrance to the river, again the Norse set to the water. They headed southward urgently, in quest of the small river and the healer who lived alongside it, but darkness began to gloom, and so did the storm surge.

The Norse woman wrapped in skins behind them, now laying down and in obvious pain was in need desperate need of healing. Her dire need was the only reason the Norsemen would have left their gifted village location at Gungywamp.

The woman, who was with child, was in fact one of the only four women of their small clan, an important wife of one of the clan leaders. The child to be born would be essential to the continued heritage of their people in this new land. The Norsemen needed to risk the travel to seek out the Nehantucket healer shaman woman, Mahkiwasie, who they had heard about through the Nehantuckets in the area of Gungywamp.

It was almost by some divine intervention that their small craft ended up on Tauabakono or what we now call Plum Island, to be repaired with a driftwood tiller, and then under a moonlit night to navigate the narrow gut river inlet. All this had occurred with no real idea if they were anywhere close to the intended shoreline they sought! Their makeshift map was vague at best and certainly not to scale!

The reunion continued with dialog of hand gesture and sand drawings, telling the tale of the Nordic's three day journey. The Nordic chieftain finally had his men carry the ailing woman forward and lay her down in front of the Nehantucket men.

With hand gestures and a broken Algonkin pronunciation, the other Norse woman repeated the mispronounced name "Mahkiwasie" numerous times. Bewildered by her broken language and foreign tongue, the group of five natives tried to decipher her words, asking each other what she meant.

Finally Kajagen, the Abenaki scout stood up, moving to the forefront, "it is our shaman healer she is asking for! I am sure of it. They are trying to say Mahkiwasie! They wish for her to help this ill woman." He then pointed at the sick women lying there and looked at the Norse woman repeating "Mahkiwasie, Mahkiwasie." Then he gestured with both his hands upon the ill woman as Medicine Girl would do in a healing session, repeating the name Mahkiwasie each time he placed his hands on the woman. "These Nordics are here to ask our great shaman healer to help this women!" The Norse woman came over and kneeled, pronouncing the name correctly this time, nodding her head in agreement.

Tibamahgan called for the messenger boy Kimozika!

64   Of Pipe and Peace

By the time the sun had burned off the morning mist, almost every villager from the immediate clans had gathered upon the ancient pine point. Word had spread rapidly during the waking hour and no one could resist the temptation to witness the men with hair coming out of their faces. For the two fishermen brothers it was the large "canoe" craft they arrived in, that drove their curiosity. They had to see for themselves how this was crafted! Lined up just behind the chieftain group, they obtained Bird's attention. He waved permission for them to come closer than the others but to remain back so as not to interfere. He whispered, "The time will come for you soon my friends, to know why they are here."

Kimozika, the running messenger boy, arrived, striding up just behind Kijibashie, who stopped the boy with his open hand upon his chest. Had he not done so the boy would have interrupted the dialog of signing and drawings in the sand.

Kijibashie liked the young runner, his enthusiasm and swiftness, similar traits as his own. He would soon teach the boy tricks and techniques to use while running distance through forest and trail. He would have special foot coverings made, moccasin style with thick hide sole pads, for the boy to protect his feet from sharp stones or shells at the shore.

Tibamahgan had Nashkid relay instructions to the boy to run a message to Mahkiwasie and escort her straight to the Nordic location. She would need to bring her medicine pouch! The boy did not have to run very far, Mahkiwasie was already en route. When the boy intercepted her, he excitedly told Mahkiwasie all about the arrival and the ailing Norse woman. "I am to escort you directly to them." After a moment of contemplation, Mahkiwasie said, "Kimozika, you must run to gather the Abenaki women and have them bring their birthing tools. You will escort them, while I proceed on my own. I know the way as I lived there when I was young.

It was the most exciting event in their lifetimes for the Nehantucket villagers, these alien Norsemen. Their watercraft, their bearded facial hair, and their implements were of great mystery to the villagers. Word soon spread of how and why by sheer luck, without divination, they had arrived. Villagers had heard about them and the earlier arrival at Pawtucket many months ago, but to view them in person held the villagers in awe!

Mahkiwasie arrived. She walked directly to the circle, where Bird and Kijibashie escorted her to the forefront. Briefly, she hesitated at the appearance of the Nordic men, their strange clothing, and heavily bearded faces. The Nordic men all stood up from the circle in respect of her presence, sensing immediately that she was in fact the great medicine master healer they were seeking.

They could not help but gaze at her. Her adornments and her headpiece with the small blue bird feathers hanging down flowing with the small braids in her hair were unlike any of the other Nehantucket women. Her medicine pouch hung naturally over her shoulder nestled into her side as she stood, gazing back at them. She then spoke in a whispered tone, not taking her eyes off of them. She asked Lone Wolf where the ailing woman was in her Algonkin tongue. Mahkiwasie needed no formality of introduction. Still Nashkid gestured with his hand toward Medicine Girl and spoke her name "Mahkiwasie." Not sure the Nordic leader understood the introduction, he did it again. This time the Nordic leader, still standing, gestured a welcome and then, glancing at Tibamahgan, Bird, Kijibashie, and Nashkid as if for permission, he motioned toward the shaded side of the boat.

The Nordic chieftain motioned again for them all to follow him toward the sandy side of the boat. There lay the ailing Nordic woman with the other woman tending to her. In his Nordic tongue, he pronounced "Mahkiwasie" the best he could, followed by words in his Norse language. The tending woman stood and walked over to embrace Medicine Girl with joy, then led her by the hand as she kneeled next to the woman sweating from fever. Wiping her brow, she looked at Mahkiwasie with concern, worry overflowing as tears upon her face. Medicine Girl put two fingers to her lips, signaling the Norse woman to be still.

Mahkiwasie knelt over the ill woman, making many different symbols with her hands in the air over her head and abdomen. Then she placed her hands upon the woman's forehead ever so gently. The laying of hands lasted a few moments. She then moved her hands gently down upon the woman's chest, over her heart, again holding them in place. Finally she moved her hands to the distended belly. Mahkiwasie whispered words and phrases barely legible to the Norse men still standing in distance. It was as if she was talking to others not seen. The Nehantucket men knew that she was!

Much time was spent with hands on upon the pregnant belly area, but eventually her hands moved down upon the pelvis, legs, and feet. Mahkiwasie noticed the wound on the heel of the woman's foot: a slight cut that penetrated deep into the flesh, it was purple with infection.

The session continued with Mahkiwasie's hands back upon the sick woman's head, with gentle strokes that reached to the base of her neck upon the adrenal gland. Mahkiwasie's hands made more symbols in the air as she whispered and chanted some closure phrases, giving thanks to the spirit guides. Finally, she placed both hot hands upon the Nordic woman's cheeks, and with that the woman opened her eyes!

Medicine Girl sat back quietly. She gestured toward the tending Norsewoman and gazed out upon the menfolk, as she spoke in her own tongue, "Now we shall wait for the other healers to arrive. Spirit has shown me what will be needed for this woman and her child."

The native crowd began to encroach closer, not being able to resist a chance to view these visitors up close. The Nehantucket leaders all resumed their attempts to communicate with the Norsemen. Meanwhile Bird motioned to his woman Abanimie, who was amongst the forefront of the viewers, to bring food and fresh water to the council, mostly for the famished Nordics. She and six other women left and returned laden with armloads of bounty in the baskets, way more than any small group could ever eat!

The Norse finally were able to tell their tale of the broken rudder and the midnight storm out on the bay, the story of miracle that landed them not only inside the river's narrow entrance but in the heart of the tribal village of the great sachem healer medicine woman Mahkiwasie, the one that they set out to seek!

The tall, weathered Norseman leader expressed gratitude with his hand gestures to the "one who walks with the wolf," the obvious leader chief of the entire native people, who with his soft spoken words commanded such power, for their kindness and hospitality. He did this by drawing with his fingertip in the sand, a silhouette of the monolithic axe. The picture he drew was over a foot in length and proportional in height. Only the members of the elite group could see it clearly and knew its meaning. The symbol was in fact a significant bond between them all, all that were members of the secret elite group.

The men continued to have an improvised dialect. With Bird in the lead, the two curious fishermen brothers were allowed to come in closer and inspect the Nordic boat's craftsmanship. It was then when the Abenaki healing energy women appeared and were brought to the forefront by Kimozika, the young messenger runner, who, finally was allowed to remain there, in full view of the Norsemen.

Nashkid led the women down to where Mahkiwasie was in attendance to the ailing woman, still lying under the makeshift shelter at the rear of the vessel. After a brief counsel of her condition and Mahkiwasie's spiritual assessment, they all sat around the woman implementing hands-on energy work as a group. The attending Norse woman was allowed to sit in as well for her healing intention was strong. At the conclusion of the session, Mahkiwasie determined that this young women should be relocated to a quiet remote area so as to initiate the vibrational healing frequencies in private, without prying eyes. She whispered softly, "This work will require us to call her ancestral guides."

A litter was assembled by some of the villagers and four strong young men were assigned to help carry it. Mahkiwasie explained the best she could to the Nordic elder that she was to be brought to a quiet hut not too far from this site. The hut turned out to be Lone Wolf's own "bachelor" wigwam located just at the southerly entrance of "Oswegatchie" hills. The Norsemen were asked to remain camped with their vessel for just a few more nights and days. It took a while for the explanation to be understood, but the Nordic men knew that their clanswoman was in better hands now and agreed to the directive.

The men would remain there on the beach head and continue to interact with the Nehantuckets, allowing them to come closer into view. This would go on for another couple days, with the tribal folk presenting food stuff and gifts and tokens of their trade.

Meanwhile at the healing hut, an eerie sound, a faint monotoned frequency, could barely be heard, as the tones emitted from the secluded hovel. The quartz singing bowl, the deep hollow tube, the log drum, and voice all harmonized into one vibrational earth tone. It was very soothing, more a deep feeling within, than a sound heard with just the ear. To experience it would move one's soul to a quiet realm. And so it was with for the ailing Nordic woman.

A poultice of *usnea* lichen that grows in the forest upon the branches of certain trees near ponds and bodies of water was prepared. It was packed into her wound on the heel of her foot. Also, the bearded lichen was simmered into a tea to be sipped. Mahkiwasie knew both applications would work effectively towards the bacteria and fungi of the infection.

Mahkiwasie knew not of any science of it, nor did she know of the details of bacterial or fungal intrusions on a human body. She did know spiritually of the magic power of a healthy immune system. She discerned through the hands-on energy work that this woman and her unborn baby's bodies were in danger and compromised by the intrusion. She was shown the cure through vision, how the use of the bearded lichen would boost and enhance the sick woman's natural immune system. Wild blueberries were squashed into a juice and mixed with the lichen tincture, and this was the diet for the ailing Nordic woman for the next four days. The other Norse women was not allowed into the hut during the frequency sessions that endured an hour twice a day for two days. She was however grateful for being allowed to partake in the hands-on energy work, and served as the interpreter of the healing process and progress to the Norsemen. After two full days and half of the third day, the fever had broken and the Norsewoman was sitting up, speaking to her kinswoman, trying to remember what had transpired and how she had gotten to this place, while not really sure where she was!

By decree from the sachem Tibamahgan, the Norsemen would remain camped at the western shore cove inlet just below Oswegatchie hills for another three moons. The ailing woman recovered from her near-death infection and gave birth to a healthy Norse red-haired girl, with all of the hospitality the Nehantucket midwives could provide. She and the other Norsemen were very grateful to Tibamahgan, Mahkiwasie and all of the inner circle of the monolithic axe. They found the Nehantucket people to be very kind, sharing, and compassionate. They learned much of the Nehantucket ways. Lone Wolf even invited the Norse chieftain to his lodge, where they held ceremony with all eight elite members of the monolithic axe for the Nordic leader to hold and journey one more time, sealing their alliance.

With their large craft repaired and laden with food stuff and supplies, the Nordics departed back to their outpost at Gungywamp woods, partway up the current Thames River. They had extended invitations for any of the Nehantucket to be welcome in their small clan community. And so, with their long dugout canoes some Nehantuckets did just that, accompanying them, paddling with gifted supplies, along the coast and up the Thames to help them prepare for another winter season. Many seasonal visits were made thereafter as well.

65   Of Tale and Lore

The Nehantuckets had no written language in these ancient times, but what they did have were gifted members of the tribe within each clan who were the story tellers of legends and great feats and acts of bravery or spiritual power. With their "legend belts" and their parchments of birch bark picturing etchings, they would tell the tales of the great accomplishments of their ancestors, and pass the tales down intact from generation to generation. These story tellers could capture the imagination of young and old in the tale as if they were there in person! One tale would be of the great sachem, Tibamahigan, who became the first ever shaman scout to tame and walk with the spirit wolf, who rose in rank under the powerful Eagle Claw with his quiet perspectives and wisdom, scouting season after season the winter camp locations. This was the talk of he who negotiated and created peaceful long-term relations with the newly arrived Norsemen through generosity and kindness, a trait that he taught and mandated for his people for future generations. The tale told of how he fell in love with a beautiful maiden with long hair down below her knees, a maiden of powerful healing abilities; how he stole her away and made her his wife and matriarch of the tribe; and how together they effected powerful positive traditions for the people. Lone Wolf remained a powerful icon in Nehantucket lore.

Mahkiwasie, "medicine woman who heals with her touch," would be known throughout the land. Stories of her would be handed down and etched into the birch parchments and story bands for generations. Her inner beauty and power were unsurpassed. Tales of her gentle healing touch and magic inner knowingness for the many she helped will endure. Her teachings of vibration, frequency, and herbal remedies would be passed to the enlightened students for many generations and remains with us even today.

Enduring tales would also be told of the great Abenaki leader Nashkid and his gifted spirit woman Ninikiji, who, with men like Kajagen with his superior hunting skills, trekked many miles for many moons from the distant green mountains bringing earth spirit and Starr people knowledge of vibrational frequency. These tales also told how they shared crafting the bow and arrow hunting implements with the Nehantucket, and of how they helped to negotiate a peaceful coexistence with the newcomers from the land of the Norse, possibly the first Viking visitors.

Lore and stories were told of the great boy named Bird, who became known as Mammatoth Scout for his feats in tracking and hunting the powerful woolly mammoth. They included his vision quest passage to become the great shaman who was the first to defeat the massive lion cat, cousin of the saber-tooth tiger! They told how he later became a great Nehantucket sachem, using his vast wisdom, skills, and knowledge for the good of the Nehantucket people.

Kijibashie, the one who runs, would prevail to become the fastest long distance runner messenger of all time. In legend, he became the one with "wings of foot," he who relayed important messages between the distant shoreline clans, the first to interpret with the Nordic, and the first to learn their dialog fluently.

Women also became legendary. Tales told of the great spirit and medicine woman, Abanimie, the wife of the lion sachem, who became a great spirit medium and tribal matriarch, a great teacher of earth energy and Starr people knowledge. The talks told of Ninikiji, the Abenaki wife of the great shaman Nashkid, who became a renowned vibrational healer with her own special technique. Her story is etched into stone caves deep in the Nehantic forest, depicting her pure crystal singing bowl crafted in the Vermont mountains. Kijibashie's woman Ikwea, became a powerful shaman with her knowledge of manifestation, the birthright of all Nehantucket. She would teach the meditations to the children.

Legends of a "secret society" originated during the time of the Tibamahigan/Mahkiwasie sachem leadership. They were whispered about in the light of the evening fires of the Nehantuckets for another thousand years. The legend of a special artifact emerged, long since the time when it began with only eight elite original members, eight being the sign and symbol for eternity (∞). Only a select few from then forward, generation to generation, would be tasked and enlightened into the fold, into the knowledge of it. These select few were always eight and they were tasked with the protection of the special stone axe. They were the secret keepers, the teachers, passing its knowledge and power of vision and manifestation to the next generation, passing it only to those worthy few, with open mind, Starr knowledge, and Mother Earth connection.

Thus the artifact would remain a legend, the truth of it hidden by the keepers during the coming times of human ignorance and unbalance with Mother Earth. They too, these keepers, would become great sachems, great healers, and great shamans of the Nehantucket. The Nehantuckets prevailed, living on, quietly, upon the river and shores, practicing abundance, peace, and harmony.

These stories remain only as whispered legends of a peaceful tribal people, aboriginal inhabitants of a sacred place that to this day embodies their name and heritage,

Nehantucket, "on point of land."

It is with some sadness that we bring this story, "Nehantucket," to a conclusion. It is with elation that the Nehantucket story does not end here. Their heritage and people will forever continue for all those who wish to choose truth and to remember.

Then to Now

Shifts of sand and time

Nehantuckets lived for centuries in peace and harmony from before the timeline of this story, living in the abundance of all natural things that earth provides.

During glacial melt, Long Island Sound was in fact a large land-locked fresh-water lake. Through the Paleo, Archaic, and Woodland periods, the shoreline was much further out from where it is today. This was due to sea levels still on the rise from previous glacial melting. Imagine five thousand years ago where one could walk out five hundred yards or more from the shoreline of today.

Wigwam Rock just off McCook Beach in Niantic, Connecticut would be the point seen from afar to light a beacon fire for all clan villages to see to summon gatherings of council or celebration. It was used for that purpose even after the great salt sea breached the land mass of Long Island and merged into what is now called Long Island Sound. It was then when shellfish of all varieties took their place along the sandy shores. Crabs, Clams, Oyster, Lobster, to name a few. The fish life within the sound teamed with schools of salt water varieties. At night, the fire within their long dugout canoes attracted fish up to the canoe, allowing Nehantics to easily spear or net their catch.

Over many centuries migratory animals diminished shifting their routes more northward, perhaps due to the magnetic and climate shifts. Indigenous populations rose within neighboring and invasive tribes. Competition in the hunting of game became more prevalent. Still, Nehantic people thrived remaining peaceful and hospitable, trading and living with abundance upon the shores from Connecticut River to the shores of Rhode Island. The central village remained at Niantic Bay with their clan villages spread throughout the coastal shoreline and eastward beyond Pawcatuck. They lived both upon the shores and through the winters retreated into the inland forests.

Pequot Intrusion

Some 150 to 200 years before 1600, as verbal and recorded tribal records depict, the Pequot arrived. As it is written, the fiercest and most brutal of the Pequots, known as the Nameaugs, took their foothold at the Mystic River area in Connecticut. They came from the northwest attempting to infiltrate with woodland tribal nations in upper New England and again southward along the Connecticut River valley. Their aggressive, controlling nature competing for game and territory set not well with better populated tribes who forced them evermore southward. Hence their final foothold at the Stonington and Mystic Rivers.

Over the first few decades, the interaction was mostly peaceful by the Nehantics submission to them. Soon, through increased violent demands, tribute was forced upon the Nehantic clans not in compliance. These Pequot aggression during these times split the Nehantucket tribe. The eastern Nehantics integrated and allied with the western Narragansetts. In time, a great Nehantucket sachem emerged, Ninigret became a powerful leader of the clans to the east and held a semblance of peace and protection for those many years. The western Nehantics, maintaining their peaceful nature, had to endure indenture under ever harsher Pequot controls. Thus, some accounts say that the Nehantics, out of sheer defense and protection, had to learn and engage in the ways of battle tactics to ward off Pequot raiders from stealing winter stores. It is written in many documents that the name Pequot refers to Destroyers of Men. It wasn't until later colonial leaders, in favorable interaction with Nehantics, sustained Pequot aggressions trying to control all trade with the Europeans. Surrounding tribes including Narragansett, Uncas, Hamonassets and now the more docile Mohican formed a loose alliance. The brutality of Pequot War essentially annihilated the Pequot tribe at their fort at Mystic River. A war that peaceful western Nehantics played no part.

Today the current Pequot tribal nation has been reborn with all reflections of them now in the historical past. Upon their reservation, later granted to them by colonial magistrates and to their credit today, the first casino enterprise in New England was created. This institution helped to restore and continues to enhance the local economy of South Eastern Connecticut. The creation of the Mashatucket Pequot Museum has depicted one of the most accurate lifelike recreations of how they and Nehantics looked and lived in their clan villages during their time.

Today the museum is a peaceful tribute preserving the heritage of both

Pequot, and neighboring ancient indigenous tribal people of that era. It is also fair to recognize the Mohican Sun Casino Resort and museum in Norwich, Connecticut created by the current Mohican tribal council. This facility has also contributed to the local economy and their indigenous tribal heritage.

European Invasion

Many versions of how and what the Nehantic tribal people were like was documented by the first early Dutch and English sea captains and literate traders who first arrived on the Connecticut coast venturing along the southeastern rivers and inlets. Their versions of the indigenous were at first tainted somewhat by their different perspectives and influenced by their staunch religious backgrounds. At first, they could not distinguish between the friendly Nehantics and the aggressive Pequot. Eventually, the difference became clear, written accounts revealed western Nehantics to be a welcoming, sharing, and peaceful people. They were hospitable and eager to learn of these alien men bearing and introducing gifts of metallurgy, steel implements, axe, hatchet, knifes and weapons. It was however more the cooking pots and pans of copper and cast iron that induced the most interest, in exchange of a few mere furs and beaver pelts.

The Nehantics hospitality eventually was taken for granted as the influx of European colonial settlers systematically claimed large territories of acreage here on the southeastern shores. They created deeds and title to vast areas claiming it as their own with paper entitlement that no native Nehantic could conceive. The Nehantics had absolutely no concept of land ownership or coin, silver or gold values. Nor did they have any concept of exploiting land or its creatures for personal monetary gain. They did use wampum adornments made from the colorful interior parts of shell fish. This wampum was, in fact, a common base form of exchange system on which many other items could be traded, or bartered for between tribal nations. In the Nehantic culture a man's wealth was based on what he or she gifted back, and contributed to the clan. It was much like a pay it forward concept of living.

The desecration and extortion of all natural resources occurred over the following decades of European invasion. Yet the Nehantuckets remained peaceful, succumbing to and enduring the violations. While in other parts of the New England coast and inland territories, tribal tensions rose leading to native tribal alliances and acts of outright war to evict the European intruders out. There are no documents that speak of the Nehantics having participated in any conflicts during this time.

Nehantics were indentured into European society here in southeastern Connecticut. After the Pequot War, and later the King Philip War did the Europeans impose systematic extortions upon the indigenous. Nehantics were disrespected, belittled, and even owned as conquered property for their misunderstood heritage. Starting with the Puritans, European colonials placed themselves as superior entities over the indigenous. Indentured Nehantics endured the disrespectful colonial mentality.

Miles of stone walls in rectangular patterns were constructed by indentured Nehantics, walls meant to retain cattle, sheep and even geese. Vast changes affected the natural landscape and habitats of game animals. These stone walls remain today as testament to the indentured Nehantics.

Norris Bull Artifact Collection

The Monolithic Axe truly exists as part of the vast artifact collection assembled by Mr. Norris Bull. A collection of ancient Nehantic Indian points, tools utensils and implements. His lifetime work included collections of artifacts obtained from the shores and river systems in southeastern Connecticut. His vast and diverse collection is not limited to just Nehantic, however a large majority of it focuses on the Nehantic due to the countless man hours working the digs along the Niantic River and known Clan Village sites on the western East Lyme and the eastern Waterford sides of the river. Many other digs were explored along various land mass points jetting out into Niantic Bay.

The Norris Bull collection was, before his passing, entrusted in its entirety, to the University of Connecticut under conditions that it to remain on display for the general public to forever view and learn. The UConn Anthropology department still currently holds the collection. *The Monolithic Axe*, a pamphlet written by Norris Bull describes it as the only one of its kind so far found in Connecticut. Within his separate booklet he depicts photos, detailed descriptions, and possible origin concepts. He also speaks to historical comparisons of other similar stone axes throughout the continent. Within his pamphlet, *The Norris Bull Monolithic Axe*, is noted to be only one of three documented monolithic axes found so far in all of New England.

Nehantic lineage

The Nehantic tribal people are not extinct, and have never been extinct. In fact, today descendants of true bloodline Nehantics still living and walking the earth number over 150 souls. Lineage names the last 200 years. Nehantic heritage family names documented as Tatten, Jeffery, Waukeet, Sobuck,

Quasso, Nonesutch, and Occuish. Many other family bloodlines can be traced and found to be indigenous Nehantic inhabitants from the Old Lyme, East Lyme, Waterford, New London and as far east as Mystic and Pawcatuck areas along the Connecticut Shores.

Names such as Metoxin and Chesnoo appear in writings (*Last of the Nehantics*) by Mrs. Jane T. Hills Smith. Also, *The Nehantic Way* by Herb and Marilyn Davis. These texts describe how the appointed overseers (colonial settlers), appointment was to protect encroachments on behalf of the Nehantics and their reservation lands. Instead, some 199 years later these same overseers seemingly pressured a select few Nehantics to agree to a petition which asserted that they were the last sole members of the tribe.

Ambiguous Entitlement

Reservation lands granted to them in 1671 by the governing British crown in written titled documents include Winter Quarters Land northward inland from the shore, known as the Gungy Tract. Approximately in 1870 a handful of entrepreneurial white men on the basis that no Nehantics inhabited their small reservation land year-round, petitioned a colonial court to sell the Nehantic reservation lands claiming with no proof that they were extinct.

It was a deceptive and false means to extort titled land for personal monetary gain. The petitioners in 1870 knew full well that Nehantics historically lived at winter camps inland since prehistoric times. The petition was presented to a colonial court magistrate, and hastily granted.

Soon after another revised petition was filed, granted and approved, to preserve the ancient burial grounds at the hilltop at the Crescent Beach and McCook's Park area. The mere fact that it bears the mark of still living members of the Nonesuch family, many today find it very disconcerting that the same overseers were farmers leasing the same reservation land acreage at Black Point and Crescent Beach from the living local Nehantics.

Ancient Burial Grounds Desecration

Merely five years after the Nehantic John Nonesuch's passing, the sacred burial ground at today's McCook Park hilltop was sold and desecrated under a separate petition by local developers, the petition again hastily granted by a sole local magistrate. Those same burial grounds that were to be preserved forever under the petition granted by the earlier court. While hundreds of Nehantic remains were placed at this site for over hundreds of years, only eight indigenous bodies were exhumed and haphazardly interned at the

Union Cemetery into one small pit. Recorded accounts depict how bones were tossed in together in haste with no separation. A single marker was placed over the pit. Artifacts were taken and added to private collections or sold as souvenirs.

Only to Reclaim

Many attempts to reclaim their share of Black Point Reservation Land and heritage by descendants of Phillip Occuish and other Nehantics went unanswered. Walking great distance annually to return to the reservation, the descendants would gather at the fireplace of the old house at the extremity of Black Point telling tales of their Oneida cousins.

In one story of injustice, a Nehantic family who had tilled and grown their crops had petitioned a hearing before a local Magistrate over a complaint that a neighboring colonial farmer's cattle repeatedly trampled and ruined their crops. The Nehantics tried to articulate how they wanted the cows to be contained by the colonial. The colonial argued his rights to graze his cows where ever they roam. The Magistrate deliberated for some time, then finally came to a resolution. The final ruling was to grant the Nehantics crop field and land they inhabited by legal document to the colonial rancher, and evict the native Nehantic family barring them from their ancestral territory. Colonial Favoritism deliberately prevailed.

In another private journal describes a Nehantic native stripped of his authentic name, known only as Edgar Bound, an indentured Nehantic in servitude under a prominent family at the reservation land in Black Point.

Movement of Today

The current Nehantic Nation Tribal Counsel under Chief Ray Tatten, David Brule and Dr. John Pfeiffer and a coalition of supporters, East Lyme and Waterford Historical Societies, and local indigenous Nehantic advocates, are working diligently to restore the ancient burial grounds, place proper monuments, and placards. Petitions are being prepared to reinstate the ancient tribal nation Nehantics name and heritage with the Federal Government, and subsequently the State of Connecticut. This endeavor is only to overturn the seemingly illegal rulings in 1800s by a single New London Court Magistrate declaring the Nehantics extinct. A declaration that continues to raise far too many questions of truthful authenticity, and even today continues to prove otherwise.

A Name and A Place in History

Today, in the town of East Lyme, Connecticut, there are many magnificent topographical features: the shoreline areas are considered to be the jewel of the coastline, the flowing and ebbing Niantic River, the scenic blue waters of Nehantic Bay, the quaint burrow and beaches of Niantic, finally the pristine woodlands of the Nehantic State Forest.

The various derivative names and pronunciations, Niantic, Nehantic, Nehanticut, Nayanticks, and Nehantucket all stem from the original indigenous native peoples, the Algonkin-speaking Nehantucket. For thousands of years, they referred to these landmarks to describe their ancient culture and presence, and their way of life: "On Points of Land."

A Passage

The shamen foresaw the storm
strange men will come ashore
time will shift our sands
wind of change upon our land
The shamen foresaw the storm
strange men shall come ashore
from a land so far away
shall forever change our ways
The shamen foresaw the storm
years of sixteen hundred and four
shifting our beaches sand
harsher winds upon our lands
We give thanks to those who remember
our tribal people of ancient ways
now a village by ebbing Nehantic river
overlooking the pristine Nehantic bay
Ten thousand years we lived on points of land
barefoot leaving our footprints upon the sand
on "point of land" its meaning and so it remains
our tribal name, a river, a forest, and a bay
To bear our name "Nehantic" so be it the same we the
Nehantucket indigenous tribal people upon these shore's
since time began
"Nehantucket" forever we shall remain

Robert S. Foster

Photo Gallery

Cooking Utensils

Mortise and grinding stone found at the Pattangansett River Creek. From a private collection.

 A Nehantucket bowl from a side view and top. It was found along the Pattangansett River in Nehantic. This is estimated to be about 3,000 years old. From a private collection.

  Pounding stone used to break bone or shells. Shaped to fit one's hand perfectly. Author's collection.

A stone bowl from a dig on the west side of the Nehantic River.

Mounds, Stones & Cairns

The snake cairn's body and head. Located in East Lyme.

Salmon Head Stone   Offering Stone
Located in Nehantic State Forest and Lyme.

The back of a stone ceremonial pedestal points due west.

A directional marker also off a private trail in Lyme.

Norris Bull Collection

The Norris Bull Monolithic Axe is noted to be only one of three documented monolithic axes found so far in New England

This is a pestle (left) and the enlargement is of the head of the pestle to the right

A ceremonial stone mound in the shape of a tortoise

Tortoise-shaped offering chamber. From the Markham Starr collection.

Tools

Arrowheads

Three collections of arrowheads and shark teeth used as tools, and points, some found along the shore of the Nehantucket River. From the author's private collection.

Dedication

While there are many folks currently deserving dedications for this writing who have tirelessly studied, researched, and shared inspirations and insights over these past many years. I would like to recognize all those who have walked and hiked, traveled, and worked the earthen sites with me and those who came before me who have worked tirelessly and passionately to preserve this culture's history.

My gratitude includes the earliest of colonial settlers who took the effort to set pen to parchment, documenting their descriptions and their understanding of the aboriginal natives, the Nehantuckets. Their sketches and simple maps depict points of land and ancient trail systems meandering throughout the shoreline and inland areas, that today we unwittingly travel over. My appreciation extends to the historians of our local townships who have preserved the tales and lore, landmarks, and descriptions of how our Nehantuckets lived and prospered, enjoying the bounties and beauty of the region.

The anthropologists and archaeologists, both professional and amateur, are certainly deserving for their efforts, labors, and passions in preserving artifacts and documenting locations. Their work and digs have clarified and dated the Nehantucket culture with timelines that extend to thousands of years prior to European contact.

These passionate people include some of the simple quiet folks who have written or preserved old letters, or documented a stone tool, point, or arrowhead. Perhaps even a small collection found in great Grandpa's attic has piqued their curiosity to look and learn more about our native inhabitants.

Still, there is no one better suited for this dedication than the ancient peaceable Nehantucket native men and women themselves. They lived and prospered here, on this very ground that many of us take for granted. They walked the very pathways now paved over and obscured even within our own backyards. The Nehantuckets enjoyed the very same beaches and sandy points that jut out to touch the bay and the Niantic River waters.

Imagine one-hundred-fold the ancient summer breezes of our shores and rivers, the abundance of fish and shellfish within the ocean and fresh waters, and the migratory wildlife within the lush upper woodland forests. They cultivated ancient seeds of the "three sisters," (squash, maize, and beans) in small fields of fertile growing mounds. They also harvested native herbs, berries, and plants.

They gave homage, tribute and, gratitude for all their bounties, including the spirit of earth, sun, and stars that nurtured all and provided ancient universal knowledge. They possessed and taught an ancient birthright of a knowingness and use of harmonic earth energies. They possessed personal powers of manifestation and spiritual connection.

The effigies of stone throughout our wooded areas remain as testaments. Ancient offering chambers and tributes to sacred animals, along with mounds and circles of stone endure as ritual sites. Other ancient mounds are situated in sophisticated patterns, not unlike star clusters and constellations. They lived by all accounts in peace and harmony with the earth, ocean, rivers, forest, and each other for thousands of years without animosity, hatred, or war.

There is no one person to dedicate this book to, no group, organization, or institution. The only true dedication belongs to none other than the memory, history, lore, lives, and essence of the actual tribal people of a time now long past.

Ultimately and sincerely, this dedication is to the ancient Nehantucket tribal people.

Acknowledgments

Special thanks to a host of folks and friends who contributed a wealth of information, knowledge, and insights in the preparations as well as inspirations that helped to formulate and nurture this writing. UConn Anthropology Department curator Sarah Sportman helped to locate and provided sample copies of the Norris Bull collection his work, and writings archived and displayed at UConn and the Thomas J. Dodd Center. Norris Bull was the foremost private exploratory archaeologist and anthropologist, a researcher of Nehantic Indian artifacts. His outstanding work includes a vast collection now displayed at the UConn anthropology department. His photographs, notations, articles, documentation, research, displays of tools and implements can bring the viewer back in time! His document, "Monolithic axe found in Connecticut," depicts an ancient artifact that opens one's imagination to a possible Nordic or Viking interaction with the Nehantucket tribal people. William Beebe was a contributor to Norris Bull's work.

Other important authors include:

Markham Starr, whose work, *Ceremonial Stonework*, is a wonderful and educational depiction of ancient coastal Indian sites and works, including Nehantic and surrounding tribal cultures. The outstanding photos of stone effigies and ceremonial stone sites truly open one's mind as to who these natives were. Markham Starr's work resonates with the real and actual belief system of our ancient coastal indigenous cultures, who were predominately the Nehantic throughout the southeastern coastline of Connecticut. His recent archaeological videos are incredible.

William Cronon, whose book, *Changes in the Land*, provides a vast understanding of the New England native ancient culture, with eloquent clarity of how the land once was; along with the colonial interaction cultural misunderstandings of indigenous peoples.

Herb and Marilyn Davis, whose book, *The Nehantic Way*, provides a simple historical rendition of ancient Nehantic trail systems, and a cultural understanding taking place prior to white European contact and prior to the

Pequot invasion. It provides simple insights of how the Nehantucket peoples lived and prospered from over three thousand years ago here on the southeastern Quonoktacut (Connecticut) shore.

As a special notation, there exist many forms of pronunciations and spellings for the 'living river' and points of land along the bay, which ancients referred to as Nehantucket. Today, the area is called Niantic, but other past and perhaps more authentic forms are Neyahantik, Neyahantuket, Niantikut, and Nehantic as described in the historical writings.

Early settlers, colonists, and Dutch and English traders formed their versions of the original native pronunciation as it was difficult for them for it to roll off the tongue or to spell it in their journals. So today the final filtered version remains Niantic. This author prefers and will use the original Algonquin pronunciation throughout the manuscript if only to honor the culture of the natives who were known to inhabit 'on the point of land,' as they called this pristine place and themselves, the Nehantucket.

Old soul inspiring friends

My gratitude goes out to

Lewis Bull, historian, musician
Howard Estes, teacher, gardener and mariner
Sue Perry, herbalist
Pete and Millie Caron, friends of like mind
James Littlefield, author and historian
Susan McTigue Ryan, author and editor
Debora Hastings, intuitive adviser
John "Woody" Wood, song writer and musician
Clayton Allen, song writer and musician, Penobscot
Debora Kraft Smyth, caregiver, Penobscot
Melissa Turner, vibrational healer herbalist, musician
Mike Eramo, lifelong friend, fly fisherman, woodsman
Mark Starr, author, archaeologist, woodsman, historian.
Kitty Werner, publicist, advisor, and really smart friend.
Susan Leppla, artist, song writer, musician.
Mary D. Foster, wife, friend, spiritual healer and soul mate

So much thanks to these friends for their encouragement and inspiration.

About the Author

Robert S. Foster, known by his nickname Butch by his friends and acquaintances, spent the last forty-plus years as an excavation and site development contractor in East Lyme, Connecticut. His passions over the years have included beekeeping, aviation, woodsman ship, playing guitar and blues harps, song writing, fly fishing and upholding "old school" New England values and traditions.

Along with his wife Mary, he developed a farmstead known as Old Orchard Farm, hosting an antique cider mill, bakery, and sound stage for homespun folk music events—a place where folks can sense the simplicity of old traditions and a bit of quiet serenity.

Today, Butch enjoys making music, writing, restoring old things, ancient native Indian cultures along with the quiet natural beauty and being in the energy of Vermont's Green Mountains.

www.ingramcontent.com/pod-product-compliance
Lightning Source LLC
Chambersburg PA
CBHW030600080526
44585CB00012B/441